The Englishwoman in Egypt

Portrait of Sophia Poole by her brother Richard Lane,
made around the time of her stay in Egypt

The Englishwoman in Egypt

Letters from Cairo
Written during a residence there in 1842–46

by
Sophia Poole

Edited with an Introduction and Notes by
Azza Kararah

The American University in Cairo Press
Cairo   New York

Copyright © 2003 by
The American University in Cairo Press
113 Sharia Kasr el Aini, Cairo, Egypt
420 Fifth Avenue, New York, NY 10018
www.aucpress.com

First published in London in three volumes in 1844–46 by Charles Knight

Dar el Kutub No. 3251/03
ISBN 977 424 799 X

Printed in Egypt

Contents

Introduction

by Azza Kararah

It is high time for a new edition of Sophia Poole's *The Englishwoman in Egypt* to be published. The letters that make up the work were originally serialized by the London publisher Charles Knight in *The Monthly Volume*[1] before he collected them for publication in two volumes in London in 1844 (Letters I–XVI in Volume I; Letters XVII–XXX in Volume II); he later published the third volume (labeled "Second Series," with new numbering: Letters I–XI) in 1846; an American book club edition of volumes I and II (in one volume, but omitting Letters IX and XVI) was published in Philadelphia in 1845 by G.B. Zieber & Co. No other editions or printings were made. We are told that Sophia Poole was "more dismayed than pleased" when a copy of the first volume arrived in Cairo.[2] She had not been sent the proofs, so had not had a chance to correct some obvious typographical errors; the publisher had changed the title (from her original, and preferred, "Letters from an English Hareem in Egypt") without consulting her; and the frontispiece illustration of the mosque of Ibn Tulun was wrongly identified as Bab Zuweila.

Notwithstanding Sophia Poole's own disappointment with the publication, *The Englishwoman in Egypt* was highly acclaimed when it first appeared,[3] and recently several critics have scrutinized Poole's work and examined it in the light of modern critical theories. It therefore seems essential that the original text be available for the reader to be able to verify the words of the author and to check occasional misquotations and possible distortions.[4] I am very grateful to the American University in Cairo Press for granting me the privilege of editing Poole's work and of introducing her in a few words to the public. I had previously published an Arabic translation of *The Englishwoman in Egypt*.[5]

Sophia Poole was the youngest child of the Rev. Theophilus Lane, D.C.L., prebendary of Hereford, where she was born on 16 January 1804. Her mother, who seems to have been a remarkable woman, was a grandniece of Thomas Gainsborough, the painter. Sophia had three older brothers: Theophilus, Richard (who later became a well-known lithographer), and Edward, the great Orientalist. In 1829, she married Edward Richard Poole (the eldest son of John Poole, Esq., of Great Ormond Street, London), a barrister with a degree from Trinity Hall, Cambridge, who had taken holy orders. We do not know when he was born, but, as he was admitted as a pensioner to Trinity Hall in 1823, he and Sophia were probably of more or less the same age.[6] He was ordained deacon at Rochester in 1829 and from that time onward he seems to have been constantly on the move: from Rochester to London, to Yorkshire, to Nottinghamshire, to Derbyshire; finally, he disappeared from Crockford's *Clerical Directory* in 1885.[7] As far as I know, no mention of him appeared in any of the private letters of the Lane family.

Sophia and Edward Poole had two sons: Edward Stanley Poole (born in 1830) and Reginald Stuart Poole (born in 1832). Both became notable scholars, the elder as an Orientalist and the younger as an Egyptologist and numismatist.[8] Nothing has come to light thus far about Sophia's life with her husband, and it seems that she and her children had moved in with her mother and her brother Edward by 1840.[9] Also living with them was Nefeeseh, a young slave girl Edward had brought back with him from Egypt after his first visit (1825–28). Of Greek origin, she was nine years old when Lane's friend Robert Hay bought her and gave her to him. Lane's mother undertook her education and she seems to have fitted well into the English way of life.[10]

Edward Lane was so absorbed in his work that it is remarkable he took time off to marry Nefeeseh in Kensington Parish Church on 8 July 1840. In the letter to Hay in which he announced his marriage he writes: "I was obliged to fag very hard to be able to leave home for three days. To-morrow evening I hope to be at home again, & then I shall have to work hard again to make up for my frolic."[11] His marriage had the full approbation of his mother and Sophia,[12] while Nefeeseh, in a letter to Hay in June, shortly before her wedding, expressed her feelings by saying, "I am sure I have your prayers united with mine that I may with the blessing of Almighty God prove a source of happiness to one so dear to me, and a real blessing to a family for whom I feel the same affection as if they were my *own* dear Mother, Sister and Brothers."[13] This she certainly proved to be, as years later Lane imparted in a letter to Hay: "Never . . . has there existed a more affectionate wife."[14]

Early in January 1841, Lane's mother died, and shortly afterward he himself became gravely ill and was advised by his doctors to go to a warmer climate. Toward the end of that year, he received an offer of an annual grant of £150 from his friend Lord Prudhoe, the future Duke of Northumberland, whom he had met during his first visit to Egypt, to support him in the preparation of an Arabic–English lexicon.[15] Understandably, Lane eagerly accepted the generous offer. Later, in 1848, it would be supplemented by an annual government grant of £100 from the Fund for Special Services.[16] Lane's grand-nephew, Stanley Lane Poole, reported that "it was this sore trouble [the death of her mother] that decided Mrs. Poole, who had lived in late years always with her mother, on accompanying her brother to Egypt, and from this time to his death she never left him for more than a few days at a time, unless summoned by the illness of her own sons."[17]

On 1 July 1842, Sophia Poole and her two sons sailed for Alexandria on the P&O steamer *Tagus*, with her brother Edward and his wife Nefeeseh. On 19 July they reached Alexandria, from where they soon sailed up the Mahmudiya Canal and the Nile to Cairo. There, after a strange experience in a "haunted" house (described in Letters XIV and XVII), they finally settled down in a comfortable dwelling in January 1843, where they remained until the beginning of 1845, when they moved for the last time to the house they lived in until their return to England in 1849. Once more in Cairo, Lane settled down to his tremendous task of composing his Arabic–English lexicon.[18] He had decided to rely basically on Sayyid Murtada's *Taj al-'Arus*, so he engaged Shaykh Ibrahim al-Desuqi, who brought him manuscripts from the libraries of different mosques and with whom he worked incessantly.[19]

From an early breakfast to near midnight he was always at his desk, the long hours of work being broken only by a few minutes for meals—he allowed himself no more—and a scanty half-hour of exercise, spent in walking up and down a room or on the terrace on the roof. For six months he did not cross the threshold of his house, and during all the seven years he only once left Cairo, and that was to take his wife and sister for a three-day visit to the Pyramids. At first he used to devote a short time every day to the classical education of his nephews, but even this was taken off his hands after a time by the kindness of the Rev. G.S. Cautley, and the ready counsel of Mr. Charles Murray.[20]

In his previous two visits to Egypt (1825–28 and 1833–35), Lane had conformed in many ways to the Egyptian way of life, and now his family followed suit. We know from Poole's letters that both she and her sister-in-law always wore the *habara* and the veil when they went out of doors and that their table manners at home were eastern. For Lane, however, there was a difference this time. During his first two visits, especially the second, when he was occupied with writing his *Account of the Manners and Customs of the Modern Egyptians*, he had felt that the nature of his work imposed on him a certain way of life and that he must attempt to metamorphose himself into an oriental in order to be completely accepted by the people he wished to examine, understand, and write about. He therefore isolated himself from the resident Frank community except for the few who were congenial and in harmony with his ideas. He became Mansur Efendi and only felt comfortable when he sat cross-legged and smoked the *nargileh*, to which he had become addicted.[21]

On his third visit, however, work on the lexicon required quite a different way of life. Lane worked at home and, as Stanley Lane Poole remarked, "it was a time of unremitting, exhausting labour: but it was a happy time."[22] Lane enjoyed the home atmosphere he dearly loved with his wife and sister and, though he had no children of his own,[23] it is clear from some of Sophia's letters that his two young nephews filled the house with fun and laughter.

Friday was their 'at home' day, when a mixture of European and Egyptian friends would meet at Lane's house. The "less exclusively Oriental friends and the few ladies who visited Cairo, such as Harriet Martineau, would betake themselves to the other side of the house, where Mrs. Lane and Mrs. Poole were 'at home.'"[24] On the list of names Stanley Lane Poole provides of the "pleasant little society they entered into, for the seven years of their stay in Cairo," English and European names far exceed the Egyptian ones.[25] One of the names he mentions is "Hagee Hasan El-Burralee, the poet," who may be the poet referred to in one of Poole's letters, whose house she visited and whose wife reminded her "of an Englishwoman."[26]

The reason I have presented a rather exhaustive account of Edward Lane is that in her preface, and in the first two volumes of her book, Sophia Poole never fails to express not only her admiration for, but also her debt to, her brother. What is of interest, however, is to examine to what extent Lane in fact helped her with her work.

To begin with, as she proudly acknowledged in her preface, it was her brother who proposed the idea to her of occupying her time in an enjoyable fashion by "obtaining an insight into the mode of life of the higher classes of the ladies in this country . . . accessible only to a lady," and he further encouraged her to write a book on the subject, with the idea probably in mind that it would complement his own *Modern Egyptians*, which was deficient in that aspect: he, as a man, could not supply this insight. To facilitate a task for her wherein she was so far a novice, he advised her to use the epistolary form, which, besides being fashionable among women writers at the time, was also less demanding than what was then considered more serious writing. Furthermore, as she writes, "to encourage me . . . he placed at my disposal a large collection of his own unpublished notes, that I might extract from them, and insert in my letters whatever I might think fit." These notes were, of course, his unpublished manuscript of *Description of Egypt*, which he had written during his first visit to Egypt. Through diligent work, Jason Thompson has finally brought *Description of Egypt* to publication after it remained for many years in manuscript form.[27]

To a large extent, I have availed myself of Thompson's edition in pointing out in my notes the passages that Poole wrote herself and those that she drew from *Description*. In many cases, she starts off by describing in her own voice a place she has visited but then reverts to what her brother had written in *Description* and copies his words. In particular, Letters V, VI, IX, XVI, XXVI, and XXVIII are taken almost verbatim from *Description*.

Poole followed Lane's example of wearing local costume, swathing herself in a *habara* whilst carefully hiding her face behind a veil. Thus disguised, she gained an anonymity that allowed her to wander freely through the streets of Cairo on her donkey. She entered mosques, visited the *maristan* (public hospital) and a public bath, and witnessed such events as the procession of the Mahmal and the Dosa, as well as weddings and funerals: places and events to which she would not have had access had she remained in western garb. She also visited her neighbors and frequented the homes of some middle-class Egyptian families. Sophia claimed that she had no difficulty in imitating the manners and customs of Egyptians and in so doing, had pleased them and secured for herself "invariable polite attention and respect."[28] This was the way Lane himself had gained access to Egyptian society and won the confidence of the people, who readily imparted to him their affairs.

Sophia Poole would talk to the women in Arabic, a language she had learned since her arrival in Egypt to prepare herself for her intended visits to the "hareems of the great."[29] It is true that Turkish was the language usually spoken in those hareems, but Arabic was also understood and spoken, especially by the younger generation. In one of her letters,[30] she describes an animated conversation "about the question of liberty of conscience on religious subjects," which took place during a visit to the hareem of Habib Effendi, and she makes the point that the ladies in the hareem are "particularly well informed and the conversation during our visit takes often a lively and a political turn." The discussion was no doubt in Arabic, for when the chief lady entered the room, "she listened with extreme interest to our conversation, which was translated to her into Turkish by her daughters." Thereupon, Poole comments that "in common with all the Turkish ladies I have seen in this country, the wife of Habeeb Effendi speaks sufficient Arabic for the usual purposes of conversation; but when any particularly interesting topic is discussed, they all like it explained in their own language." In addition to conversations on politics in some of the hareems, Poole could converse easily and with feeling about more homely matters: "The subject of the number, health, and age of each lady's children is always the darling theme of conversation in the hareems, and truly to a mother ever agreeable."[31] It also seems that Poole could translate easily from Arabic to English, for she tells how during the wedding festivities, "Nezleh Hánum . . . requested me to return the compliment for her" from one of the foreign ladies.[32]

Her feelings for her own two boys made her especially sensitive to the condition of children, and wherever she was, her attention was always drawn to them. Likewise, she would interrupt any account to comment or reflect on the state of Egyptian children. She was horrified at the numerous cases of blindness among the local children and ascribes them to the ignorance of parents and their adherence to superstitions and incorrect beliefs. She also comments on the foolishness of parents who harmed their children out of misguided fondness. While witnessing the festival of the departure of the Mahmal to Mecca, she noticed that "on one point all denominations of people seemed agreed; viz. in purchasing something for their children from almost all the venders of sweets . . . therefore their poor children kept up a continual system of cramming during the whole procession; and here my eyes were opened to a new manner of accounting for the generally wretched appearance of the children of this country. Their parents put anything and everything that is eatable into their mouths, without the slightest regard to its being wholesome or otherwise. How then can they be strong and healthy?"[33] Sophia also relates, as an instance of how children are wrongly trained, a case in which a mother pretended that she was about to beat a cat and a slave for a small boy's amusement. Her comment is succinct: "Though neither slave nor cat was a sufferer on the occasion, the effect must have been equally bad on the mind of the child."[34]

But Poole's aim was not to deal with the women of Egypt in general. Her brother had done that adequately in *Modern Egyptians*. Rather, she intended to provide an insight into the life of the hareems of the upper echelon of Egyptian society where the Turkish element predominated, which Lane was unable to provide.

The domain of the hareems would have remained a mystery were it not for women travelers who could gain access to them and were able to recount what they saw and experienced there. These visits sometimes proved rather disappointing, as can be imagined when people of different cultures briefly meet and exchange smiles and a few polite words through an interpreter. When Harriet Martineau visited a hareem in Cairo and another in Damascus, for example, she was able to see nothing there but what was apparent on the surface. Unable to converse with the women in their own language, she could find "no trace of mind" in the hareems, and what most irritated and distressed her was the vacuity and idleness of hareem life: the women appeared to her "dull, soulless, brutish or peevish."[35] Likewise, Florence Nightingale felt oppressed by what she saw as the empty, enclosed life of the hareem of Said Pasha at Alexandria. "Oh," she exclaimed, "the ennui of that magnificent palace, it will stand in my memory as a circle of hell!"[36] Both, as so many others, lacked the ability to communicate directly and did not have the time to bridge the formality of a first visit. Therein lay Sophia Poole's great advantage, as she was a resident in Egypt and had the time for more than a casual visit, as well as being able to converse in Arabic.

Poole was neither a Harriet Montague nor a Lucie Duff Gordon. She was a typical Victorian Englishwoman who shared the patriotic sentiments and religious beliefs of her countrywomen. There is no doubt that England was very interested in Egypt in the early part of the nineteenth century, and biding its time, "waiting for the plum to ripen a little more before it was finally ready to be plucked."[37] Anything, therefore, that revealed more about the country would be welcomed, and it was probably with this in mind that the Society for the Diffusion of Useful Knowledge proposed to publish Lane's *Modern Egyptians* and agreed to give him an advance to enable him to return to Egypt for additional material. On the other hand, England and the English occupied a special status in the estimation of Muhammad 'Ali, viceroy of Egypt, and this attitude was no doubt reflected in his hareems. Poole was flattered by the respect and courteous welcome she always received in the "High Hareems" and for these visits she did not wear the "Turkish dress" which she usually wore at home and when visiting ladies of the middle class, but resumed her English dress because, she maintained, "as an Englishwoman, I am entertained by the most distinguished, not only as an equal, but generally as a superior."[38] Poole underscores this observation when she writes: "I find the feeling very strong in favour of England in hareems; and I conclude that I hear general opinions echoed there. I judge not only from the remarks I hear, but from the honourable manner in which I am treated; and the reception, entertainment and farewell I experience are in every respect highly flattering."[39]

Muhammad 'Ali's wish to impress the European powers was reflected, as Poole remarked, by the attitude the ladies of his harem showed toward her. "Were I a person of rank, there would be nothing remarkable in the honourable attentions I receive; but as a private lady, I confess they are extremely beyond my anticipations."[40] But Poole served the viceroy's purpose much more than "a person of rank" would have been able to do. She was the sister of Edward Lane, whose *Modern Egyptians* had received wide acclaim not only in England but also in Europe, and it was probably a well known fact that his sister was writing a companion book about the high hareems. Every courtesy and attention, therefore, was given to the author and she was shown all that it was hoped would impress her.[41]

A clear indication of this can be seen during the eight days of festivities for the wedding of the youngest daughter of the pasha. Over a hundred European ladies were guests of the pasha's hareem, but only a few were invited to spend the nights at the palace, among them Poole and her friend Mrs. Lieder (the wife of the resident missionary, with whom Sophia had become very friendly and whose name recurs frequently in the later letters). But it was Poole alone who was singled out by Nezleh Hánum to see and handle the wedding gifts, which included priceless jewels. She was expected to give a report on what she had witnessed, and she did not fail them. Poole had only praise for the ladies, admiration for their comportment and behavior, and fascination for their jewelry, which consisted mainly of diamonds.[42] She had also been made to understand that it would be a "breach of etiquette, and contrary to hareem laws" were she to "describe *particularly* the persons of the wives of the Páshá, or any lady after distinguishing her by her name, or her situation in a family."[43] She had to be on her guard.

Undoubtedly, Lane laid at his sister's disposal the manuscript notes of his unpublished *Description of Egypt*, with occasional marginal remarks that would help her.[44] She copied freely from them, as the book was in manuscript form and there was little hope then of it ever being published. She also used *Modern Egyptians*, of course, to which she referred whenever she found herself in need of her brother's more authoritative voice on any particular subject. But it is noticeable that in a number of instances Poole, when writing in her own voice, misunderstood certain situations and fell into misconceptions through a lack of knowledge that Lane would most certainly have corrected had he seen them. For example, when she writes about the law of triple divorce in one of her stories, she entirely confuses the issue,[45] whereas, at the end of the Second Series (third volume) of *The Englishwoman in Egypt*, an appendix added by the publisher but drawn from Lane's notes to his translation of *The Thousand and One Nights* contains a passage "On Marriage," in which Lane clearly and simply explains this question. In *Modern Egyptians*, Lane also explains this matter in several places.[46] Why then would he have withheld that information from Sophia, if he had been guiding her closely?

Lane, as Poole mentioned in her preface, had promised "that he would select those letters which he should esteem suitable for publication, and mark them to be copied." This he scrupulously did and, as she acknowledges, "the present selection has been made by him." The question is, how carefully had he read them? He may have gone over them cursorily, marking them as he went, but it is very doubtful that he perused each letter carefully. After all, we must never forget that he was extremely busy at the time with his lexicon and could little afford to spare any time on anything else.

There is a lapse of eight months between the last letter of the second volume of *The Englishwoman* in April 1844 and the first letter of the Second Series (i.e., the third volume), written in January 1845.[47] This was a period of anxiety and sorrow for Lane and his family. According to Stanley Lane Poole, the news reached them in 1844 of the death of Edward and Sophia's elder brother, Theophilus Lane. Worse was to come, when both Sophia and Nefeeseh "lay dangerously ill with Cholera and typhus fever."[48] This would account for the break in her correspondence. It must have been a difficult time for the family, with Lane anxious to get on with his work, two boys in their teens needing care and attention, and the two women bedridden, needing medical attention and nursing and unable to cope with household affairs. The English physician, Dr Abbott, "to whose friendly services Lane owed much,"[49] probably provided the necessary medical care, while Mrs. Lieder may have rendered her assistance in nursing the patients and running the household.

When Poole resumed writing in 1845, her work was sporadic and heterogeneous. She started her first letter in January, her second and third were written in March, and three more appeared in April and May, to be followed by
a very long gap until December. She finally concluded her letters in March
1846. Her main contribution in this Second Series is undoubtedly her eyewitness account of the royal wedding of Zeyneb Hanum, the youngest daughter of
Muhammad 'Ali Pasha, which took place in the palace in the citadel and lasted for eight days, starting on Thursday, 18 December 1845.[50] Poole, accompanied by Mrs. Lieder, spent most of the wedding at the palace, except the
three nights between Saturday and Tuesday, in order to be with their families
on Sunday. They returned to the festivities on Tuesday and remained until two
o'clock Thursday morning, which was Christmas morning, when they drove
home through the deserted streets of Cairo. The *zaffa*, or procession of the
bride from the citadel to her own palace in the Azbakiya, took place after
church on Christmas Day but Poole was "so completely tired" that she could not
go to see it and gave a description that she had received from friends.[51]

Sophia Poole, who was meticulous in her attention to details, was at her
best when she described things she saw and experienced. Her account is
unique: there is no other description available of this historic event, and certainly not of the festivities that took place within the precincts of the viceroy's
hareem. She rendered a careful account of the inside of the palace, of the
furnishings, the guests, their clothes, their jewelry, the entertainment, and the
way European guests were made comfortable. It is surprising that Poole was
invited to view the jewelry. "I have since ascertained from the best authority
that the cost of all the diamonds given by the Páshá to his daughter on this
occasion has been 200,000*l*., and of these ornaments the girdle and a necklace are the most costly and splendid. The girdle cost 40,000*l*., the necklace
37,000*l*., the ear-rings 12,000*l*., and the bracelets 10,000*l*. sterling!"[52] As
noted above, Sophia was the only guest privileged to see these fabulous
treasures. Through her vivid word-painting, she fulfilled her wish that the
"fairy-like scenes" she was witnessing could be "transferred to canvas" so
that her friends in England might be able "to form some idea of Eastern
magnificence."[53] And after more than 150 years, we can still transform her
words into mental images.

We know that farces were performed as entertainment during the times of
the Mamluks and Muhammad 'Ali, but we learn from Poole that "a company
of European actors" gave a performance in "an apartment which had been
fitted up as a theatre."[54] This was part of the entertainment the pasha provided
for his male guests. It is a great pity that Poole does not elaborate on the subject. Knowledge of the nationality of the company and the play they presented
would have been of great value to us today.

Lane, of course, was too busy working on his lexicon to spend time at weddings and such like frivolities; and Poole, who wished to complete her picture
of a grand wedding by presenting not only the female festivities but also those
provided for the men, had to draw on the notes her brother had taken at a
"public ceremonial" ten years previously on the occasion of the marriage of a
sister of Ahmad Pasha, a nephew of the viceroy.[55] The account is verbatim from

Lane and relates events that took place over eight nights, with only a few intro-
ductory words by Poole, and a final paragraph in which she remarks on the
elegance of the "equipages of the present day in Cairo" relative to the "shabbiness of the carriages used by the grandees ten years since," as described by
her brother.[56]

It is a great pity that Sophia Poole, with the unique opportunities she
enjoyed, did not write more than she did about her experiences in Egypt. But
as it stands, *The Englishwoman in Egypt* is a mine of information and furnishes
valuable knowledge, scarcely found elsewhere, about conditions in the country
during the first half of the nineteenth century. We should be thankful to have her
book as a complement to Lane's *Modern Egyptians*, to give us a picture of some
aspects of that crucial historical time that initiated the birth of modern Egypt.

A Note on the Text

A number of appendices were added to the second and third volumes of *The
Englishwoman in Egypt* by the London publisher Charles Knight, who took them
from Edward Lane's *Modern Egyptians* and his notes to his translation of *The
Thousand and One Nights*. Since they were neither written nor selected by
Sophia Poole, I have omitted them from this edition.

The Second Series (third volume) carried an errata note to Volumes I and II,
and I have made those corrections in this edition. Most of them are minor:
'Arabian' for 'Arabic'; 'El-Kal'ah' for 'El-Kat'ah'; 'Lepsius' for 'Lipsius'; 'mezz'
for 'nurz'; 'Libyan Desert' for 'Syrian Desert.' One was more serious: "Page
206, line 16, and subsequently throughout the work, for 'Mrs. Sieder,' read
'Mrs. Lieder.'" I have also corrected a very few other evident misprints, such as
the date in Letter XV from 1833 to 1843.

Volume I of the *The Englishwoman in Egypt* contained eleven illustrations,
Volume II fifteen, and the Second Series (third volume) none. The illustrations
were selected from those in *The Thousand and One Nights* and *Modern
Egyptians* and the ones Lane had prepared for *Description of Egypt*.[57] As the
illustrations were not originally made for *The Englishwoman in Egypt*, and as
they are not of a good quality, I have dispensed with them in this edition.

Sophia Poole's original footnotes are numbered on each page; my own
comments are footnoted with asterisks and daggers.

Acknowledgments

My thanks and gratitude go to those who will always be associated in my mind
with the preparation of this edition: Amin Morsi Kandeel, Amr El-Abbadi,
Abdelsalam Heddaya, Dorothy Thompson, Hala Halim, Hind Kararah, Jason
Thompson, Lionel Thompson, Mohammed Awad, Nadia Zeitoun, Roger
Bagnall, and first and foremost, Mostafa El-Abbadi.

Notes

1. Charles Knight was among the pioneers of the publication of "cheap literature," first publishing the letters in monthly installments, selling at 2s.6d.each. See Leila Ahmed, *Edward W. Lane*, 150.
2. Jason Thompson, "Edward William Lane's 'Description of Egypt,'" 565–83.
3. Alexander Kinglake, "The Rights of Women," 108.
4. For example, Sahar Sobhi Abdel-Hakim, in her essay "Sophia Poole: Writing the Self, Scribing Egyptian Women," 107–26, suggests "the accessibility of the naked premier to imperial males" (118) by telling the story of the two Europeans who, she says, while wandering in the Shubra palace gardens, "ended up in the presence of Mohammad Ali, naked in his bath." Poole, however, mentions this incident only to show that "the houses of the grandees, separate from their hareems, are generally accessible; and the liberty of ingress is sometimes not a little abused." The Europeans, writes Poole, at length "entered the bedroom of the Páshá, where sat his highness, nearly undressed! Although taken by surprise, his Turkish coolness did not forsake him: calling for his dragoman, he said, 'Enquire of those gentlemen where they bought their tarbooshes.' The Europeans replied, 'They were purchased in Constantinople;' 'and *there*,' rejoined the Páshá, 'I suppose they learned their manners. Tell them so.' Judging from this retort that their presence was not agreeable, the Franks saluted the viceroy and withdrew" (Letter XXII). The same writer again misunderstands the text when she claims that Sophia and Lane "co-authored the narrative of the wedding of Zeinab Hanem" (109). It is true that Sophia described the celebrations in the 'hareem' while Lane delineated those of the men (Letter VI, Second Series), but they were two different weddings with a gap of ten years between them.
5. Kararah, *Harim Muhammad 'Ali Basha.*
6. Venn, *Alumni Cantabrigienses.*
7. Crockford's *Clerical Directory* recorded that he was first curate and then vicar of Boulton and Alvaston, near Derby. There is no mention of him after that date.
8. Reginald was one of the founding members, with Amelia Edwards, of the Egypt Exploration Fund (now the Egypt Exploration Society).
9. Lane Poole, *Life of Edward Lane*, 111. When referring to the death of Lane's mother in 1841, Lane Poole mentions "Mrs. Poole, who had lived in late years always with her mother." On page 135, when referring to the death of his own father, Edward Stanley Poole, in 1867, he writes: "Twenty-seven years before, [Lane] had taken to his home his sister and her sons."
10. Ahmed, *Lane*, 33–34.
11. Ahmed, *Lane*, 38–40.
12. Ahmed, *Lane*, 38 n.66.
13. Lane, MS Letters, no. 61, 30 June 1840; cf. Ahmed, *Lane*, 49 n.73.
14. Lane, MS Letters, no. 78, 17 December 1844; cf. Ahmed, *Lane*, 50 n.74.
15. Ahmed, *Lane*, 42.
16. Ahmed, *Lane*, 43; Lane Poole, *Life*, 125–26.
17. Lane Poole, *Life*, 111. In a letter on 1 June 1842, Theo, the eldest brother, wrote to Richard, saying: "In expectation of a letter from dearest Sophy . . . Very anxious to know whether they have succeeded in obtaining the means of going with dear Ned to Egypt as I consider it to be conducive to their mutual comfort and happiness, that they should if practicable be together. . . . Give my best love to her and thanks for the presents, also to Nefeeseh for hers. I shall depend upon being given all particulars as to dearest Sophy . . . and how often and by what means I can write to Egypt" (Edward Lane Papers, Univ. Library, Cambridge, Add. 8843).
18. Lane Poole, *Life*, 103–7.

19. "The Pasha himself, Mohammad 'Alee, was anxious to further the work by any means in his power, and the Prime Minister, Arteen Bey, called upon Lane with the view of discovering in what manner the Government could assist him. But the loan of manuscripts from the Mosques was a request beyond the power even of Mohammad 'Alee to grant; and Lane had to submit to the tedious process of borrowing through his Sheykh a few pages at a time, which were copied and then exchanged for a few more" (Lane Poole, *Life*, 118).
20. Lane Poole, *Life*, 116–17.
21. Leila Ahmed recounts how Lane had disconcerted Charles Knight (his publisher) when at a dinner of the "best society" he had turned to him and whispered, "I can not endure these chairs, I will tuck my legs under me and then I shall be comfort able." Ahmed, *Lane*, 33.
22. Lane Poole, *Life*, 120.
23. Lane, *MS Letters*, no. 78, 17 December 1844; cf. Ahmed, *Lane*, 40.
24. Lane Poole, *Life*, 116.
25. Lane Poole, *Life*, 113–15.
26. Letter XX, July 1843.
27. Lane's *Description of Egypt* was eventually published by the American University in Cairo Press in 2000.
28. Letter XVII, April 1843.
29. Letter IV, August 1842.
30. Letter XXX, April 1844.
31. *Ibid.*
32. Letter IX (Second Series), December 1845.
33. Letter VIII, 26 November 1842.
34. Letter XXIV, February 1844. Lisa Bernasek ("Unveiling the Orient, Unmasking Orientalism," 75) misrepresents Poole when she writes that the "chief lady . . . orders a cat and a slave beaten for the entertainment of her infant son."
35. Harriet Martineau, *Eastern Life Present and Past*, as quoted by Joan Rees, *Writings on the Nile*, 42–43. Martineau considered hareem life a form of slavery, as did many other European women travelers. Cf. the German Ida Hahn-Hahn, who talks about the "Joch des Harems" and condemns the "Reich der Despotie und Sclaverei" in her 1842 *Orientalische Briefe*, as quoted in Deeken and Bösel, *An den süssen Wassern Asiens*, 103.
36. Florence Nightingale, *Letters from Egypt*, as quoted in Rees, *Writings*, 66.
37. James Aldridge, *Cairo*, 187.
38. Letter XV, February 1843.
39. Letter XX, July 1843.
40. Letter XXIII, January 1844.
41. Later, in 1870, Khedive Ismail invited a German writer, Louise Mülbach, with her daughter and a maid, to visit Egypt as "auteur distinguée," in order to write about the new developments in the country and, in particular, about his grandfather Muhammad 'Ali. Deeken and Bösel, *An den süssen Wassern Asiens*, 173–79.
42. Letter VII (Second Series), 16 December 1845.
43. Letter XXI, September 1843.
44. Jason Thompson, "Editor's Introduction" to Lane, *Description*, xxiii–xxiv.
45. Letter I (Second Series), January 1845.
46. Lane, *Modern Egyptians* 98–100, 179.
47. A note by the London editor of *The Englishwoman* appears at the end of Volume II: "This Series of Letters abruptly terminates. The last letter, dated April, 1844, with several others, arrived from Cairo in May, and were delivered for publication. Since then, through some accidental circumstances, the communication has been interrupted."

48. Lane Poole, *Life,* 120–21.
49. Lane Poole, *Life,* 113.
50. Letter VII (Second Series), 16 December 1845.
51. Letter IX (Second Series), December 1845.
52. Letter VII (Second Series), 16 December 1845.
53. Letter VIII (Second Series), December 1845.
54. *Ibid.*
55. Letter VI (Second Series), May 1845.
56. *Ibid.*
57. See Jason Thompson, "Editor's Introduction" to Lane, *Description,* xxix–xxx.

Bibliography

El-Abbadi, Mostafa, *Life and Fate of the Ancient Library of Alexandria* (Paris: Unesco, 1990).

Abdel-Hakim, Sahar Sobhi, "Sophia Poole: Writing the Self, Scribing Egyptian Women" (*Alif* 22, Cairo: The American University in Cairo Press, 2002).

Ahmed, Leila, *Edward W. Lane* (Longman: London & Beirut, 1978).

Aldridge, James, *Cairo* (Boston: Little, Brown, 1969).

Bernasek, Lisa, "Unveiling the Orient, Unmasking Orientalism: Sophia Poole's *The Englishwoman in Egypt,*" *Cairo Papers in Social Science,* vol. 23, no. 3 ("Egyptian Encounters"), edited by Jason Thompson (Cairo: The American University in Cairo Press, 2002).

Breccia E.V., *Alexandrea ad Aegyptum* (Bergamo: Instituto Italiano d'Arti Grafiche, 1922).

Crockford's *Clerical Directory* (London, 1841–84).

Damer, G.L., *Diary of a Tour in Greece, Turkey and Egypt* (London, 1841).

Deeken, A. and M. Bösel, *An den süssen Wassern Asiens* (Frankfurt: Campus Verlag, 1996).

Duff Gordon, Lucie, *Letters from Egypt (1862–69)* (London: Virago Press, 1983).

Farid, Zeinab, "Ta'lim al-bint fi Misr," M.A. thesis, Faculty of Education, Ain Shams University 1961.

Forster, E.M., *Alexandria: A History and a Guide* (Alexandria: Whitehead Morris Limited, 2nd ed. 1938, 1st ed. 1922).

Hahn-Hahn, Ida, *Orientalische Briefe* (Berlin, 1842).

al-Jabarti, Abd al-Rahman, 'Aja'ib al-athar fi-l-tarajim wa-l-akhbar (Bulaq: Dar al-Tuba'a, 1880).

Kararah, Azza, *Harim Muhammad 'Ali Basha* (Cairo: Sutoor, 1999; revised edition 2000).

Khalifa, Iglal, *al-Haraka al-nisa'iya al-haditha.* (Cairo, 1973).

Kinglake, Alexander, "The Rights of Women," *Quarterly Review* (December, 1844).

Lane, Edward William, *An Account of the Manners and Customs of the Modern Egyptians: Written in Egypt during the Years 1833, —34, and —35, Partly from Notes Made during a Former Visit to That Country in the Years 1825, —26, —27, and —28* (first published by Charles Knight in London in 1836; fifth edition, 1860, reprinted with an introduction by Jason Thompson: Cairo: The American University in Cairo Press, 2003).

——, *Description of Egypt: Notes and views in Egypt and Nubia, made during the years 1825, —26, —27, and —28,* edited and with an introduction by Jason Thompson (Cairo: The American University in Cairo Press, 2000).

——, MS Letters, Bodleian Library, Letters to Robert Hay, MS Eng. lett. d. 165.

——, *The Thousand and One Nights, commonly called in England The Arabian Nights' Entertainments.* A new translation from the Arabic, with copious notes, by Edward William Lane (London: Charles Knight, 1839).

Lane Poole, Stanley, *Life of Edward Lane* (London: Williams and Norgate, 1877).

Malval, B. and G. Jondet, *Le Port d'Alexandrie* (Cairo: Imprimerie Nationale, 1912).

Martineau, Harriet, *Eastern Life Present and Past* (London: E. Moxam, 1848).

Montagu, Lady Mary Wortley, *The Turkish Embassy Letters* (London: Virago Press, 1994).

Nightingale, Florence, *Letters from Egypt* (London: Spottiswood, 1854).

Rees, Joan, *Writings on the Nile* (London: The Rubicon Press, 1995).

Thompson, Jason, "Edward William Lane's 'Description of Egypt,'" *International Journal of Middle East Studies*, 28 (1996).

Urquhart, D., *The Spirit of the East* (London, 2nd ed. 1839).

Venn, J.A., *Alumni Cantabrigienses: a biographical list of all known students, graduates and holders of office at the University of Cambridge from the earliest times to 1900, Part 2 1752–1900* (Cambridge: Cambridge University Press, 1922–54).

Wilkinson, Sir John Gardner, *Manners and Customs of the Ancient Egyptians* (London, 1837).

The Englishwoman in Egypt

Contents

or Castle of the Ram—Sebeels, or public fountains—Hods, or watering-places for beasts of burden—Hammáms, or public baths—Kahwehs, or coffee-shops

Second Series

Polite attention of Nezleh Hánum—More dancing and a farce—Winter wrappers of ladies—Night arrangements in the hareem—The Páshá dropping gold coins in the hareem—Little Eastern lady—Eunuchs clearing the apartments—Throng of visitors—Passage of the bride on the seventh day of the feast—Her gorgeous dress—Child trodden to death during a shower of gold—The procession of candles—Procession of the bride from the citadel to her own palace

PREFACE

THE desire of shortening the period of my separation from a beloved brother, was the first and strongest motive that induced me to think of accompanying him to the country in which I am now writing, and which he was preparing to visit for the third time. An eager curiosity, mainly excited by his own publications, greatly increased this desire; and little persuasion on his part was necessary to draw me to a decision; but the idea was no sooner formed than he found numerous arguments in its favour. The opportunities I might enjoy of obtaining an insight into the mode of life of the higher classes of the ladies in this country, and of seeing many things highly interesting in themselves, and rendered more so by their being accessible only to a lady, suggested to him the idea that I might both gratify my own curiosity and collect much information of a novel and interesting nature, which he proposed I should embody in a series of familiar letters to a friend. To encourage me to attempt this latter object, he placed at my disposal a large collection of his own unpublished notes, that I might extract from them, and insert in my letters whatever I might think fit; and in order that I might record my impressions and observations with less restraint than I should experience if always feeling that I was writing for the press, he promised me that he would select those letters which he should esteem suitable for publication, and mark them to be copied. The present selection has been made by him; and I fear the reader may think that affection has sometimes biassed his judgment; but am encouraged to hope for their favourable reception, for the sake of the more solid matter with which they are interspersed, from the notes of one to whom Egypt has become almost as familiar as England.

SOPHIA POOLE

LETTER I

Alexandria, July, 1842

MY DEAR FRIEND,

THE blessing of going into port, at the conclusion of a first long voyage, awakens feelings so deep and so lasting, that it must form a striking era in the life of every traveller. Eagerly, during a long morning, did I and my children[†] strain our eyes as the low uninteresting coast of Egypt spread before our view, that we might catch the first glimpse of one or more of those monuments of which we had hitherto only heard or read. The first object which met our view was the Arab Tower,[‡] which stands on a little elevation; and shortly after, the new lighthouse on the peninsula of the Pharos, and the Pasha's army of windmills, showed our near approach to Alexandria, and the Pillar (commonly called Pompey's) seemed to rise from the bay.

The coast presents to the Mediterranean a long sandy flat, bearing throughout a most desolate aspect, and in no part more so than in the neighbourhood of Alexandria. To the west of this town we see nothing but a tract of yellowish calcareous rock and sand, with here and there a few stunted palm-trees, which diversify but little the dreary prospect.

The old or western harbour (anciently called Eunostos Portus) is deeper and more secure than the new harbour (which is called Magnus Portus).[††] The former, which was once exclusively appropriated to the vessels of the Muslims, is now open to the ships of all nations; and the latter, which was "the harbour of the infidels," is almost deserted. The entrance of the old harbour is rendered difficult by reefs of rocks, leaving three natural passages, of which the central has the greatest depth of water.[‡‡] The rocks occasion a most

---

[†]Edward Stanley Poole (1830–79) and Reginald Stuart Poole (1832–95).

[‡]Abusir, the Taposiris Magna of antiquity.

[††]Portus Magnus is the Eastern Harbor, where the battle between Caesar and Ptolemy XIII took place in 48/47 B.C.

[‡‡]Sophia, following Lane, calls the western harbor "old" and the eastern harbor "new," cf. Lane, *Description of Egypt*, 3. This appellation corresponds with the map of the two ports of Alexandria produced in the *Description de l'Egypte* 1798–1802 (E.M. vol. II, pl. 84), where the eastern harbor is called "neuf" and the western "vieux." Cf. B. Malval and G. Jondet, *Le Port d'Alexandrie*. To call the eastern harbour 'new' and the western 'old' may surprise the modern reader who is familiar with the city only after the changes started by Muhammad Ali circa 1818, when he abandoned the Portus Magnus of the ancients and embarked upon ambitious plans for the renovation and restoration of the western harbor so that it has become ever since the main, modern

13

unpleasant swell, from which we all suffered, but I especially; and I cannot describe how thankfully I stepped on shore, having passed the smooth water of the harbour. Here already I see so much upon which to remark, that I must indulge myself by writing two or three letters before our arrival in Cairo,[†] where the state of *Arabian* society being unaltered by European innovations, I hope to observe much that will interest you with respect to the condition of the native female society. I do not mean to give you many remarks on the manners and customs of the male portion of the people, my brother having written so full a description of them, the correctness of which has been attested by numerous persons, who cannot be suspected (as his sister might be) of undue partiality.

To tell you of our landing, of the various and violent contentions of the Arab boatmen for the conveyance of our party, of our really polite reception at the custom-house, and of our thankfulness when enjoying the quiet of our hotel, would be to detain you from subjects far more interesting; but I long to describe the people by whom we were surrounded, and the noisy crowded streets and lanes through which we passed. The streets, until we arrived at the part of the town inhabited by Franks, were so narrow that it was extremely formidable to meet anything on our way. They are miserably close, and for the purpose of shade the inhabitants have in many cases thrown matting from roof to roof, extending across the street, with here and there a

---

harbor of Egypt (cf. Malval and Jondet, *Le Port.* 17, 27 ff.) In agreement with this, Breccia in his *Alexandrea ad Aegyptum*, 77, calls Port Eunostos, i.e., the western harbor, "our modern harbor." An explanation for calling the eastern harbour "new," may be found in what Gratien Le Père mentions in *Description de l'Egypte* about the development of the city of Alexandria prior to the French expedition. He says that a new "modern city" was constructed on the alluvium accumulated on the shore of the eastern harbor, south of the rock of Pharos, in the middle of the sixteenth century, a few years after the Ottoman conquest of Egypt by Sultan Selim in 1517 (now known as the Turkish City). A new quay was no doubt constructed for the landing of ships and the name "new" could therefore also have been applied to the harbor. Le Père also remarked that Leo Africanus (Hasan al-Wazaan), who visited Alexandria in 1517, the very year of the Ottoman conquest, called the eastern harbor "Marsa al-Silsila" ('harbour of the chain'), in accordance with the ancient custom of closing the entrance of the harbor by night with a chain (*Description de l'Egypte*, "Memoire sur la Ville d'Alexandrie," 487). The ancient Cape Lochias is known nowadays as al-Silsila ('the chain').

[†]The first three letters Sophia wrote, about her landing in Alexandria with her brother Edward Lane, his wife Nefeeseh, and her two sons Stanley and Stuart, aged 12 and 10 respectively, and their further journey to Cairo, merely state the month and the year (July 1842) without specifying the exact date. This implies that they were written later on in Cairo, when she had settled down and had had leisure to examine the manuscript notes of Lane's *Description of Egypt*, which he had placed at her disposal.

small aperture to admit light; but the edges of these apertures are generally broken, and the torn matting hanging down: in short, the whole appearance is gloomy and wretched. I ought not, however, to complain of the narrowness of the streets, for where the sun is not excluded by matting, the deep shade produced by the manner in which the houses are constructed is most welcome in this sunny land; and, indeed, when we arrived at the Frank part of the town, which is in appearance almost European, and where a wide street and a fine open square form a singular contrast to the Arab part of the town, we scarcely congratulated ourselves; for the heat was intense, and we hastened to our hotel, and gratefully enjoyed the breeze which played through the apartments. I hear that many persons prefer the climate of Alexandria to that of Cairo, and pronounce it to be more salubrious; but a Caireen tells me that their opinion is false—that it is certainly cooler, but that the air is extremely damp, and although the inhabitants generally enjoy a sea breeze, that luxury involves some discomfort.

But I must tell you of the people; for there appeared to my first view none but dignified grandees, in every variety of costume, and miserable beggars, co closely assembled in the narrow streets that it seemed as though they had congregated on the occasion of some public festival. On examining more closely, however, I found many gradations in the style of dress of the middle and higher classes; but the manner of the Eastern (even that of the well-clothed servant) is so distinguished, and their carriage is so superior, that a European glancing for the first time at their picturesque costume, and observing their general bearing, may be perfectly at a loss as to what may be their position in society.

I believe that I have already seen persons of almost every country bordering on the Mediterranean, and I can convey but a very imperfect idea of such a scene. The contrast between the rich and gaudy habits of the higher classes, and the wretched clothing of the bare-footed poor, while many children of a large growth are perfectly in a state of nudity, produced a most remarkable effect. The number of persons nearly or entirely blind, and especially the aged blind, affected us exceedingly, but we rejoiced in the evident consideration they received from all who had occasion to make room for them to pass. I should imagine that all who have visited this country have remarked the decided respect which is shown to those who are superior in years; and that this respect is naturally rendered to the beggar as well as to the prince. In fact, the people are educated in the belief that there is honour in the "hoary head," and this glorious sentiment strengthens with their strength, and beautifully influences their conduct.

Many of the poor little infants called forth painfully my sympathy: their heads drooped languidly; and their listless, emaciated limbs showed too plainly that their little race was nearly run; while the evident tenderness of their mothers made me grieved to think what they might be called on to

endure. You will naturally infer that I expect few children to pass the season
of infancy, and you will conclude justly; for I cannot look at these little creatures, and suppose that they will survive what is here the most trying time,
the season of dentition. I may have been unfortunate; for among the numerous
infants we have passed, I have only seen two who were able to hold their
heads in an erect position, and indeed, of those past infancy, most were
wretched-looking children. Over their dark complexions there is a white lep-
rous hue, and they have a quiet melancholy manner, and an air of patient
endurance, which affected me sensibly.

It is sad to see the evident extreme poverty of the lower orders; and the
idle, lounging manner of the working class surprised me: and yet when
called on to larbour, I am informed that no people work so heartily, and so
patiently. I rather think they are very like their good camels in disposition,
with the exception that the latter scold often if an attempt be made to
overload them, and in some cases will not rise from their knees until
relieved of part of their burden, while the Arabs really suffer themselves to
be built up with loads as though they had no more sense of oppression than
a truck or wheelbarrow. The Arab groom, too, will run by the side of his
master's horse for as many hours as he requires his attendance without a
murmur. The physical strength of these people is most extraordinary. I had
an opportunity of remarking this during the removal of our luggage from
the boat.

The windows of our hotel command a view of the great square, and I can
scarcely describe to you the picturesque attraction of the scene. Among the
various peculiarities of dress, feature, and complexion, which characterize the
natives of Africa and the East, none are more striking than those which distinguish the noble and hardy western Bedawee, enveloped as he is in his
ample woollen shirt, or hooded cloak, and literally clothed suitably for a
Russian winter. You will believe that my attention has been directed to the
veiled women, exhibiting in their dull disguise no other attraction than a
degree of stateliness in their carriage, and a remarkable beauty in their large
dark eyes, which, besides being sufficiently distinguished by nature, are rendered more conspicuous by the black border of kohl round the lashes, and by
the concealment of the rest of the features. The camel-drivers' cries "O'a,"
"Guarda," and "Sákin,"[1] resound every where, and at every moment, therefore, you may imagine the noise and confusion in the streets.

In the open space before the hotel there are long trains of camels laden
with water-skins, or with bales of merchandise, winding slowly and cautiously along even in this wide place, while their noiseless tread, and their
dignified (I might almost say affected) walk, at once distinguishes them from
all other beasts of burden.

---

[1]"Take care," in Arabic, Italian, and Turkish.

I must not omit mentioning the shops of Alexandria, for they resemble cupboards rather than rooms; and this I understand to be the case in most Turkish and Arabian cities. A raised seat of brick or stone about three feet high, and the same or more in width, extends along each side of the street, and upon this the tradesman sits before his shop, either smoking or at work. It is really amusing to see how easily they appear to gain their livelihood: the fact is, that they are an exceedingly contented people, and there is much of real philosophy in their conclusions. They are seldom disposed, when working on their own account, to labour for more than enough, and have the quality, so rarely found in Europe, of considering that enough is as desirable as abundance: therefore they are happy, and "their best riches, ignorance of wealth." I have observed, at corners of the streets, or wherever else there was sufficient space, groups of men and women seated on the ground, with baskets before them containing bread and vegetables for sale.

The quarter occupied by the Europeans is the south-eastern part of the town, by the shore of the new harbour. This situation I conclude was chosen for the convenience of landing and shipping their merchandise; but now that the old harbour is open to their vessels, the situation is not so advantageous for them. On the east side of the great square is a large building called the New Wekáleh (by the Europeans Occále), for the reception of merchants and others, on the shore of the new harbour. It surrounds a spacious square court; and the ground-floor of the building consists of magazines towards the court, and shops and the entrances of the dwellings towards the exterior.

My brother has given me a piece of information with regard to the present Pharos, which you shall receive in his own words:—[†]

"The modern Pharos is a poor successor of the ancient building, erected by Sostratus Cnidius, from which it derives its name; though from a distance it has rather an imposing appearance. Several Arab historians mention the telescopic mirror of metal which was placed at the summit of the ancient Pharos. In this mirror, vessels might be discerned at sea at a very great distance. El-Makreezee[1] informs us that the Greeks, being desirous of effecting the destruction of the Pharos, or of obtaining possession of the wonderful mirror, employed a deep stratagem. One of their country-men repaired to the sovereign of the Arabs, El-Weleed the son of 'Abd-el-Melik, and professed himself a convert to the faith of El-Islám, pretending that he had fled from his king, who would have put him to death. He informed the prince that he had acquired, from certain books in his possession, the art of discovering where treasures were concealed in the earth, and had thus ascertained that there was a valuable treasure, consisting of money and jewels, deposited beneath the foundations of the Pharos of Alexandria. The prince, deceived by

---

[†]Lane, *Description*, 7–8.
[1]El-Makreezee flourished in the 14th and 15th centuries.

this artful tale, sent a number of workmen with his crafty adviser to pull down the Pharos; and when more than half the building had been destroyed, the Greek made his escape to his own country, and his artifice thus became manifest. The same author relates that part of the Pharos was thrown down by an earthquake in the year of the Flight 177 (A.D. 793–4); that Ahmad Ibn-Tooloon surmounted it with a dome of wood; and that an inscription upon a plate of lead was found upon the northern side, buried in the earth, written in ancient Greek characters, every letter of which was a cubit in height, and a span in breadth. This was perhaps the inscription placed by the original architect, and which, according to Strabo, was to this effect—'Sostratus Cnidius, the son of Dexiphanes, to the protecting Gods, for the sake of the mariners.' It is also related by Es-Sooyootee,[1] that the inhabitants of Alexandria likewise made use of the mirror above mentioned to burn the vessels of their enemies, by directing it so as to reflect the concentrated rays of the sun upon them."

The causeway of stone which connects the fort and lighthouse with the peninsula of Pharos, is now called Ródat-el-Teen (or the Garden of the Fig), on account of a few fig-trees growing there. Its south-western extremity is called Rás-et-Teen (or the Cape of the Fig). Upon this rocky peninsula are a palace of the Pasha, and some other buildings, with the burial-ground of the Muslims, adjacent to the town.[†]

I must endeavour in my next letter to give you a brief general account of the town, and must close this by remarking on the affecting sound of the Mueddin's chant or Muslim call to prayer. I should be grieved to think that we are impressed by the solemnity of their sonorous voices, simply because we hear them for the first time; and trust we may always feel a mixture of pity and admiration when we believe our fellow-creatures to be in earnest in the service of God, however mistaken their opinions.[‡] The sight of the Muslim engaged in his devotions I think most interesting; and it cannot fail, I should hope, in impressing the beholder with some degree of veneration. The attitudes are peculiarly striking and expressive; and the solemn demeanour of the worshipper, who, even in the busy market-place, appears wholly abstracted from the concerns of the world, is very remarkable. The practice of praying in a public place is so general in the East, and attracts so little notice on the part of Muslims, that we must be charitable, and must not regard it as a result of hypocrisy or ostentation.

---

[1] A celebrated Arab theologian and historian, so called from his birth-place Usyoot or Suyoot (commonly pronounced Asyoot), in Upper Egypt.
[†] Known nowadays as the Turkish part of the city.
[‡] The following remarks are verbatim from Lane, *Description*, 5.

LETTER II

Alexandria, July, 1842

MY DEAR FRIEND,

WE find little to interest us in this place, excepting by association with bygone times; therefore our stay will not be long. But I will give you concisely an account of all that has excited our curiosity.

I am not disappointed in Alexandria (or, as it is called by the natives, El-Iskendereeyeh), for I did not imagine it could possess many attractions. It is built upon a narrow neck of land, which unites the peninsula of Pharos to the continent, and thus forms a double harbour, as did anciently the causeway, which, from its length of seven stadia,† was called the Heptastadium.

The ground which is occupied by the modern town has been chiefly formed by a gradual deposit of sand on each side of the Heptastadium; and the present situation is more advantageous for a commercial city than the ancient site. The houses are generally built of white calcareous stone, with a profusion of mortar and plaster. Some have the foundation walls only of stone, and the superstructure of brick. They generally have plain or projecting windows of wooden lattice-work; but the windows of some houses, viz., those of Europeans, the palaces of the Pasha, the governor of Alexandria, and a few others, are of glass. The roofs are flat and covered with cement. There is little to admire in the interior architecture of the houses, excepting that they have a substantial appearance. Many ancient columns of granite and marble have been used in the construction of the mosques and private dwellings.

The water here is far from good; the inhabitants receive their supply from the cisterns under the site of the ancient city (of which I must tell you by and by). These are filled by subterranean aqueducts from the canal during the time of the greatest height of the Nile; but in consequence of the saline nature of the soil through which it passes from the river, the water is not good. Almost every house has its cistern, which is filled by means of skins borne by camels or asses; and there are many wells of brackish water in the town.

As the northern coast of Egypt has no harbour, excepting those of Alexandria, it is a place of considerable importance as the emporium and key of Egypt; but otherwise it appears to me in no respect a desirable residence, and around it nothing but sea and desert meets the eye, excepting here and

---

†One stadium (pl. stadia) equaled approximately 190 meters.

there the house of a rich man, and scattered in every direction extensive mounds of rubbish. Ancient writers have extolled the *salubrity* of the air of Alexandria. This quality of the air was attributed, according to Strabo, to the almost insular situation of the city, the sea being on one side, and the lake Mareotis on the other. The *insalubrity* of climate, of late years, has been regarded as the result of the conversion of the lake into a salt marsh. The English army, in 1801, made a cut by which the water of the sea was admitted from the lake of Aboo-keer into the bed of the lake Mareotis; and the operation was repeated by Mohammed 'Alee in 1803, and again by the English in 1807: on each occasion, as you will have supposed, military policy dictated the measure; and as soon as the object in view had been attained, the gap was speedily closed, as it cut off the supply of fresh water from Alexandria by interrupting the course of the canal. While the communication between the two lakes remained open, it was not found that the climate of Alexandria was at all improved; and the evaporation of the waters of the lake Mareotis afterwards must have had a pernicious effect. The damp and rain during the winter here, and the heavy dew at night throughout the year, have a particularly baneful influence. Cases of fever are very general; and it is always observed that this town is one of the places where the plague makes its appearance many days earlier than in the interior of Egypt. With all these objections to Alexandria as a place of residence, it is wonderful that any persons should prefer it, and consider the climate more agreeable than that of the valley of the Nile, which all allow to be so salubrious.

There is a series of telegraphs from Alexandria to the metropolis, a distance of more than a hundred and twenty British miles. The towers composing this series are nineteen in number; the first is on the peninsula of Pharos, and the last in the citadel of Cairo.

The wall which surrounds the site of the old Arab city was rebuilt not many years since. This work was commenced in 1811. Mohammed 'Alee, fearing another invasion of the French, deemed it necessary to strengthen this place; for the wall I have mentioned defends the town on the land-side, and surrounds the cisterns from which the inhabitants derive their supply of fresh water. The wall has four gates, and I cannot describe to you the complete scene of desolation which presented itself on entering the enclosure by that gate which is nearest to the modern town, the "sea-gate;" indeed, it can scarcely be conceived: for mounds of rubbish and drifted sand occupy nearly the whole site of the ancient city. Within the area surrounded by the present wall, besides some monuments of the ancient city, are two convents and a synagogue, several groups of houses and huts, with a few walled gardens containing chiefly palm-trees.

You will think it strange when I tell you that there are also two lofty hills of rubbish, each of which is surmounted by a fort, commanding an extensive view. It appears to me most extraordinary that any persons should choose such a foundation; but I understand it is far from remarkable, and that these accidental eminences are improved to advantage in this flat country, the face of which in a course of years has undergone important changes, from the habit of the people of leaving crumbling ruins to accumulate. Here the line of the principal street can be traced extending in a straight direction from the shore of the old harbour to the Gate of Resheed,[1] which is at the eastern extremity of the enclosure; and the direction of the other great street, which crossed the former at right angles, is observable.

It must have been an extensive city, but it is impossible to mark its precise limits. Certainly its remains alone convey an idea of its having been a flourishing town, and considerably more important than the Arab city which succeeded it.

Desiring to see the Obelisks before the heat of the day, we set out early, and having passed the great square, we entered the field of ruins, and found a number of peasants loitering among miserable huts, while a few children, in a state of nudity, and extremely unsightly in form, were standing or sitting in the entrances of their dwellings. I was grieved to see that the bodies of these poor little children were distended to a most unnatural size; while their limbs, which were very thin and small, appeared, from the contrast, to be sadly emaciated.

Among the mounds we observed the mouths of some of the ancient cisterns; each, with few exceptions, having the hollowed marble base of an ancient column placed over it. The cisterns seem to have extended under a great part of the ancient city; and there remain a sufficient number of them open and in good repair for the supply of the modern town. They have arched or vaulted roofs, which are supported by columns or by square pillars, and some of them have two or three ranges of pillars and arches, one above another, and are very extensive.[†]

We saw little worthy of remark until we reached the Obelisks, which are situated at an angle of the enclosure, almost close to the shore of the new harbour; I mean those Obelisks called Cleopatra's Needles. Each is composed of a single block of red granite, nearly seventy feet in length, and seven feet and a half wide at the base. And here I wondered, as so many have done before me, that the ancient Egyptians contrived to raise such solid masses, and concluded that their knowledge of machinery, of which they have left such extraordinary proofs, must have been remarkable indeed.

Three lines of hieroglyphics adorn each of the four faces of either monument. My brother tells me that the central line bears the title and name of

---

[1]Resheed is the name of the town which the English call Rosetta.
[†]Breccia, *Alexandrea ad Aegyptum*, 81, informs us that at the time of the French expedition there were still 308 cisterns in use, and that Mahmoud al-Falaki knew of 700 in 1872.

Thothmos the Third, who appears, from strong evidence, to have reigned
shortly before the departure of the Israelites from Egypt: the lateral lines
were sculptured at a later period; for they bear the name of Rameses the
Great, or Sesostris. The inscriptions near the base of the erect Obelisk seemed
nearly obliterated, and the prostrate one is so encumbered with rubbish, that
much of it is concealed. Pliny relates that Ramses erected four obelisks at
Heliopolis: those of Alexandria are perhaps two of the four thus alluded to.
Their antiquity being so much greater than that of Alexandria, suggests the
probability of their having been taken from Heliopolis to adorn a temple or
palace in the new city. The fact of the name of Ramses the Great being sculptured on them may have given rise to the tradition that they were *erected* by
that king. An adjacent fort occupies the site of an old tower which belonged
to the former wall (that is, to the *old* wall of the *Arab* city), and which was
called by European travellers "the Tower of the Romans;" as it was apparently
of Roman origin. Near this, standing on a mound of rubbish, we saw the
shore of the new harbour, behind the wall on the left of the fort.

When the British army was in Alexandria in 1801, operations were commenced for transporting the fallen obelisk to England; but the commander-in-
chief refusing to sanction the undertaking, it was abandoned, and nothing is
said of its being resumed, although Mohammed 'Alee offered the monument
to us some years ago.[†]

After viewing the Obelisks, we thankfully turned homewards, for the sun
had risen, and the heat became intense.

Not far from the eastern gate (perhaps two miles and a half) is the field of
the memorable battle of the 21st of March, 1801, in which Sir Ralph
Abercrombie, who commanded our victorious army, received his mortal
wound.[‡] At the spot where the battle raged most furiously, by the sea-shore,
is a quadrangular enclosure, surrounded by substantial, but now ruined
walls, constructed of calcareous stone and large bricks, in distinct layers, like
many other Roman buildings. The ruin is called Kasr-el-Káyasireh (or the
Pavilion, or Palace, of the Cæsars). It marks the site of a small town, which
received the name of Nicopolis, in commemoration of a famous victory
obtained there by Octavius Cæsar over Antony.

The Pillar called Pompey's is undoubtedly a magnificent monument. The
shaft of the column is a single block of red granite, sixty-eight feet in
height, and nine feet in diameter at the bottom, according to my brother's

---

[†]Breccia, *Alexandrea ad Aegyptum*, 92, tells us that "as far back as the Middle Ages,
one of these obelisks had fallen down. This was the one which was given to England
by Mohamad Aly, but it was not transported to the bank of the Thames until 1877.
The other, granted to the United States in 1879, is at present in Central Park, New
York."

[‡]He died a week after the engagement with Napoleon's French army in Alexandria.

measurement. The capital is a block of the same kind of stone, and is ten feet high. The base, plinth, and pedestal are likewise of red granite, and each is a single block. The combined length of these three pieces is seventeen feet. The total height of this superb monument is therefore ninety-five feet; and the substructure, which is partly modern, is four feet in height.[†] The shaft is beautifully wrought, but sadly disfigured by numerous names inscribed in very large characters, with black paint. They have mostly been written by persons who have ascended to the summit. This they have contrived by flying a large paper kite, and causing it to descend so that the cord rested on the top of the capital; by these means, they succeeded in drawing a stout rope over it; and having accomplished this (to use the naval term) they easily "rigged shrouds," by which to ascend. This exploit has been performed several times, generally by naval officers, who have caused the name of their ship to be painted on the shaft.

Among the adventures, an English lady once ascended to the summit. There is a Greek inscription on the pedestal, but it can only be faintly seen when the rays of the sun fall obliquely upon the surface of the stone. Every traveller who examined the Pillar since the time of Pococke[‡] believed the inscription to be entirely obliterated, until Colonel Squire again discovered it. That gentleman with Mr. Hamilton and Colonel Leake deciphered (with the exception of a few characters) the lines, four in number, which record the dedication, by a "Prefect of Egypt" (whose name is almost illegible), to the "most revered Emperor, the protecting divinity of Alexandria, Diocletian the Invincible." The name of the "Prefect" also has since been deciphered by Sir Gardener Wilkinson[††]—it is Publius.[‡‡] This inscription certainly proves that the column, or the building in which it stood, was *dedicated* to the Roman emperor whose name is thus recorded, but not that the column was *erected* in honour of that individual, any more than the lateral lines on the Obelisks which I have described prove that they were erected in the reign of Sesostris.

[†]Breccia, *Alexandrea ad Aegyptum*, 116, gives the following measurements: "The total height of the column including the base and the capital is 26 metres 85 (88 feet). The shaft measures 20 m.75 and it has a diameter of 2 m.70 at the base and 2 m.30 at the top."

[‡]Richard Pococke visited Egypt in 1737.

[††]Sir John Gardner Wilkinson (1797–1875), author of *Manners and Customs of the Ancient Egyptians*.

[‡‡]Breccia, *Alexandrea ad Aegyptum*, 116, gives the name of the prefect of Egypt who erected the monument as "Postumus." Forster, Alexandria, 161, gives the translation of the four-line Greek inscription on the base as follows: "To the most just Emperor, the tutelary God of Alexandria, Diocletian the invincible: Postumus, prefect of Egypt." He dates the pillar about A.D. 297, "after the Emperor had crushed a rebellion and was a god to be propitiated; the Pillar, erected in the precincts of Serapis, would celebrate his power and clemency and presumably bore his statue on the top."

I may here briefly give you the tradition respecting the burning of the Alexandrian library (deriving my information from my brother), which took place in the time of 'Omar, as it is connected with the history of the great pillar. 'Abd-el-Lateef and El-Makreezee affirm, that this pillar originally belonged to a magnificent building, containing a library, which 'Amr, the Arab general, burned by the command of 'Omar. A particular account of the burning of this library is given by Abu-l-Faraj; but the statement of that author has been disbelieved, because the story is related by few other writers; yet why should they record what they considered an event of scarcely any importance? It is evident from the slight manner in which 'Abd-el-Lateef and El-Makreezee mention the fact, that they regarded it as a very unimportant occurrence. They allude to it merely as connected with the history of the great Pillar. The former says, "Here was the library which 'Amr Ibn-el-'A's burned by permission of 'Omar." El-Makreezee says, "The Pillar is of a red speckled stone; hard and flinty. There were around it about four hundred columns which Karaja, Governor of Alexandria in the time of the Sultán Saláh-el-Deen Yoosuf Ibn-Eiyoob (called by Europeans "Saladin"), broke, and threw them into the sea, near the shore, to prevent the vessels of an enemy from approaching the walls of the city. It is said (he adds) that this pillar is one of those which stood in the portico of Aristotle, who there taught philosophy; and that this academy contained a library, which 'Amr Ibn-el-'A's burned by direction of 'Omar." The Arab General 'Amr, having taken Alexandria, was solicited by one Johannes, surnamed "the Grammarian," to spare the library above mentioned, and to suffer it to remain in the possession of its former owners. 'Amr, willing to oblige the philosopher, wrote to his sovereign, desiring to know his pleasure respecting these books, and received the following answer:– "As to the books which you have mentioned, if they contain what is agreeable with the book of God, in the book of God is sufficient without them; and if they contain what is contrary to the book of God, there is no need of them; so give orders for their destruction." They were accordingly distributed about the city, to be used for heating the baths, and in the space of six months they were consumed." "Hear what happened," writes Abu-l-Faraj, "and wonder!" The author here quoted does certainly speak of this event as one of lamentable importance; but he was a Christian writer. The Muslims, though they love and encourage many branches of literature, generally imagine that the books of the Christians are useless, or of an evil tendency.[†]

I must now leave Alexandria and its environs, saying a few words respecting the ancient Necropolis, or "City of the Dead," which I have *not* seen, being satisfied with my brother's account of it, and being anxious to proceed to Cairo.

[†]For the definitive opinion on that question, cf. El-Abbadi, *Life and Fate of the Ancient Library of Alexandria*.

The name of Necropolis has been given to a tract of nearly two miles in length, on the southwest of the site of the ancient city, between the old harbour and the bed of the Lake Mareotis. The sepulchres are all excavated in the rock, which is calcareous, or rather soft. Those my brother saw were small and rudely cut, without painting or any other decorations. One of the catacombs is very spacious. It is the only one that is well worthy of being examined. The principal chamber is described as being of a circular form; and the roof is excavated like the interior of a dome. Around it are three recesses, which were doubtless receptacles for mummies; and around each of these are three troughs cut in the rock, designed to serve as sarcophagi. In other chambers are similar receptacles for the dead. The entrance of the principal, or circular, apartment being ornamented with pilasters and a pediment, it is evident that the period of the formation of the catacomb was posterior to the founding of Alexandria. Along the shore of the harbour are many other excavations, but of small dimensions, which are also sepulchres. Many of them, being partly below the level of the sea, are more or less filled with water; the part of the rock which intervened having crumbled away, and left the interior exposed to the waves. Some of these have been called "the baths of Cleopatra," though evidently sepulchres like the rest.

And now, if my account of Alexandria and its monuments has been too brief, I must plead as my apology, my anxiety to pursue our route; but I must add, that although the modern Alexandria is the successor of one of the most illustrious cities of ancient times, it disappoints me, and occasions only melancholy reflections.

Truly history confers a deep interest on this spot, once the chief seat of Egyptian learning, the theatre of many wars and bloody tragedies, the scene of the martyrdom of St. Mark, the birthplace and residence of many of the most eminent fathers of the church, and the hot-bed of schisms and heresies. But it is only in retrospect we find that on which our minds can rest, and which can give rise to reflections which may be pursued to advantage.[†]

[†]Letter II relies heavily on Lane, *Description* (Chapter II), from which Sophia copies or paraphrases whole paragraphs, adding occasional personal reflections of her own or leaving out some remarks Lane makes, such as one reference to the destruction of the monuments of Alexandria: "Much of the work of demolition must be attributed to the fanatic zeal of the Christians during the reign of the Emperor Theodosius, and in subsequent periods" (*Description*, 18).

LETTER III

Cairo, July, 1842

MY DEAR FRIEND,

TO-DAY we have arrived with thankful hearts at Cairo, our voyage by sea and by river completed for a time.

On leaving Alexandria, we engaged an iron track-boat, used chiefly for the conveyance of travellers on their way to India from Alexandria, by the canal called the Mahmoodeeyeh, to the Nile. The boat was very large, containing two large cabins, the foremost of which was furnished with benches and tables, and apparently clean; and being drawn by four horses, passed so rapidly along, that we enjoyed, from the current of air, a feeling of freshness, which led us at nightfall into a grievous mistake; for we laid down and expected rest without arranging our musquito curtains. Those who had fitted up the boat had covered the wide benches with carpet. Imagine *such* a couch in *such* a latitude! we were positively covered by fleas, and swarmed by black beetles, and the latter of such a growth as are never seen in England. Too late we repented of our error, and I should strongly recommend any person travelling in Egypt to sleep under musquito curtains winter and summer. There is certainly a consciousness of heat and want of air, for perhaps a quarter of an hour after the curtain is closely tucked in, but what is that compared to the constant attacks of vermin of an extraordinary variety? Our first night in the track-boat, without musquito-curtains, will not be easily forgotten.[1]

On the following morning we arrived at the point where the canal enters the Nile, and found that the boat which we expected would be ready for our voyage to Cairo, had conveyed a party towards the scene of a festival, and might not return for some days. Here our situation was one of severe suffering. We were stationed between two high ridges, composed of mud thrown up in forming the bed of the canal, very dry of course, and exceedingly dusty, and covered with mud huts. The intense heat, the clouds of dust, and the smell of this place, where we were hemmed in by boats and barges for two days and

---

[1] Since I wrote the above, the Peninsular and Oriental Steam Navigation Company have, I believe, undertaken the conveyance of travellers from Alexandria to Suez. Be this as it may, it is due to the Company to say, that our voyage from England to Egypt was rendered as pleasant as a splendid vessel, excellent attendance, and every desirable accommodation could make it; and the manner in which travellers are brought through Egypt, on their way to India, is now, I am told, as comfortable as any reasonable person could desire.

nights, without being able to improve our situation (because it was necessary in order to be ready for the Nile-boat to continue near the entrance of the canal), was infinitely worse than sea-sickness, or anything else in the way of inconvenience we had hitherto experienced. Indeed the sea-sickness was welcome to me, for it confined me to my bed, and spared me the pain of seeing my own dear country, which holds so many and so much we love, fade from my sight. However long or however short may be the time proposed by any person for the purpose of visiting other countries, however pleasurable their expectations, however full of hope their prospects, there are regrets—there is a pang—on *quitting* England, which must be felt by the wayfarer, but can never be described, and is never fully anticipated. But I must not wander from my proper subject.† Where the canal runs along the narrow neck of land between the salt marsh of Mareotis and that of Aboo-keer, the sides are formed by solid masses of stone, to prevent in some degree the filtration of salt water into the Mahmoodeeyeh, as it supplies the cisterns of Alexandria. In scarcely any part does this canal occupy the bed of the *ancient* canal of Alexandria, which it crosses in several places. More than three hundred thousand men were employed to dig it; and about twelve thousand of these are said to have died in the course of ten months; many of them in consequence of ill-treatment, excessive labour, and the want of wholesome nourishment and good water. Their only implements in this work were the hoes which are commonly used in Egyptian agriculture; and where the soil was moist they scraped it up with their hands, and then removed it in baskets. The whole length of the canal is nearly fifty British miles, and its breadth about eighty or ninety feet. It was commenced and completed in the year 1819. The name of Mahmoodeeyeh was given to it in honour of Mahmoud, the reigning sultan.‡

In two days our promised boat arrived, and we joyfully left the Mahmoodeeyeh, and its gloomy prospect, where the peasants appeared to be suffering from abject poverty, and where the mud huts, rising one above another, many of them being built in a circular form, bore the appearance by moonlight of the ruined towers of castles, with here and there a gleam of red light issuing from the apertures.

---

†Here Sophia starts copying from Lane's, *Description*, Chapter III, interspersing the narrative with her own observations and reflections. She skips Chapters IV (Physical Sketch of Egypt) and V (Rashee'd or Rosetta) and resumes her narrative with excerpts from Lane when describing the various towns they pass by, though she leaves out remarks Lane makes about "courtesans," dancing-girls, and their performances, which "consist in various amorous gestures and particularly in a wriggling motion of the hips" (*Description*, 55).

‡Mahmud II (1785–1839), Sultan of Turkey, son of Abdul-Hamid I and successor of his brother Mustafa IV in 1808. He was succeeded in 1839 by his son Abdul-Mejid. Sophia in 1842 copied this passage verbatim from Lane, who was describing his journey in 1825; she should have said "the then reigning sultan."

The communication between the canal and the Nile was closed, therefore we walked for a few minutes along the bank, and we rejoiced on entering our boat to feel the sweetest breeze imaginable, and to look upon the green banks (especially on the Delta side) of one of the most famous rivers in the world.

The boats of the Nile are admirably constructed for the navigation of that river. Their great triangular sails are managed with extraordinary facility, which is an advantage of the utmost importance; for the sudden and frequent gusts of wind to which they are subject, require that a sail should be taken in almost in a moment, or the vessel would most probably be overset. On many occasions one side of our boat was completely under water, but the men are so skilful that an accident seldom happens, unless travellers pursue the voyage during the night.

We ordered that our boat should not proceed at night, therefore we were three days on the Nile.

A custom which is always observed by the Arab boat-men at the commencement of a voyage much pleased me. As soon as the wind had filled our large sail, the Reyyis (or captain of the boat) exclaimed "El-Fát-'hah." This is the title of the opening chapter of the Kur-'an (a short and simple prayer), which the Reyyis and all the crew repeated together in a low tone of voice. Would to Heaven that, in this respect, the example of the poor Muslim might be followed by our country-men, that our entire dependence on the protecting providence of God might be universally acknowledged, and every journey, and every voyage, be sanctified by prayer.

On the first day we passed the town of Fooweh, where I could distinguish eleven mosques with their picturesque domes and minarets, and a few manu-factories; the dwellings are miserable, but when viewed from a little distance the whole has a pleasing appearance, for the minarets are white-washed, and the houses, for a town in Egypt, *have been* good. Numbers of women and girls belonging to this town were filling their pitchers on the bank as we passed; while others were washing clothes; which done, each proceeded to wash her hands, face, and feet, and immediately returned with her pitcher or bundle on her head. A piece of rag rolled in the form of a ring, and placed upon the head, served to secure the pitcher in its erect position; and I constantly saw, during our stay on the Mahmoodeeyeh, large and heavy pitchers carried by the women on their heads, without a hand upraised to keep them steady.

Fooweh, like Matoobis, is celebrated for the beauty of its women; but as our boat kept in the middle of the stream, I had no opportunity of pro-nouncing on their personal attractions.[†] The lower orders are mostly, I think, remarkably plain. Their usual dress (and indeed frequently, their only article of clothing, except the head veil) is a plain blue shirt, differing little from that

---

†Lane, on the other hand, from his cabin windows, could admire at his "leisure . . . the fine figures and handsome countenances of most of the girls" (*Description*, 54–55).

of the men, which is also commonly blue. It is a general custom of the Egyptian women of this class to tattoo some parts of their persons, particularly the front of the chin and the lips, with blue marks; and like the women of the higher classes, many of them tinge their nails with the dull red dye of the henna, and arrange their hair in a number of small plaits which hang down the back.

I must not omit telling you that Fooweh is also famous for its pomegranates, which are both plentiful and excellent in flavour.

We reached the village of Shubra Kheet shortly after sunset, and as our boatmen recommended that our boat should be made fast under this place, we remained there until the morning. It was then curious to see the various occupations of the peasants, and to observe the lassitude with which they labour. During our voyage several poor fellows floated towards the boat, sitting as it were upright on the water, paddling with their feet, and bearing each three water-melons, one in each hand, and one on their heads. Their manner of swimming is extraordinary—they seem perfectly at their ease.

On the second day we passed renowned Sais, and afterwards had a glimpse of the great desert, and its almost immeasurable sea of sand.[†] Sais was the ancient capital of the Delta, one of the most celebrated cities of Egypt, and the reputed birthplace of Cecrops, who, it is said, led a colony of Saites to Attica, about 1556 years before the Christian era, founded Athens, and established there the worship of Minerva (the Egyptian Neith), the tutelar goddess of his native city. This place is so choked up with rubbish that its ruins are scarcely worth visiting; but the labour of excavation would probably be rewarded by interesting discoveries. The modern name of the place is "Sá-el-Hagar," that is, "Sais of the Stone," probably allusive to the great mono-lithic chapel described by Herodotus as the most remarkable of the monu-ments here existing in his time. The remains of Sais, viewed from the river, appear merely like lofty and extensive mounds. They chiefly consist of a vast enclosure, about half a mile in length, and nearly the same in breadth. This is formed by walls of prodigious dimensions, being about fifty feet thick, and, in several parts, considerably more than that in height, constructed of large crude bricks, fifteen or sixteen inches in length, eight in breadth, and seven in thickness. The rains, though very rare even in this part of Egypt, have so much decayed these walls, that from a little distance they are hardly to be distinguished from the rubbish in which they are partly buried. Within the enclosure are only seen some enormous blocks of stone, and the remains of some buildings of unburnt brick, which appear to have been tombs, and several catacombs, which have been explored and ransacked. The enclosure contained the famous temple of the Egyptian Minerva, described by Herodotus, the portico of which surpassed in its colossal dimensions all other works of a similar nature, and was adorned with gigantic figures and

[†]Lane, *Description*, 56.

enormous androsphinxes. Before it was the famous monolithic chapel I have mentioned, which was twenty-one cubits long, fourteen wide, and eight high. It is related by Herodotus that two thousand boatmen were employed during the space of three years in transporting this monolith down the Nile from Elephantine. There was also, before the temple, a colossus, in a reclining posture (or, more probably, a *sitting* posture[†]), seventy-five feet in length, similar to that before the temple of Vulcan at Memphis, which latter colossus was the gift of Amasis. Behind the temple was a sepulchre, but for whom it was destined the historian declines mentioning. Lofty obelisks were likewise raised within the sacred enclosure, near a circular lake, which was lined with stone. This lake served as a kind of theatre for nocturnal exhibitions of solemn mysteries relating to the history of the unnamed person above alluded to, who was, probably, Osiris; for, from feeling of religious awe, many of the Egyptians abstained from mentioning the name of that god. Many other towns in Egypt disputed the honour of being regarded as the burial-place of Osiris. All the Pharaohs born in the Saitic district were buried within the enclosure which surrounded the sacred edifices of Sais; and one of those kings, Apries, founded here a magnificent palace. Of the grand religious festivals which were periodically celebrated in Egypt in ancient times, the third, in point of magnificence, was that of Sais, in honour of Neith; the most splendid being that of Bubastis, and the next, that of Busiris, both in Lower Egypt. That of Sais was called "the festival of burning lamps," because, on the occasion of its celebration, the houses in that city, and throughout all Egypt, were illuminated by lamps hung around them.[‡]

I mentioned that the boat we had been promised at the Mahmoodeeyeh had conveyed a party towards the scene of a festival; and you may be surprised to hear that the manners of the modern Egyptians are not wholly different from those of the ancient Alexandrians, who flocked to the licentious festivals celebrated at Canopus in honour of the god Serapis. Innumerable boats covered the canal by night as well as by day, conveying pilgrims of both sexes, dancing, singing, and drinking, and availing themselves in every way of the religious licence afforded them. So, in the present day, vast numbers of the male inhabitants of the metropolis of Egypt, and persons from other parts, with numerous courtesans, repair to the festivals celebrated in commemoration of the birth of the seyyid[1] Ahmad El-Bedawee (a celebrated Muslim saint), at Tanta, in the Delta, where swarms of dancing-girls and singers contribute to their amusement, and where, I am told, brandy is drunk almost as freely as coffee.[††]

[†]Sophia adds Lane's footnote 1 to the text *(Description,* 57).
[‡]Lane, *Description,* 57.
[1]Seyyid is a title given to the descendants of the Prophet.
[††]Lane, *Description,* 24

We passed, to-day, by the village of Kafr-ez-Zeiyát, which exhibited a busy scene: numerous visitors of the seyyid landing there, on their way to Tanta, and others embarking to return to their homes.

We arrived late at the village of Nadir, under which we remained for the night. In the morning we found ourselves surrounded by fine buffaloes standing in the water. Their milk is chiefly used, and the butter made from it is very white and sweet. We often saw numbers of these animals standing or lying in the water, for the Nile is in many parts extremely shallow, and abounds with moving sandbanks. Hence the boats frequently run aground, but they are generally pushed off without much difficulty by means of poles, or the crew descend into the water and shove the vessel off with their backs and shoulders. In a calm, the boat is towed by the crew; and in several cases during our voyage, the whole boat's crew, consisting of ten men, were thus drawing it, while no one remained with us but the Reyyis. It was astonishing to see how well they performed this laborious task, in the heat of July[†]; very seldom stopping to take rest, and then only for a short time. The boatmen generally sing while the vessel is under sail, and they often accompany their songs with the rude music of the darebukkeh and zummárah, which are a funnel-shaped earthen drum and a double reed-pipe. There is something very agreeable in the songs of the boatmen, although the airs they sing are most strange. There is so much of contentment in the tones of their voices that it does one good to hear them.

The most common kind of passage-boat, or pleasure-boat, is called a kangeh, also pronounced kanjeh. It is long and narrow, and does not draw much water. It has two masts, with two large triangular sails, and a low cabin, which is generally divided into two or more apartments, having small square windows, which are furnished with blinds, or glasses, and sliding shutters in the inside. In our boat we were exceedingly worried by beetles, bugs, and fleas; and these seriously annoyed me on account of my poor children, whose rest was sadly disturbed, and their very patience and cheerfulness increased our sympathy. Indeed, these young wayfarers made us cast many a longing wish for their sakes towards the comforts of a home.

During the nights our musquito curtains diminished but did not remove the inconvenience; but they are invaluable, as they prevent all attacks from large reptiles, although bugs and fleas are proof against all precaution.

The boats belonging to the Turkish grandees are very gay: bunches of flowers are commonly painted on the panels of the cabin, both within and without; and the blood-red flag, with its white crescent and star or stars, waves at the stern. Other boats are more simple in their decorations, and all extremely picturesque.

[†]Lane, *Description*, 20–21. Sophia changes Lane's "in the very hottest weather" to "in the heat of July," to correspond with the date of her letter.

On this day of our voyage, we passed little worthy of remark, excepting, indeed, the groups of noble and graceful palm trees, which form a characteristic and beautiful feature in every Egyptian landscape. The villages presented a curious effect, from almost every hut being crowned with a conical pigeon-house, constructed of earthen pots. With these cones, frequently as large as the huts themselves, almost every village hereabouts abounds.

We observed many carcasses of cattle floating upon the water, or lying by the banks of the river, for Egypt is at present visited by a severe murrain.[1]

During our voyage we saw several instances of mirage (called by the Arabs seráb); but the apparent clearness of the mock water destroyed the illusion; for the Nile, generally turbid, was then particularly so; and it was impossible to strain the imagination so far as to conceive that a *clear* lake should exist near the banks of the river. Yet it was an interesting and curious phenomenon, and indeed rendered painfully interesting by the knowledge that many a perishing wanderer in the desert had bitterly tasted the disappointment its mimicry occasions.

I can say little of the beauty of the banks of the Nile. They are in many places sufficiently high to obstruct the view, and broken and perpendicular. The Delta side certainly often presented to the eye a sloping bank of refreshing green, but with scarcely any diversity. I am not disposed to underrate the prospect; but you have doubtless heard that the borders of the Nile are seen in all their beauty about a month after the decrease of the river, which has left its fertilizing soil for a considerable space on either side, when its banks seem covered with a carpet of the brightest emerald green, and its little islands are crowned with the most brilliant verdure.

Our voyage was made during its increase; and when, on the third night, our boat was made fast to a sandy island, no village being in the neighbourhood under which the Reyyis thought we could safely pass the night, we all congratulated ourselves and each other that our boating was nearly at the end.

Early on the following morning we descried the venerable Pyramids, but the undulations of the heated atmosphere on the surface of the intermediate plain prevented their being distinctly visible. They were three leagues distant.

We shortly after arrived at Boulak, the principal port of Cairo, and with our arrival came the necessity that I and my sister-in-law should equip ourselves in Eastern costume. There was no small difficulty in this ceremony, and when completed, it was stifling to a degree not to be forgotten. Imagine the face covered closely by a muslim veil, double at the upper part, the eyes only uncovered, and over a dress of coloured silk an overwhelming covering of black silk, extending, in my idea, in every direction; so that, having nothing free but my eyes, I looked with dismay at the high bank I must climb, and

[1] This murrain lasted more than three months, and reminded us of that in the time of Moses.

the donkey I must mount, which was waiting for me at the summit. Nothing can be more awkward and uncomfortable than this riding dress; and if I had any chance of attaining my object without assuming it, I should never adopt it; but in English costume I should not gain admittance into many hareems: besides, the knowledge that a Muslim believes a curse to rest on the "seer and the seen," makes one anxious not to expose passers-by to what they would deem a misfortune, or ourselves to their malediction.

My brother, in his 'Modern Egyptians,' has represented the manner in which the hábarah is worn by the native ladies of Egypt. The Turkish ladies close it in front, esteeming it improper to show the colour of the sebleh or tób beneath.

The house dress is well suited to the climate and extremely picturesque, but the walking dress is grotesque and curious.

With a short account of our ride of nearly two miles from Boulak to Cairo, I shall conclude.

All mounted, and preceded by a janissary, we looked in wonder, as we rode through Boulak, at the dilapidated state of this suburb. There are, indeed, good houses there, I am assured, but we had not the good fortune to see them, and we emerged gladly from its narrow streets to an open space, where soon, however, the dust (which rose in clouds from the tread of our easy-paced donkeys) so annoyed us, that for the first time I felt it desirable that nothing but the eyes should be uncovered. At length we fairly entered Cairo, and my astonishment increased tenfold.

I wrote to you that the streets of Alexandria are narrow; they are wide when compared with those of Cairo. The meshreebeeyehs, or projecting windows, facing each other, above the ground-floors, literally touch in *some* instances; and in *many*, the opposite windows are within reach.

The first impression received on entering this celebrated city, is, that it has the appearance of having been deserted for perhaps a century, and suddenly repeopled by persons who had been unable, from poverty or some other cause, to repair it, and clear away its antiquated cobwebs. I never saw such cobwebs as hung in many apertures, in gloomy dark festoons, leading me to consider the unmolested condition of their tenants. I wish I could say that I do not fear these creatures; but surely in the insect world there is nothing so savage-looking as a black thick-legged spider.

After passing through several of the streets, into which it appeared as though the dwellings had turned out nearly all their inhabitants, we arrived at an agreeable house situated in the midst of gardens, in which we are to take up our temporary abode.[†] Graceful palm-trees, loaded with their fruit, meet our eyes in every direction, while acacias, bananas, orange and lemon trees, pomegranate trees, and vines, form a splendid variety, and but for one

---

†The consul-general's residence. Cf. Lane Poole, *Life of Edward Lane,* 112.

essential drawback, the coup d'œil would be charming. This drawback is the want of refreshing showers. The foliage on which we look is perfectly covered with dust, and the soil of the gardens is watered by a wheel worked by a patient bullock who pursues his round-about with little intermission, and thrives in his persevering labour.

The plan of the gardens is very curious; they are divided by long parallel walks, with gutters on either side, and subdivided into little square compartments, each about two yards wide, by ridges of earth about half a foot high, and the water is admitted into these squares, one after another. When I looked upon the little ditches and squares of water, remaining for some time without absorption, I could not but remember our bright pretty gardens in England, and how carefully in watering our flowers we avoided saturating the mould, both because it would be injurious to them, and displeasing to the eye—and these recollections almost brought me to the conclusion that a garden in Egypt is not worth the trouble of cultivation—so much for national prejudice and love of home scenes. Adieu!

LETTER IV

Cairo, August, 1842

MY DEAR FRIEND,

ALTHOUGH prepared by the motley groups at Malta, and the changing scene and variety of costume at Alexandria, for much that is more astonishing to the European in Cairo, I find the peculiarities of this place and people are beyond my most extravagant expectations. The Shubra road passes very near our windows, and I am constantly attracted by the various processions which wind their way to and from this city.

The wedding processions, in which the poor bride walks under a canopy of silk, not only veiled, but enveloped in a large shawl, between two other females, amuse me much; while the tribe before the "destined one," occasionally demonstrate their joy by executing many possible, and, to our ideas, many impossible feats, and the rear is brought up by the contributions of children from many of the houses en route. The bride must, indeed, be nearly suffocated long before she reaches her destination, for she has to walk, frequently almost fainting, under a mid-day sun, sometimes a long distance, while a few musicians make what is considered melody with drums and shrill hautboys, and attending females scream their zagháreet (or quavering cries of joy), in deafening discord in her train.

The funeral processions distress me. The corpse of a man is carried in an open bier, with merely a shawl thrown over the body, through which the form is painfully visible. The body of a woman is carried in a covered bier over which a shawl is laid; and an upright piece of wood, covered also with a shawl and decorated with ornaments belonging to the female head-dress, rises from the forepart. The corpses of children are borne on this latter kind of bier.

One sound that I heard as a funeral procession approached, I can never forget; it was a cry of such deep sorrow—a sob of such heartfelt distress, that it was clearly distinguished from the wail of the hired women who joined the funeral chorus. We were immediately drawn to the windows, and saw a man leading a procession of women, and bearing in his arms a little dead infant, wrapt merely in a shawl, and travelling to its last earthly home. The cry of agony proceeded, I conclude, from its mother, and could only be wrung from a nearly bursting heart. Contend against me who may, I must ever maintain my opinion, that no love is so deep, no attachment so strong, as that of mother to child, and of child to mother.

The funerals that pass are very numerous; but other spectacles that I see from my windows afford various and endless entertainment, and make me long to look into the houses of this most curious city, as well as into the streets and roads. After much consideration, however, I have determined to defer my intended visits to the hareems of the great, until I shall have acquired some little knowledge of Arabic; for although Turkish is the language usually spoken in those hareems, Arabic is generally understood by the inmates, and as the latter is the common language of Egypt, some knowledge of it is indispensable to me.

But our first object has been to find a comfortable dwelling; and notwithstanding the kind assistance of numerous friends, my brother has experienced great difficulty in attaining this object. The friendly attention that has been shown to us all is most highly gratifying; and I have already had some experience of the manners and usages of the hareem; two Syrian ladies[†] having devoted themselves in the most amiable manner to render us every possible service.

After having searched for a house here during a month in vain, we were delighted by the offer of an exceedingly good one, which appeared in almost every respect eligible, and in which we are now residing. But our domestic comfort in this new abode has been disturbed by a singular trouble, which has obliged us to arrange as soon as possible for a removal. The house is an admirable one, being nearly new, though on the old construction; therefore I shall endeavour to give you an idea of the better houses of Cairo by describing this, and some knowledge of the plan of its interior will enable you more fully to understand the annoyance to which we are subjected.

On the ground-flour is a court, open to the sky, round which the apartments extend, gallery above gallery. Round the court are five rooms; one large room (a mandarah) intended for the reception of male guests, with a fountain in the centre; a winter room; a small sleeping-room, for any male guest; a kitchen, and a coffee-room, for servants. On the right hand, immediately on entering the street-door, is the door of the hareem, or the entrance to the stairs leading to the ladies' apartments; the whole of the house, excepting the apartments of the ground-floor, being considered as the "hareem." On the first floor is a marble-paved chamber, with a roof open towards the north, and sloping upwards, conveying into the chamber generally a delightful breeze. There are also five other rooms on the first floor; and in each of the two principal apartments, the greater portion of the floor, forming about three-fourths, is raised from five to six inches, the depressed portion being paved with marble. The reason for thus laying the floor is, that the outer slippers are left on the depressed portion, and the raised part, which is matted, is not to be defiled with anything which is unclean. The feet are covered, in addition to the stockings, with a kind of inner slippers, the soles of which,

---

[†]Syria in the nineteenth century comprised Syria, Lebanon, Palestine, and Jordan. Many Syrians emigrated to Egypt at that time.

as well as the upper leathers, are of yellow morocco: they are called mezz; and the outer slippers, which are without heels, are styled báboog. The latter, by the way, I am often losing, and I fear I shall continue to do so, for I despair of learning to shuffle, like the ladies of the country. When wearing the riding or walking dress, the mezz are exchanged for a pair of high morocco socks, and the báboog are worn as usual. They are always pale yellow. The walls throughout are whitewashed, and the ceilings composed of fancifully carved woodwork, in some instances extremely tastefully arranged. Besides the rooms I have mentioned, there are three small marble-paved apartments, forming, *en suite*, an antechamber, a reclining chamber, and a bath. We little thought, when we congratulated ourselves on this luxury, that it would become the most abominable part of the house. Above are four rooms, the principal one opening to a delightful terrace, which is considerably above most of the surrounding houses; and on this we enjoy our breakfast and supper under the clearest sky in the world; but we always remember that the sweet air which comforts us in the mornings and evenings of our sultry days, blows from the direction of our own dear country; and the thought renders it the more welcome.

We were much surprised, after passing a few days here, to find that our servants were unable to procure any rest during the night; being disturbed by a constant knocking, and by the appearances of what they believed to be an 'Efreet, that is, "an evil spirit," but the term 'Efreet is often used to signify "a ghost." The manner of the servants' complaint of the latter was very characteristic. Having been much annoyed one morning by a noisy quarrel under our windows, my brother called one of our servants to ascertain how it had arisen, when he replied, "It is a matter of no importance, O Efendee, but the subject which perplexes us is that there is a devil in the bath." My brother being aware of their superstitious prejudices, replied, "Well, is there a bath in the world that you do not believe to be a resort of evil spirits, according to the well-known tradition on that subject?" "True, O my master," rejoined the man, "the case is so; this devil has long been the resident of the house, and he will never permit any other tenant to retain its quiet possession; for a long time no one has remained more than a month within these walls, excepting the last person who lived here, and he, though he had soldiers and slaves, could not stay longer than about nine months; for the devil disturbed his family all night." I must here tell you that during our short stay in the house, two maids had left us, one after another, without giving us any idea of their intentions, and had never returned, and the cause of their sudden disappearance was now explained by the men, their fellow-servants. Certainly our own rest had been grievously disturbed; but we had attributed all the annoyance to a neighbour's extraordinary demonstrations of joy on the subject of his own marriage, and whose festivities were perhaps the more extravagant because he is an old man, and his bride a young girl: but as I hope to give you a particular account, on a future occasion, of the manner in which the people of this country celebrate a marriage, suffice it to say at present, the noise was deafening during the *whole* of eight nights, and that, when we were becoming accustomed to the constant din, we were roused by three tremendous reports of fire-arms, which rung through the apartments of our own and the neighbouring houses, and shook our dwelling to the very foundation. It is therefore not remarkable that we did not hear the noises which disturbed our poor servants, in addition to the sufficient uproar without.

It appeared, on inquiry, that the man to whom this house formerly belonged, and who is now dead, had, during his residence in it, murdered a poor tradesman who entered the court with his merchandise, and two slaves: one of these (a black girl) was destroyed in the bath, and you will easily understand how far *such* a story as this, and a *true* one too, sheds its influence on the minds of a people who are superstitious to a proverb. We can only regret that my brother engaged the house in ignorance of these circumstances; had he known them, he would also have been aware that the prejudice among the lower orders would be insurmountable, and that no female servant would remain with us. The sudden disappearance of our maids was thus quaintly explained by our door-keeper. "Why did A'mineh and Zeyneb leave you? Verily, O my master, because they feared for their security. When A'mineh saw the 'Efreet she said at once, 'I must quit this house; for if he touch me, I shall be deranged, and unfit for service;' and truly," he added, "this would have been the case. For ourselves, as men, we fear not; but we fear for the hareem. Surely you will consider their situation, and quit this house." This (he thought) was putting the matter in the strongest light. "Try a few nights longer," my brother said, "and call me as soon as the 'Efreet appears to-night; we might have caught him last night, when you say he was so near you, and after giving him a sound beating, you would not have found your rest disturbed." At this remark it was evident that the respect of both servants for their master had received a temporary shock. "O Efendee," exclaimed one of them, "this is an 'Efreet, and not a son of Adam, as you seem to suppose. He assumed last night all imaginary shapes, and when I raised my hand to seize him, he became a piece of cord, or any other trifle." Now these men are valuable servants, and we should be sorry to lose them, especially in our present predicament; therefore my brother merely answered, that if the annoyance did not cease, he would make inquiry respecting another house. But to obtain a house, excepting in the heart of the city, is no easy matter; and on account of my children, we feel it to be indispensable for the preservation of their health that we should reside on the west side of the city, and close to the outskirts, where the air is pure and salubrious, and where Ibraheem Pasha has caused the mounds of rubbish to be removed, and succeeded by extensive plantations of olive, palm, cypress, acacia, and other trees. These plantations are open to the public, and form a charming place of resort for children.

I have not mentioned to you that the inhuman wretch to whom this house belonged bequeathed it to a mosque, perhaps as an expiation for his crimes, but left it, for the term of her life, to the person who is our present landlady; and now a circumstance was explained to our minds which we had not before fully understood. On the day before we desired to remove here, we sent one of our servants to hire some women, and to superintend the clearing of the house; and on his arrival there, the landlady (whose name is Lálah-Zár, or bed of tulips) refused him admission, saying, "Return to the Efendee, and say to him that I am baking cakes in the oven of his kitchen, that I may give them away *to-morrow* at the tomb of the late owner of the house, to the poor and needy. This is a meritorious act for your master's sake, as well as for my own, and your master will understand it."

Poor woman! it is now evident to us that she hoped by this act of propitiation to prevent further annoyance to her tenants, and consequent loss to herself.

The morning after the conversation I have related took place, the servants' report was considerably improved. They had passed, they said, a comfortable night, and we hoped we might arrange to remain here, but the following day a most singular statement awaited us. The door-keeper, in a tone of considerable alarm, said that he had been unable to sleep at all; that the 'Efreet had walked round the gallery all night in *clogs!*[1] and had repeatedly knocked at his door with a brick, or some other hard substance. Then followed the question why one of the men had not called my brother, evidently because neither of them dared pass the gallery round which the supposed 'Efreet was taking his midnight walk, striking each door violently as he passed it. For many nights these noises continued, and many evenings they began before we retired to rest, and as we could never find the offender, I sadly feared for my children; not for their personal safety, but lest they should incline to superstition, and nothing impoverishes the mind so much as such a tendency.

Another singular circumstance attending this most provoking annoyance was our finding, on several successive mornings, five or six pieces of charcoal laid at the door leading to the chambers in which we sleep; conveying in this country a wish, or rather an imprecation, which is far from agreeable; viz. "May your faces be blackened." However, under all these circumstances, I rejoiced to find my children increasingly amused by these pranks, and established in the belief that one or more wicked persons liked the house so well, that they resolved to gain possession, and to eject by dint of sundry noises, and other annoyances, any persons who desire its occupation. It is however, a more serious matter to poor Lálah-Zár than to us; for it is very certain that

---

[1]Clogs are always worn in the bath.

the legacy of the late possessor will never prove a great benefit either to her or to the mosque. You will be surprised when I tell you that the rent of such a house as this does not exceed £ 12 per annum. It is a very superior house, and infinitely beyond the usual run of houses, therefore always styled by the people of the country, the house of an Emeer (a Noble-man).

One thing we much regretted, that A'mineh (whom I mentioned early in this letter) had taken fright. She was the best of our maids; and her gentle respectful manners, and the perfect propriety of her demeanour, made her a very desirable attendant. I am sorry to say we have met with no other, but those who have proved themselves in every respect inefficient. The men-servants are excellent, and become attached to their masters almost invariably, when treated as they deserve; but as to the maids, I scarcely know how to describe them. I really do not think they hardly ever wash themselves, excepting when they go to the bath, which is once in about ten days or a fortnight. On these occasions a complete scouring takes place (I can find no other term for the operation of the bath), and their long hair is arranged in many small plaits: from that time until the next visit to the bath, their hair is never unplaited. I speak from having watched with dismay all we have had, excepting A'mineh, who was a jewel among them, and from the information of all our friends in this country. These maids are extremely deceitful, and when directed with regard to their work, will answer with the most abject sub-mission, although really disheartened by the most ordinary occupation. They sleep in their clothes, after the manner of the country, and the habit of doing so, coupled with the neglect of proper washing, involving a want of that freshness produced by a complete change of clothes, is especially objectionable. Were they strict in their religious observances, their cleanliness would be secured, as frequent ablutions are ordered in their code of law; but the lower orders of the women have seldom any religion at all.

Believe me, you are fortunate in England, in this respect, as well as many others, and I hope you will prize our English maids, if you have not done so already.

LETTER V

September, 1842

MY DEAR FRIEND,

THAT you may be better prepared for future letters, you wish me to give you a general physical sketch of this most singular country, which is distinguished by its natural characteristics, as well as by its monuments of antiquity, from every other region of the globe. As my own experience will not enable me to do so, my brother has promised to furnish me with the necessary information.

The country (as well as the metropolis) is called Masr, by its modern inhabitants. It is generally divided into Upper and Lower. Upper Egypt, or the Sa'eed, may be described as a long winding valley, containing a soil of amazing fertility, bounded throughout its whole length by mountainous and sandy wastes.

Lower Egypt is an extensive plain, for the most part cultivated, and copiously supplied with moisture by the divided streams of the Nile, and by numerous canals. All the cultivable soil of Egypt owes its existence to the Nile, by which it is still annually augmented: for this river, when swollen by the summer rains which regularly drench the countries between the northern limits of Sennár and the equinoctial line, is impregnated with rich earth washed down from the mountains of Abyssinia and the neighbouring regions; and in its course through Nubia and Egypt, where rain is a rare phenomenon, it deposits a copious sediment, both in the channel in which it constantly flows, and upon the tracts which it annually inundates. It is every where bordered by cultivated fields, excepting in a few places, where it is closely hemmed in by the mountains, or the drifted sand of the desert. The mud of the Nile, analyzed by Regnault, was found to consist of 11 parts in 100 of water: 48 of alumine; 18 of carbonate of lime; 9 of carbon; 6 of oxide of iron; 4 of silex; and 4 of carbonate of magnesia.

The Nile is called in Egypt "El-Bahr" (or "the river"); for bahr signifies a "great river," as well as the sea. It is also called "Bahr en Neel" (or "the river Nile"), and "Neel Masr" (or "the Nile of Egypt"). The Arabs, generally, believe the "Neel Masr" to be a continuation of the "Neel es-Soodán" (or "Nile of the Negroes").

Of the two great branches, called "El-Bahr el-Azrak" (or "the blue river"), and "El-Bahr el-Abyad" (or "the white river"), which, uniting, form the Nile of Nubia and Egypt, the former (though less long than the other) is that to which Egypt principally owes its fertility. Its chief characteristics (its colour, the banks between which it flows, &c.) are similar to those of the Nile of Egypt. Its dark colour, arising from its being impregnated with soil during the greater part of the year, has caused it to receive the name of "the blue river," while the other branch, from the opposite colour of its waters, is called "the white river." The latter is considerably wider than the former; its banks are sloping lawns, richly wooded, and very unlike the steep and broken banks of the Nile of Egypt.

At its entrance into the valley of Egypt, the Nile is obstructed by innumerable rocks of granite, which cause a succession of cataracts, or rather rapids. The mountains on the east of the river, as well as the islands in it, are here of granite: those on the western side are of sandstone. From this point, to the distance of thirty leagues southward, sandstone mountains of small altitude extend on each side of the river. The valley, so far, is very narrow, particularly throughout the upper half of the sandstone district; and there is but very little cultivable land on the banks of the river in that part; in some places the mountains are close to the stream; and in others, only a narrow sandy strip intervenes. At the distance of twelve leagues below the cataracts, the river is contracted to little more than half its usual width, by the mountains on each side. Here are extensive quarries, from which were taken the materials for the construction of many of the temples in the Thebais. This part is called "Gebel es-Silsileh," or "the Mountain of the Chain." Where the calcareous district begins, are two insulated hills (El-Gebeleyn) on the west of the Nile; one of them close to the river, and the other at a little distance behind the former. The valley then becomes wider, and more irregular in its direction; and the Nile winds through the middle of the cultivable land, or nearly so. Afterwards the valley assumes a less serpentine form, and the river flows along the eastern side; in many places washing the sides of the precipitous mountains. The calcareous district continues to the end of the valley, where the mountains on both sides diverge; the Arabian chain running due east to Suez, and the western hills extending in a north-west direction, towards the Mediterranean. Near the termination of the valley is an opening in the low western mountains, through which a canal conveys the waters of the Nile into the fertile province of El-Feiyoom. On the north-west of this province is a great lake, which receives the superfluous waters during the inundation. The length of the valley of Egypt, from the cataracts to the metropolis, is about 450 geographical miles. The distance by the river is above 500 miles from the cataracts to the metropolis, and about 400 miles from Thebes to the same point. The difference in latitude between the cataracts and the metropolis is six degrees, or 360 geographical miles; and the distance from the latter point to the sea, in a straight line, is rather more than ninety miles. The width of the valley is in few parts more than eight or ten miles; and generally less than that. The width of that part of Lower Egypt which constituted the ancient Delta, is about 120 miles from east to west.

The whole of the fertile country is very flat; but the lands in the vicinity of the river are rather higher than those which are more remote. This has been supposed to result from a greater deposit of mud upon the former; which, however, cannot be the case, for it is observed that the fields near the river are generally above the reach of the inundation, while those towards the mountains are abundantly overflowed; but while the latter yield but one crop, the former are cultivated throughout the whole year; and it is the constant cultivation and frequent watering (which is done by artificial means) that so considerably raise the soil; not so much by the deposit of mud left by the water, as by the accumulation of stubble and manure. The cultivable soil throughout Egypt is free from stones, excepting in parts immediately adjacent to the desert. It almost everywhere abounds with nitre.

Between the cultivable land and the mountains, there generally intervenes a desert space, too high to be inundated. This tract partly consists of sand and pebbles, covering a bed of rock, and partly of drifted sand which has encroached on the cultivable soil. In some places, this desert space is two or three miles in width.

The extent of the cultivated land in Egypt, my brother calculates to be equal to rather more than one square degree and a half: in other words 5,500 square geographical miles.[2] This is less than half the extent of the land which is comprised within the confines of the desert; for many parts within the limits of the cultivable land are too high to be inundated, and consequently are not cultivated; and other parts, particularly in Lower Egypt, are occupied by lakes, or marshes, or drifted sand. Allowance also must be made for the space which is occupied by towns and villages, the river, canals, &c. Lower Egypt comprises about the same extent of cultivated land as the whole of Upper Egypt.[2]

The annual inundation irrigates the land sufficiently for one crop; but not without any labour of the fellah (or agriculturist): for care must be taken to detain the water by means of dams, or it would subside too soon. The highest rise of the Nile ever known would scarcely be sufficient if the waters were allowed to drain off the fields when the river itself falls. A very high rise of the Nile is, indeed, an event not less calamitous than a very scanty rise; for it overflows vast tracts of land which cannot be drained, it washes down

---

[1]He made this calculation from a list of all the towns and villages in Egypt, and the extent of cultivated land belonging to each. This list is appended to De Sacy's "Abd Al-latif." It was made in the year of the Flight 777 (A.D. 1375–6); and may be rather underrated than the reverse. The estimate of M. Mengin shows that in 1821 the extent of the cultivated land was much less; but since that period, considerable tracts of waste land have been rendered fertile.

[2]The term "sharákee" is applied to those lands which are above the reach of the inundation, and the term "rei" to the rest.

many of the mud-built villages, the huts of which are composed of unburnt bricks, and occasions an awful loss of lives as well as property. Moreover the plague seldom visits Egypt excepting after a very high rise of the Nile. It is, however, far from being an *invariable* consequence of such an event. When the river begins to rise, all the canals are cleared out, each is closed by a dam of earth at the entrance, and opened when the Nile has nearly attained its greatest height, towards the end of September. When the river begins to fall the canals are closed again, that they may retain the water. The lands that are not inundated by the overflowing of the Nile are irrigated artificially, if sufficiently near to the river, or to a canal.

As all the cultivable soil of Egypt has been deposited by the river, it might be expected that the land would at length rise so high as to be above the reach of the inundation; but the bed of the river rises at the same time, and in the same degree.

At Thebes, the Nile rises about thirty-six feet; at the cataracts about forty; at Rosetta, owing to the proximity of the mouth, it only rises to the height of about three feet and a half. The Nile begins to rise in the end of June, or the beginning of July; that is to say, about, or soon after, the summer solstice, and attains its greatest height in the end of September, or sometimes (but rarely) in the beginning of October; that is, in other words, about or soon after the autumnal equinox. During the first three months of its decrease, it loses about half the height it had attained; and during the remaining six months, it falls more and more slowly. It generally remains not longer than three or four days at its maximum, and the same length of time at its minimum: it may therefore be said to be three months on the increase, and nine months gradually falling. It often remains without any apparent increase or diminution, at other times than those of its greatest or least elevation, and is subject to other slight irregularities. The Nile becomes turbid a little before its rise is apparent, and soon after it assumes a green hue, which it retains more than a fortnight. Its water is extremely delicious even when it is most impregnated with earth; but *then* the Egyptians (excepting the lower orders) usually leave it to settle before they drink it, and put it in porous earthen bottles, which cool it by evaporation. While the Nile is green, the people generally abstain from drinking the water fresh from the river, having recourse to a supply previously drawn, and kept in cisterns.

The width of the Nile where there are no islands is in few parts more than half a mile. The branches which enclose the Delta are not so wide, generally speaking, as the undivided stream above; and the river is as wide in most parts of Upper Egypt as in the lower extremity of the valley.

The rapidity of the current when the waters are low is not greater than the rate of a mile and a quarter in an hour; but during the higher state of the river, the current is very rapid, and while vessels with furled sails are carried down by the stream with great speed, others ascend the river at an almost equal rate, favoured by the strong northerly winds, which prevail most when the current is most rapid. When the river is low, the wind from the north is often more powerful than the current, and vessels cannot then descend the stream even with the help of oars.

I believe that I shall have occasion to add a few more words on the Nile some days hence, when I hope to send you the remainder of the general sketch.

Meanwhile, believe me to remain, &c.

LETTER VI

October, 1842

My Dear Friend,

SINCE I last wrote to you, the weather has continued intensely hot; but during the last three days almost constant lightning throughout the evening, though succeeded by excessive heat during the nights, has given us hope of speedy relief. This heat is attributed to the present state of the Nile, which has continued most unusually increasing up to this time (the 13th of October), and given rise to serious apprehensions; for unless the water drain quickly off the land when the river begins to fall, it is feared that a severe plague may ensue. In such a case, we propose going up to Thebes for four months, but we earnestly hope it may please Almighty God to avert so dreadful a calamity as a pestilence must inevitably prove. I now resume the sketch I left unfinished in my last letter.

The climate of Egypt is generally very salubrious. The extraordinary dryness of the atmosphere (excepting in the maritime parts) is proved by the wonderful state of preservation in which bread, meat, fruits, &c. have been found in the tombs of ancient Thebes, after having been deposited there two or three thousand years. The ancient monuments of Egypt have suffered very little from the weather: the colours with which some of them are adorned retain almost their pristine brightness. There arises from the waters of the fields a considerable exhalation (though not often visible), during the inundation, and for some months afterwards; but even then it seems perfectly dry immediately within the skirts of the desert, where most of the monuments of antiquity are situated.[1]

The heat in Egypt is very great; but not so oppressive as might be imagined, on account of that extreme dryness of the atmosphere of which I have spoken, and the prevalence of northerly breezes.[2]

Rain is very rare phenomenon in the valley of Egypt. In the Sa'eed, a heavy rain falls not oftener, on the average, than once in four or five years. My

---

[1]The damp at this period, slight as it is, occasions ophthalmia, diarrhoea, and dysentery, to be more prevalent now than at other times.

[2]The general height of the thermometer (Fahrenheit's) in Lower Egypt during the hot season, at noon, and in the shade, is from 90° to 100°; in Upper Egypt, from 10° to 11°; and in Nubia, from 110° to 120°, and even 130°, though in few years. In the latter country, if placed in the sand and exposed to the sun, the thermometer often rises to 150° or more. The temperature of Lower Egypt in the depth of winter is from 50°to 60°.

brother witnessed such an occurrence at Thebes, a tremendous storm of lightning and rain, in the autumn of 1827. Lightning is frequently seen, but thunder is seldom heard. On that occasion it was quite terrific, and lasted throughout a whole night. The torrents which pour down the sides and ravines of the naked mountains which hem in the valley of Egypt, on these occasions, though so rare, leave very conspicuous traces. Here, in Cairo, and in the neighbouring parts, there fall on the average four or five smart showers in the year, and those generally during the winter and spring. Most unusually (but this is in every respect an unusual season), it rained heavily on the night of the 30th of September. A heavy rain very rarely falls, and when it does, much damage is done to the houses. In the maritime parts of Egypt, rain is not so unfrequent.

The prevalence of the north-westerly wind is one of the most remarkable advantages of climate the Egyptians enjoy. The north-west breeze is ever refreshing and salubrious, beneficial to vegetation, and of the greatest importance in facilitating the navigation of the Nile at almost every season of the year, and particularly during that period when the river is rising, and the current consequently the most rapid. During the first three months of the decrease of the river, that is, from the autumnal equinox to the winter-solstice, the wind is rather variable; sometimes blowing from the west, south, or east; but still the northerly winds are most frequent. During the next three months, the wind is more variable; and during the last three months of the decrease of the river, from the vernal equinox to the summer solstice, winds from the south, or south-east, often hot and very oppressive, are frequent, but of short duration.

During a period called "El-Khamáseen," hot southerly winds are very frequent, and particularly noxious. This period is said to commence on the day after the Coptic festival of Easter-Sunday, and to terminate on Whit-Sunday; thus continuing forty-nine days. It generally begins in the latter part of April, and lasts during the whole of May. This is the most unhealthy season in Egypt; and while it lasts the inhabitants are apprehensive of being visited by the plague; but their fears cease on the termination of that period. It is remarkable that we have already suffered much from hot wind, for it is most unusual at this season. During July and August it was frequently distressing; and I can only compare it to the blast from a furnace, rendering every article of furniture literally hot, and always continuing three days. Having, happily, glass windows, we closed them in the direction of the wind, and found the close atmosphere infinitely more bearable than the heated blast. This was a season of extreme anxiety, being quite an unexpected ordeal for my children; but, I thank God, excepting slight indisposition, they escaped unhurt.

The "Samoom," which is a very violent, hot, and almost suffocating wind, is of more rare occurrence than the Khamáseen winds, and of shorter duration;

its continuance being more brief in proportion to the intensity of its parching heat, and the impetuosity of its course. Its direction is generally from the south-east, or south-south-east. It is commonly preceded by a fearful calm. As it approaches, the atmosphere assumes a yellowish hue, tinged with red; the sun appears of a deep blood colour, and gradually becomes quite concealed before the hot blast is felt in its full violence. The sand and dust raised by the wind add to the gloom, and increase the painful effects of the heat and rarity of the air. Respiration becomes uneasy, perspiration seems to be entirely stopped; the tongue is dry, the skin parched, and a prickling sensation is experienced, as if caused by electric sparks. It is sometimes impossible for a person to remain erect, on account of the force of the wind; and the sand and dust oblige all who are exposed to it to keep their eyes closed. It is, however, most distressing when it overtakes travellers in the desert. My brother encountered at Koos, in Upper Egypt, a samoom which was said to be one of the most violent ever witnessed. it lasted less than half an hour, and a very violent samoom seldom continues longer. My brother is of opinion that, although it is extremely distressing, it can never prove fatal, unless to persons already brought almost to the point of death by disease, fatigue, thirst, or some other cause. The poor camel seems to suffer from it equally with his master; and will often lie down with his back to the wind, close his eyes, stretch out his long neck upon the ground, and so remain until the storm has passed over.

Another very remarkable phenomenon is the "Zóba'ah," and very common in Egypt, and in the adjacent deserts. It is a whirlwind, which raises the sand or dust in the form of a pillar, generally of immense height.[1] These whirling pillars of sand (of which my brother has seen more than twelve in one day, and often two or three at a time during the spring) are carried sometimes with very great rapidity across the deserts and fields of Egypt, and over the river. My brother's boat was twice crossed by a zóba'ah; but on each occasion its approach was seen, and necessary precautions were taken: both the sails were let fly a few moments before it reached the boat; but the boxes and cushions in the cabin were thrown down by the sudden heeling of the vessel, and everything was covered with sand and dust.

The "Saráb," called by Europeans "mirage," which resembles a lake, and is so frequently seen in the desert, tantalizing the thirsty traveller, I mentioned

---

[1]"I measured" (says my brother) "the height of a zóba'ah, with a sextant, at Thebes, under circumstances which insured a very near approximation to perfect accuracy (observing its altitude from an elevated spot, at the precise moment when it passed through, and violently agitated, a distant group of palm-trees), and found it to be seven hundred and fifty feet. I think that several zóba'ahs I have seen were of greater height. Others which I measured at the same place were between five and seven hundred feet in height."—*Modern Egyptians*, 3rd Edition, Part I. chap. x.

to you in a former letter. The illusion is often perfect, the objects within and beyond the apparent lake being reflected by it with the utmost precision. You probably know that the reflection is produced by a heated stratum of air upon the glowing surface of a plain, and you may have seen something of the same kind in England.

The fields in the vicinity of the river, and of the great canals, are irrigated by means of machines at all seasons of the year, if not subject to the natural inundation. For a description of these, I refer you to the 'Modern Egyptians,' 3rd edition, Part II. chap. i.; and I will now conclude this letter with a concise physical and agricultural *calendar* of Egypt, drawn up by my brother from Arabic works, and from his own observations.

January.—The mean temperature in the afternoon during this month at Cairo is about 60°. The waters which, during the season of the inundation, had been retained upon the fields by means of dams, have now sunk into the soil; but water still remains in some of the large canals, their mouths having been stopped up. The river has lost about half the height it had attained; that is to say, it has sunk about twelve feet in and about the latitude of Cairo. The wind at this season, and throughout the winter, is very variable; but the northerly winds are most frequent. People should now abstain from eating fowls, and all crude and cold vegetables. The poppy is sown. It is unwholesome to drink water during the night at this season, and throughout the winter. The fifth Coptic month (Toobeh) begins on the 8th or 9th of January.[1] Now is the season of extreme cold. Beef should not be eaten at this period. The fields begin to be covered with verdure. The vines are trained. Carrots plentiful. Onions sown. The date-palm sown. The ripe sugarcanes cut.

February.—The mean temperature in the afternoon during this month at Cairo is about 66°. End of the season of extreme cold.[2] The fields everywhere throughout Egypt are covered with verdure. The sixth Coptic month (Amsheer) begins on the 7th or 8th of February. Warm water should be drunk fasting at this season. The wind very variable. The harvest of beans. The pomegranate tree blossoms. Vines are planted. Trees put forth their leaves. The season of the winds which bring rain, called el-Lawakeh. The cold ceases to be severe.

March.—Mean temperature in the afternoon during this month, at Cairo, about 68°. End of the season for planting trees. The seventh Coptic month (Barmahát) begins on the 9th of March. Variable and tempestuous winds. The Vernal Equinox. During the quarter now commencing the river continues

[1] See a note on the beginning of the first Coptic month, in September. The Egyptians (Muslims as well as Christians) still divide the seasons by the Coptic months; but for dates, in their writings, they generally use the lunar Mohammedan months.
[2] Such is the statement of the Egyptian almanacks; but there are generally as cold days in the month of Amsheer as in Toobeh, and sometimes colder.

decreasing; the wind often blows from the south or south-east; and the samoom winds (from the same quarters) occur most frequently during this period; the plague also generally visits Egypt at this season, if at all. The weather becomes mild. Northerly winds become prevalent. The wheat-harvest begins. Lentils are reaped; cotton, sesame, and indigo sown; and the sugar-cane planted. The barley-harvest begins.

April.—Mean temperature in the afternoon during this month, at Cairo, about 76°. Time for taking medicine. The eighth Coptic month (Barmoodeh) begins on the 8th of April. Samoom winds. Time for the fecundation of the date-palm. Rice sown. The wheat-harvest in Lower Egypt. Beginning of the first season for sowing millet. The Khamáseen winds generally commence in this month.

May.—Mean temperature in the afternoon during this month, at Cairo, about 85°. The Khamáseen winds prevail principally during this month; and the season is consequently unhealthy. Winter clothing disused. The ninth Coptic month (Beshens) begins on the 8th of May. Time for taking medicine, and losing blood. Season of the yellow water-melon. Cucumbers sown. The apricot bears; and the mulberry. Turnips sown. End of the first season for sowing millet. The apricot ripens. Beginning of the season of great heat. Beginning also of the season of the hot winds, called "el-bawáreh," which prevail during forty days.

June.—Mean temperature in the afternoon during this month, at Cairo, about 94°. Strong northerly winds prevail about this time. The water of the Nile becomes turbid, but does not yet begin to rise. The tenth Coptic month (Ba-ooneh) begins on the 7th of June. The banana sown. Samoom winds. Strong perfumes (as musk, &c.) are disused now, and throughout the summer. The yellow water-melon abundant. The plague, if any existed previously, now ceases. Honey collected. People should abstain from drinking the water of the Nile at this season for fifteen days,[1] unless first boiled. "The drop" (en nuktah) descends into the Nile, and, according to popular belief, causes it to increase soon after:[2] this is said to happen on the 11th of Ba-ooneh, which corresponds with the 17th of June: it is the day before the Coptic festival of Michael the Archangel. The flesh of the kid is preferred at this season, and until the end of summer. Samoom winds blow occasionally during a period of seventy days, now commencing. THE SUMMER SOLSTICE; when the day is fourteen hours long in Lower Egypt. During the quarter now beginning (i.e. during the period of the increase of the Nile) northerly winds prevail almost uninterruptedly, excepting at night, when it is generally calm. Though the heat is great, this quarter is the most healthy season of the year. The Nile begins to rise now, or a few days earlier or later. The season for grapes and figs commences. Peaches plentiful.

---

[1] Commencing from the 10th of Ba-ooneh (or the 16th of June).
[2] It is really a heavy dew which falls about this time.

July.—Mean temperature in the afternoon during this month, at Cairo, about 98°. The rise of the Nile is now daily proclaimed in the metropolis. Locusts die, or disappear, in every part of Egypt. The eleventh Coptic month (Ebeeb) begins on the 7th of July. Violent northerly winds prevail for fifteen days.[1] Honey abundant. People should abstain from eating plentifully at this season. The noonday heat is now excessive. Ophthalmia prevails now, but not so much now as in the autumn. The bawáheer, or seven days of extreme heat, fall at the end of this month.[2] Grapes and figs abundant. Maize is now sown. Harvest of the first crop of millet. The date ripens.

August.—Mean temperature in the afternoon during this month, at Cairo, about 92°. Season for pressing grapes. The last Coptic month (Misra) begins on the 6th of August. Onions should not be eaten at this time. Radishes and carrots sown. Cold water should be drunk, fasting. Watermelons plentiful. The season for gathering cotton. The pomegranate ripens. Violent northerly winds. Sweetmeats should not be eaten at this time. "The wedding of the Nile" takes place on the 14th, or one of the five following days of the month of Misra (the 19th to the 24th of August); this is when the dam of earth which closes the entrance of the canal of Cairo is broken down; it having been first announced that the river has risen (in the latitude of the metropolis) sixteen cubits, which is an exaggeration.[3] Second season for sowing millet. Musquitoes abound now. End of the seventy days in which samoom winds frequently occur.

September.—Mean temperature in the afternoon during this month, at Cairo, about 88°. White beet and turnip sown. Windy weather. The beginning of the month Toot—the first of the Coptic year; corresponding with the 10th or 11th of September, according as five or six intercalary days are added at the end of the Coptic year preceding.[4] Ripe dates abundant, and limes. Windy weather. THE AUTUMNAL EQUINOX. The Nile is now, or a few days later, at its greatest height; and all the canals are opened. During the quarter now commencing (i.e. during the first three months of the decrease of the river), the wind is very variable; often blowing from the west, and

---

[1]Fleas disappear now; and if you can form a just idea of the annoyance they occasion, you will not think the insertion of this information unimportant.

[2]They are said to commence on the 20th of Ebeeb, or 26th of July.

[3]The true rise at this period is about 19 or 20 feet; the river, therefore, has yet to rise about 4 or 5 feet more, on the average.

[4]"Five intercalary days are added at the end of three successive years; and six at the end of the fourth year. The Coptic leap-year immediately precedes ours: therefore, the Coptic year begins on the 11th of September, only when it is the next after their leap-year; or when our next ensuing year is a leap-year: and consequently after the following February, the corresponding days of the Coptic and our months will be the same as in other years. The Copts begin their reckoning from the era of Diocletian, A.D. 284."—*Modern Egyptians*, Part I., chap. ix.

sometimes from the south. The exhalations from the alluvial soil, in consequence of the inundation, occasion ophthalmia, diarrhoea, and dysentery to
be more prevalent in this quarter than at other seasons. Harvest of sesame.

October.—Mean temperature in the afternoon during this month, at Cairo,
about 80°. The leaves of trees become yellow. Green sugar-canes cut, to be
sucked. Drinking water at night, after sleep, is pernicious at this season. The
henna-leaves gathered. Winter vegetables sown. The second Coptic month
(Bábeh) begins on the 10th or 11th of October. Wheat, barley, lentils, beans,
lupins, chick-peas, kidney-beans, trefoil, fenugreek, colewort, lettuce, and
safflower are sown now, or a little later. Bleeding is injurious now. The dews
resulting from the inundation increase.

November.—Mean temperature in the afternoon during this month, at
Cairo, about 72°. The cold during the latter part of the night is now pernicious. The third Coptic month (Katoor) begins on the 9th or 10th of
November. Rain is now expected in Lower Egypt. The "mereesee," or south
wind, prevalent. The rice-harvest. The maize-harvest, and second harvest of
millet. Winter-clothing assumed. Bananas plentiful.

December.—Mean temperature in the afternoon during this month, at
Cairo, about 68°. Tempestuous and cloudy weather. Strong perfumes, as
musk, ambergris, &c., are agreeable now. The fourth Coptic month (Kiyahk)
begins on the 9th or 10th of December. The leaves of trees fall. THE WINTER
SOLSTICE; when the day is ten hours long in Lower Egypt. The wind is variable during this quarter. Beginning of the season for planting trees. Fleas
multiply. The vines are pruned. Beef is not considered wholesome food at
this season.

LETTER VII

October 18th, Ramadán, 1842

My Dear Friend,

THE leading topic of conversation in this country, at the present time, is the state of the Nile, which has hitherto (to the 18th of October) continued rising, and occasioned a general fear that a severe plague will ensue on the subsiding of the inundation. In 1818, it rose until the 16th of October; but never so late since that time, nor for a considerable period before. Our house is flooded in the lower part; and in some of the streets of Cairo, the water is within a foot of the surface, while it has entered many of the houses.

This is the 12th day of Ramadán, or the month of abstinence; and I do heartily pity those who observe the fast, for the weather is again intensely hot, and it is marvellous how any person can observe the law, denying himself from daybreak to sunset even a draught of water. I really think there are very many conscientious fasters; and it would interest you exceedingly to walk through the streets of Cairo during this month, and observe the varieties of deportment visible among the people. Some are sitting idly, holding an ornamented stick, or with a string of beads in their hands.[†] Boys, fasting for the first time, and even men, are endeavouring to distract their attention with the most childish toys; while many are exhibiting, in various ways, that fasting does not improve their tempers.

Some days since, as it drew near the hour of sunset, an aged couple were passing near our present dwelling, the old woman leading her blind husband by the hand, and carrying his pipe, that it might be ready for him as soon as the law should allow him to enjoy it. Bent as they were by age and infirmity, it was sad to see that they were evidently among the fasters, and it was a sight to excite compassion and respect; for as so many of the aged sink into their last earthly home, when the month of abstinence has passed, the fear that they too might prove martyrs to the requirements of their religion was far from groundless, and naturally present to the mind of the observer.

The great among the Muslims in general turn night into day during Ramadán; therefore they are seldom seen in the streets. Most of them sleep from daybreak until the afternoon; while others break their fast in private. I do not think that this is done by the lower orders; and no one can hear the cry of joy which rings and echoes through the city at sunset, when, in token

---

[†]A string of beads used for prayer (like a rosary).

that the fasting is over, for at least some hours, a cannon is discharged from
the citadel, without rejoicing with the people, that another day of Ramadán
has passed. But no sound is so imposing as the night-call to prayer from the
numerous menarets. I mentioned to you our impression on hearing it first at
Alexandria; but here, in Cairo, it is infinitely more striking. On some occasions, when the wind is favourable, we can hear perhaps a hundred voices, in
solemn, and indeed harmonious, concert. Here the Mueddins, raised between
earth and heaven, call on their fellow-creatures to worship Heaven's God;
and oh! as their voices are borne on the night-wind, let the silent prayer of
every Christian who hears them ascend to a throne of grace for mercy on their
behalf. They are more especially objects of pity, because they have the light
of the Gospel in their land; but how is that light obscured! prejudice, and
(shall I write it?) the conduct of many Europeans dwelling among them, and
calling themselves Christians, have blinded their eyes, and because of the sins
of others, the true Christian spends his strength in vain. Far be it from me to
cast a sweeping censure, but our respectable and respected friends here will
join me as I raise my voice against those nominal Christians, who, by their
profligacy, prove ever "rocks a-head" to the already prejudiced Muslim. This
always important city may now be ranked among "men's thoroughfares" in
a wide sense, and we must only hope that the day may come when the phrase,
"these are Christians," will no longer convey reproach.

The Mohammedan months are lunar, and consequently retrograde; and
when Ramadán[†] occurs in the summer, the obligation to abstain from water
during the long sultry days is fearful in its consequences. At sunset, the fasting
Muslim takes his breakfast; and this meal generally commences with light
refreshment, such as sweet cakes, raisins, &c.; for, from long abstinence,
many persons find themselves in so weak a state, that they cannot venture to
eat immediately a full meal. Many break their fast with merely a glass of
sherbet, or a cup of coffee. This refreshment is succeeded by a substantial
meal, equal to their usual dinner. They often retire to obtain a short sleep.
Usually, two hours after sunset, criers greet all the persons in their respective
districts, beating a small drum at the doors, and saying something compli-
mentary to the inmates of each house. Again, the morning call to prayer is
chanted much earlier than usual, perhaps an hour and a half before daybreak,
to remind all to take their second meal; and the crier also goes another round,
making a loud noise, in which he perseveres until he is answered, at each
house where his attention is required. Thus, you see, no small pains are taken
to remind the faster to avail himself of his opportunities; and it is singular to
hear the variety of noises which disturb the nights of this most unpleasant

---

[†]For an accurate and detailed exposition of Ramadan, the month of fasting, cf. Lane,
Modern Egyptians, 91, 472–79. Lane's description is of particular interest as it relates
customs now long since forgotten.

month. At daybreak, each morning, the last signal is made from the citadel, by the firing of a cannon, for the removal of all food; and on some occasions, this report seems to shake the city to the very foundations. The open lattice windows oblige us to hear all the noises I have described. Our windows are furnished with glazed frames, in addition to the carved wooden lattice-work, but the former are only closed in the winter, for those who desire to enjoy any sleep during the hot season must keep all windows (and if possible doors also) open. Judging by my own surprise at the degree of heat we have endured since our arrival, I imagine you have no adequate idea of it. On my opening, a few days since, a card-box full of sealing-wax, I found the whole converted into an oblong mass, fitting the lower part of the box.

As to the vermin of Egypt, I really think that the *flies* occasion the greatest annoyance, so abundant are they, and so distressing. Nets placed at the doors and windows exclude them; but there are days, indeed weeks and months, in Egypt, when the temperature is so oppressive, that it is not possible to allow the air to be impeded, even by a net. Musquitoes too are very troublesome in the mornings and evenings, and much reduce the comfort of early rising. This is a serious inconvenience here, for we find the most agreeable hours are in the early mornings and in the cool evenings, after sunset. The old houses abound with bugs, but in this respect we have been particularly fortunate; for we have not been annoyed by these very disgusting insects. Fleas are very troublesome during their season, I am told, but with us their season has not yet begun; and I think and hope cleanliness in our house will, in a great degree, prevent their attentions. "There are insects" (as I once heard a lecturer on natural history express himself) "which must be nameless in all polite society;" therefore, my dear friend, they must be nameless here, but of these we have seen five. These arrived at five different times in parcels of *new* linen from a bazaar, and their arrival has occasioned the closest scrutiny when anything new is brought to us.[†]

Rats, also, are extremely annoying, and nothing escapes their depredations, unless secured in wire safes, or hung up at a sufficient distance from walls. These animals run about our bedrooms during the nights; and I sometimes think they come in at the open windows. They are generally harmless, but sufficiently tiresome. Lizards too are very common, but perfectly innocuous, and occupy themselves entirely on the ceilings and windows in chasing flies, on which they seem to subsist. I told you I feared much from

---

[†]Lane does not seem to have been as susceptible or fastidious as Sophia to the vermin of Egypt. He writes: "Vermin did not trouble me so often in Egypt as to detract very much from the luxuries which the climate afforded me. From mosquitoes I was effectually secured at night by curtains; and when the flies would have been troublesome, if one hand was occupied with my pipe, the other was at liberty to shake a whisk made of palm-leaves, which at meals is generally held by a servant" (*Description*, 43).

antiquated cobwebs that spiders would be numerous. They are, truly, and so very large that I will not risk giving my opinion of their size; it is so far beyond any European specimen I have seen. But the gravest annoyances are scorpions, and of these we have found three, one of which was exactly three inches in length. I was much distressed on finding these, but comforted on hearing that if the wound they inflict be immediately scarified, and an application of sal ammoniac be made, it does not prove fatal. These applications, however, though absolutely necessary, are very painful; and I trust we may be spared the necessity of resorting to such means. Fearing for my children, for their sakes I am a coward, and I feel it is ever necessary to bear in mind that we cannot wander where we can be outcasts from the care of Heaven, or strangers to the protecting Providence of God.

I have suffered this letter to remain unfinished for a whole week, expecting daily that I might be able to tell you of the end of this year's inundation. This I am now able to do; but must first mention, that we have experienced a most extraordinary storm of wind, accompanied by such clouds of dust, that we were obliged to close our eyes and wait patiently until its fury had in some measure passed away. When it abated we looked out upon the city, and could only see the tops of its menarets above the sea of dust, and its lofty palm-trees bending before the blast. I have *heard* such a hurricane, during the night, once since our arrival in Cairo, and fearful indeed it was, but I have never seen its effects until now. This was not one of the winds to which the Easterns give a name, such as the Zóba'ah, the Khamáseen winds, or the Samoom; but a strong sweeping wind from the north-east. In looking down upon the many ruins of Cairo, I feel astonished by the fact of their withstanding such a hurricane. A storm like this is generally preceded and followed by a perfect calm.

This day (the 25th of October) is the first of the decrease of the Nile. It is usually at its greatest height, as I have already mentioned, at the end of September. It is not extraordinary that it should be a high inundation; that is well accounted for this year, as it has been in the two preceding years, by the construction of many new embankments, but it is the lateness of the inundation which is so exceedingly unusual. It rose considerably on the 23rd instant, and on the 24th slightly; and I find no one with whom we are acquainted here among the residents who remembers such an occurrence.

"A very grievous murrain," forcibly reminding us of that which visited this same country in the days of Moses, has prevailed during the last three months, and the already distressed peasants feel the calamity severely, or rather (I should say) the few who possess cattle. Among the rich men of the country, the loss has been enormous. During our voyage up the Nile, we observed several dead cows and buffaloes lying in the river, as I mentioned in a former letter; and some friends who followed us two months after, saw many on the banks; indeed, up to this time, great numbers of cattle are dying in every part of the country, and the prevailing excitement leads me to recur to the subject.

LETTER VIII

MY DEAR FRIEND,

I HAVE just returned from witnessing the curious procession of the Mahmal, preparatory to the departure of the great caravan of pilgrims to Mekkah. We were early on the way, and after riding for nearly an hour we found ourselves in the main street of the city, opposite to the khán el-Khaleelee, the chief Turkish bazaar of Cairo. I felt more than ever convinced that donkeys were the only safe means of conveyance in the streets of this city. A lady never rides but on a donkey, with a small carpet laid over the saddle. For gentlemen, horses are now more used than donkeys; but their riders encounter much inconvenience. In many cases, this morning, our donkeys threaded their way among loaded camels, where horses were turned back; and my apprehensions lest the large bales of goods should really sweep my boys from their saddles, were scarcely removed by the extreme care of their attendants, who always kept one arm round each of my children, in passing through the dangerous thoroughfares. I assure you it is an exceedingly awkward thing to ride through the streets of Cairo at any time, but especially so during a season of festivity.

We had engaged for the day a room on a first floor, commanding a good view of the street, and we had not been long seated before an extraordinary uproar commenced. This arose from crowds of boys, provided with sticks, and absolutely privileged (as is usual on the days of this procession) to beat all Christians and Jews. A poor Frank gentleman was attacked under the window we were occupying, and protected with difficulty by some Arabs, who interposed with much kindness. It was especially matter of congratulation to-day, that our party were supposed to be Easterns, and that we had so learnt to *carry* the dress that we were not suspected. On one occasion, not long since, my donkey stumbled, and a Turkish gentleman, who was passing me, exclaimed, "Yá Sátir" (O! Protector). Had he supposed I was an Englishwoman, I imagine he would not have invoked protection for me. The prejudice against Europeans is especially strong, as they are said to have enlightened the Pasha too much on matters of finance: but to-day, I will dismiss this subject, and tell you of the procession, while it is fresh in my recollection.

The first person who passed, belonging to the procession, were two men with drawn swords, who engaged occasionally in mock combat. Next came a grotesque person, well mounted, and wearing a high pointed cap, and an immense beard of twisted hemp, and clothed in sheep-skins. He held a slender stick in his right hand, and in his left a bundle of papers, on which he pretended, with a tragicomical expression of countenance, to write judicial opinions. Next followed the *gun* of the caravan, a small brass field-piece, an hour and a half before noon, preceded by a company of Nizám troops, and followed by another company, headed by their band; the musical instruments being European. I cannot praise their performance, yet it approached nearer to music than any attempt I have heard in Egypt. It remains, however, for me to hear the professional singers of this country; and I am told by persons of undoubted taste, that if I do not admire the airs they sing, I shall be surprised at their skill and the quality of their voices.

The soldiers were followed by a long procession of Darweeshes. First came the Saadeeyeh, with numerous flags, bearing, in many cases, the names of God, Mohammad, and the founder of their order, on a ground of green silk. Most of these Darweeshes were beating a small kettle-drum called báz, which is held in the left hand, and beaten with a short thick strap. Some were beating cymbals, and all repeating religious ejaculations, chiefly names and epithets of God. They were perpetually bowing their heads to the right and to the left during the whole repetition, and this motion was rendered the more apparent by many of them wearing very high felt caps; then, the variety in their costume, and, more than all, the gravity of their deportment, combined to rivet our attention. These Darweeshes were followed by a body of their parent order (the Refá-eeyeh), bearing black flags, and also beating bázes and cymbals, and repeating the like ejaculations. Their sheykh, a venerable-looking person, wearing a very large black turban, rode behind them, on horseback. Then passed the Kádireeyeh Darweeshes: their principal insignia were borne by members of their order; viz. palm-sticks, for fishing-rods; and fishing-nets strained on hoops, and raised on long poles, with many small fish suspended round them. They carried white flags. Next followed the Ahmedeeyeh, and Baráhimeh Darweeshes, bearing red and green flags; and immediately after these came "the Mahmal."

The Mahmal is a mere emblem of royalty, and contains nothing; but two copies of the Kurán, in cases of gilt silver, are fastened to the exterior. It is an imitation of a covered litter, borne on the back of a camel; and it accompanies the caravan yearly, forming, if I may use the expression, the banner of the pilgrims. Many persons have understood that it contains the Kisweh, or new covering for the temple of Mekkah; but they are mistaken. The origin of this ceremony, as related in the 'Modern Egyptians,' was as follows:— "Shegger-ed-Durr (commonly called Sheger-ed-Durr), a beautiful Turkish female slave, who became the favourite wife of the Sultan Es-Sáleh Negm-ed-Deen, and on the death of his son (with whom terminated the dynasty of the house of Eiyoob) caused herself to be acknowledged as Queen of Egypt, performed the pilgrimage in a magnificent Hódag (or covered litter), borne by a camel; and for several successive years her empty litter was sent with the caravan merely for the sake of state. Hence, succeeding princes of Egypt sent with each year's caravan of pilgrims a kind of Hódag (which received the name of Mahmal, or Mahmil) as an emblem of royalty, and the kings of other countries followed their example."[1] The usual covering of the Mahmal has been black brocade; that I have seen this morning is red, and I understand that it is shabby in comparison with those of former years: indeed each year (my brother tells me) all that is connected with this procession becomes less remarkable, and less money is expended on it by the government. But to me, and to those of us who had not previously seen it, it was extremely interesting. There were none of the great men habited in cloth of gold, who preceded it on former occasions; neither were the camels handsomely caparisoned.

The half-naked sheykh who has for so many years followed the Mahmal, incessantly rolling his head, for which feat he receives a gratuity from the government, rode on a fine horse immediately after it. If he be the same man (and I am informed he is the very same) who has year after year committed this absurdity, it is wonderful that his head has borne such unnatural and long-continued motion. There followed him a number of led camels and horses, and their decorations were extremely picturesque, but not costly. The camels were ornamented in various ways; one having small bells, strung on either side of a saddle ornamented with coloured cloth; others with palm-branches, ostrich feathers, and small flags fixed on similar saddles decorated with cowries. These were succeeded by a company of regular troops, followed by the Emeer-el-Hágg (or chief of the pilgrims). Then passed the usual collection of the presents which are distributed during the pilgrimage; and then, a number of drummers mounted on camels, and beating enormous kettle-drums: after these, some more led camels, and a numerous group bearing mesh'als, the tops of which were covered with coloured kerchiefs. "The mesh'al is a staff with a cylindrical frame of iron at the top filled with wood, or having two, three, four, or five of these receptacles for fire."[2] These were for the purpose of lighting the caravan; as the journey is mostly performed during the cool hours of night. Another company of officers and soldiers followed these; and then the litter and baggage of the Emeer-el-Hágg. His first supply of water passed next, borne by a number of camels, each laden with four skins; and these were succeeded by led camels closing the procession.

Had we gone merely with the view of seeing the spectators, we should have been amply rewarded. The shops and their benches were crowded with people of many countries; and the variety in their costume and manners formed an amusing study. The windows of the first and second floors were perfectly full of women, children, and slaves; and here and there a richly embroidered dress was seen through the lattice.

---

[1]Lane, *Modern Egyptians,* 3rd ed., part. ii, p. 203.
[2]*Modern Egyptians,* 3rd ed., part. i, p. 254

On one point all denominations of people seemed agreed; viz. In purchasing something for their children from almost all the venders of sweets, and many passed constantly on this occasion; therefore their poor children kept up a continual system of cramming during the whole procession; and here my eyes were opened to a new manner of accounting for the generally wretched appearance of the children of this country. Their parents put anything and everything that is eatable into their mouths, without the slightest regard to its being wholesome or otherwise. How then can they be strong or healthy?

LETTER IX

November, 1842

My Dear Friend,

I SHALL now endeavour to give you some account of Cairo and its environs, with the help of a series of historical notes, for which I am indebted to my brother, who has derived his information on these subjects chiefly from El-Makreezee's 'Historical and Topographical Account of Egypt and its Metropolis.' This work of El-Makreezee is chiefly a compilation from the writings of other Arab historians and geographers; and those parts of which my brother has availed himself contain observations of many authors of different ages.

The first city founded by the Arabs in Egypt was El-Fustat. It was the residence of the governors of that country for more than a century; but after the overthrow of the dynasty of the Umaweeyeh (or race of Umeeyeh), a new city called El-'Askar, adjoining El-Fustát, became the seat of government. Afterwards, another city, which received the name of El Katáë' (or El-Katáyë'), was built in the neighbourhood of El-'Askar; and the independent princes of the family of Tooloon resided there. After the extinction of this dynasty El-'Askar became again the seat of government, and continued so until the general of El-Mo'ezz obtained possession of Egypt, and founded El-Káhireh, which is now called Masr, or (by Europeans) Cairo.

El-Fustát was built upon the spot where the army of the Arabs encamped for a short time, after their conquest of Egypt, in the 20th year of the Flight (or A.D. 641). It received this name, which signifies "the Tent," from its having been founded around the tent of the Arab general 'Amr Ibn El-'A's, or (according to some authors) merely because "Fustát" is a term applicable to any city. It was, however, more commonly known by the name of Masr, which name has been lately transferred to Cairo. The appellation of Masr El-'Ateekah (or Old Masr) is now given to the small town which at present occupies a part of the site of El-Fustát. This town has been improperly called by European travellers "Old Cairo;" as well might Egyptian Babylon be called old Fustát.

The site of El-Fustát at the period of the Arabian conquest was unoccupied by any buildings, excepting a Roman fortress, still existing, called Kasr esh-Shema, on the north of the hill of Babylon; but in the neighbourhood were many churches and convents. The Nile, at that period, flowed close by the fortress above mentioned. El-Fustát is described as a very fine city, containing houses five or six stories high, constructed of brick. The primary cause of its

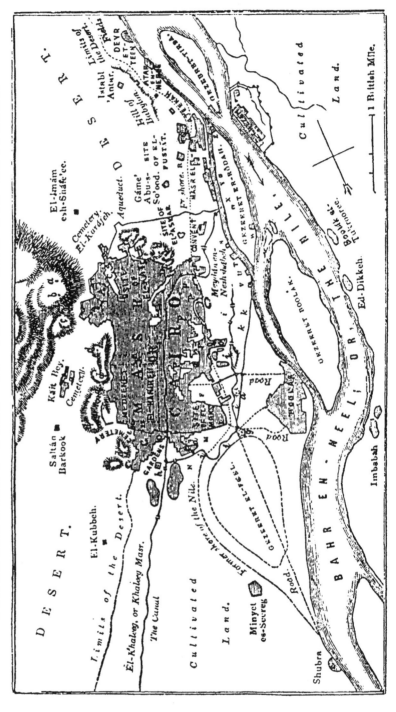

TOPOGRAPHICAL PLAN OF CAIRO AND ITS ENVIRONS.

EXPLANATION OF THE TOPOGRAPHICAL PLAN OF CAIRO AND ITS ENVIRONS

A, The Citadel.

B, Place called the Rumeyleh.

C, The Cara Meydán.

D, Kal'at el Kebsh.

E, Birket el-Feel.

F, El Ezbekeeyeh.

G, El Hoseyneeheh.

H, Space between the Báb en-Nasr of the first wall of El-Káhireh (marked by the dotted line) and that of the second wall.

I, Space between the Báb el-Futooh of the first wall and that of the second.

K, Space between the Báb Zuweyleh of the first wall and the Báb Zuweyleh of the second.

L, Báb-el-Bahr; now more commonly called Báb el-Hadeed.

M, Tract formerly called Ard et Tabbáleh.

N, Site of the Garden of El-Baal

O, El-Look, and Báb el Look.

P, Tract which was occupied by the Gardens of Ez-Zahree.

Q, Kasr es-Shema.

R, Mosque of 'Amr.

S, Convent of Darweeshes.

T, Kasr El-'Eynee.

U,V, Palace and Hareem of Ibraheem Básha.

W, Kafr 'Abd-El-'Azeez (a village).

X, Kafr Káid-Bey (a village).

Y, Kasr er-Ródah

Z, The Mikyás, or Nilometer.

a, b, Mosque and Fort on Mount Mukattam.

c, Ruin called Kubbet el-Hawa.

d, d, d d, d, d, d, d, Forts erected by the French on the mounds of rubbish.

e, Cemetery of Báb en-Nasr.

f, Birket er-Ratlee.

g, Telegraph.

h, Gáme' Ez-Záhir (a ruined mosque).

i, i, i, i, i, Western Canal, formerly called El-Khaleeg en Násiree.

k, k, New Canal.

decline was the great famine which happened in the reign of El-Mustansir, in the middle of the fifth century of the Flight, and which lasted seven years. About a century after this awful calamity, the greater part of the city was destroyed by fire, to prevent its falling a prey to an invading Christian army.[1] It was partly rebuilt, but never regained its former opulence.

El-'Askar was founded in the year of the Flight 133 (A.D. 750–1), long before the decline of El-Fustát, which continued to be the metropolis of Egypt, though the governors no longer resided there. El-'Askar was rather a suburb of El-Fustát than a distinct city. El-Katáë', or El-Katáyë, was founded in the year of the Flight 256 (A.D. 869–70). It lay immediately on the west of the hill which is now occupied by the citadel of Cairo; and was about a mile in extent, from north to south, and from east to west. In the year 292, when the dynasty of the race of Tooloon was subverted, this town was plundered, and partly destroyed by fire; and it is said that the great famine in the reign of El-Mustansir destroyed all its inhabitants, leaving it to fall to ruin. Its site has become included within the suburbs of Cairo, and its great mosque, founded by Ibn Tooloon, yet remains.

The site of another town, which was called El-Maks, and which existed before the conquest of Egypt by the Arabs, is also now included within the suburban districts of Cairo. Medeenet El-Káhireh (the city of El-Káhireh or Cairo) originally occupied a space about three quarters of a mile square. It was founded in the year of the Flight 358 (A.D. 968–9). The first wall was pulled down in the year 480 (A.D. 1087–8), and a new one built, which included a small additional space on the north and south. This was pulled down in the year 572 (A.D. 1176–7), and the citadel and a third wall were built by Saláh-ed-Deen (the Saladin of European historians). The third wall extended, from the citadel, along the eastern and northern sides of the metropolis, partly encompassing El-Maks, on the western side of which it terminated, being left unfinished. It was the intention of its builder to have made it to surround Cairo and the citadel, and El-Fustát. The suburbs of Cairo have become much more extensive than the original city.

I must now give you a brief account of the changes which have taken place in the bed of the river in the neighbourhood of El-Fustát and Cairo, chiefly since the foundation of the latter of those cities, for I think them very remarkable.

We are informed by El-Makreezee that, at the period of the conquest of Egypt by the Arabs, Er-Ródah was the only island existing in the neighbourhood of the sites of the two cities above-mentioned. It was believed that the colossal figure called Abu-l-Hól (the great Sphinx near the Pyramids of El-Geezeh), and a similar colossus on the opposite side of the Nile, were talismans contrived by the ancient Egyptians, to prevent the sands of the

---

[1] Under Amaury, King of Jerusalem, called by the Egyptians Merée.

adjacent deserts from encroaching upon the banks of the river; but in spite of the popular opinion respecting their magic influence, the latter of these colossi was demolished in the year of the Flight 711 (A.D. 1311–12); and about the year 780 (A.D. 1378–9), the face of Abu-l-Hól was mutilated by the fanatic Sheykh Mohammad, surnamed Sáim-ed-Dahr. Immediately after these periods, it is affirmed, the sands of the eastern and western deserts began to overspread the cultivable land intervening between them and the Nile, and to cause a considerable contraction of the bed of the river; in truth, however, the eastern limits of the river in the neighbourhood of Cairo had become very much contracted in the sixth and seventh centuries of the Flight, and have experienced but little change since the commencement of the eighth century.

Before the contraction of its bed, the river flowed by the walls of the Kasr-esh-Shema, and the mosque of 'Amr; to the northward of El-Fustát, its eastern limits were bounded by the town of El-'Askar, the gardens of Ez-Zahree, the eastern part of the quarter called El-Look, the town of El-Maks, the tract called Ard-et-Tabbáleh, the garden of El-Baal, and the village of Minyet-es-Seereg. Thus we see that the Nile formerly flowed close by the western suburbs and gardens of Cairo. Towards the close of the period of the dynasty of the Fawátim (the Khaleefehs of Egypt), a large vessel, called El-Feel (or the Elephant), was wrecked in the Nile, near El-Maks, and, remaining where it sank, occasioned an accumulation of sand and mud, which soon became an extensive and fertile island. This new island, from the circumstance which gave rise to it, received the name of Gezeeret el-Feel (or the Island of the Elephant). It is laid down in the plan which shall accompany this letter, according to the description of its situation and extent, given by El-Makreezee.

In the year of the Flight 570 (A.D. 1174–5), this island became united with the main land on the east; and from that period the river gradually retired from the neighbourhood of El-Maks; forming, by the deposit of soil during the successive seasons of the inundation, the wide plain upon which the town of Boolák is situated. Boolák was founded in the year of the Flight 713 (A.D. 1313–14); and the island which is named after it (Gezeeret Boolák) was formed about the same period.

Boolák is about a mile in length, and half a mile is the measure of its greatest breadth. It contains about 20,000 inhabitants. Its houses, streets, and shops, &c., are like those of the metropolis, of which I hope to give you a description in my next letter. Of the mosques of Boolák, the large one called the Sináneeyeh, and that of Abu-l-'Elë, are the most remarkable; the first for its size, the latter for the beauty of its mád'neh, or menaret. The principal manufactories are those of cotton and linen cloths, and of striped silks of the same kind as the Syrian and Indian. Many Franks find employment in them. A printing-office has also been established at Boolák by the present Viceroy. Many works on military and naval tactics, and others on Arabic grammar, poetry, letter-writing, geometry, astronomy, surgery, &c., have issued from this press. The printing-office contains several *lithographic* presses, which are used for printing proclamations, tables illustrative of military and naval tactics, &c.

The city which is known to Europeans by the name of Cairo, or Grand Cairo, is called by the Egyptians Masr;[1] and in letters and other writings, the epithet El-Mahrooseh[2] (or The Guarded) is generally added. El-Káhir (or the planet Mars), an unpropitious star, being the ascendant at the period of its foundation, it was originally called El-Káhireh,[3] whence the Italianized name Cairo. It was founded at night. Astrologers had been consulted and had fixed on a propitious moment for laying the foundations of the city-wall. They were to have given a signal at that precise moment by ringing a number of bells, which were suspended to cords supported by poles, along the whole circumference of the intended wall; but a raven happening to alight upon one of the cords, the bells were put in motion before the chosen time; and the builders, who were waiting for the signal, immediately commenced their work—thus the city was founded at an inauspicious instead of a fortunate moment.[4]

From the landing-place at Boolák to the *nearest* gates of the metropolis, the distance is a little more than one mile. The southern road leads to the Esbekeeyeh and the Frank quarters, and the northern road leads (but not in a straight course) to the gate called Báb El-Hadeed, at the north-west angle of the city. At a short distance from this gate, it passed by a high mound of rubbish, upon which was a round tower, with a telegraph. This tower commanded a magnificent view of the metropolis, the citadel, and Mount Mukattam.

The area which the metropolis occupies is about three square miles. Its extreme length is three miles, and its extreme breadth one and a half. The population is about 240,000. Some travellers (judging by the narrowness of its streets, and from the crowds that are met in the great thoroughfares), have represented Cairo as a close, overpeopled city; and have attributed to this supposed closeness the origin and spread of those epidemic diseases with which it has been visited: but the case is far otherwise; it is a less close or crowded city than London or Paris, or perhaps any European metropolis. For a population of 248,000 inhabitants, the space of three square miles is certainly very ample. The streets are made narrow for the sake of shade, but most of the houses are large enough for twice as many inmates as they contain, and are very airy, the windows being of open lattice work.

---

[1]The Turks, and many other oriental foreigners, pronounce it Misr, and thus it is pronounced in the literary dialect of Arabic.

[2]In government documents, this epithet is often used alone to designate the Egyptian metropolis.

[3]El-Káhir and El-Káhireh (masc. and fem.) signify victorious.

[4]El-Makreezee's account of the first wall

The walls by which nearly the whole of Cairo is surrounded are composed of the calcareous stone of the neighbouring mountains, and partly of the materials of some pyramidal tombs which were near the principal pyramids of El-Geezeh; but they are not of uniform strength, nor the work of one period. The metropolis is bounded on the eastern side, partly by a portion of the third wall (which was built by Saláh-ed-Deen), uniting with the walls of the citadel, and partly by modern walls of rude construction. The northern wall is well-built and lofty. The walls on the western and southern sides are irregular in their direction, low, and for the most part very ill constructed, more like the walls of a garden than those of a great city. High mounds of rubbish rise on the northern, eastern, and southern sides of the metropolis; the French erected many forts upon these mounds, which completely commanded the town, but they are now in a state of ruin. There were similar mounds on the western side; but these have been lately removed, and their site has been planted with olive trees, acacias, &c. The citadel overawes the town, but is itself commanded by the neighbouring mountain.

Three of the gates of Cairo are very fine structures. They were built with the second wall of the city, in the year of the Flight 480 (A.D. 1087–8), during the reign of El-Mustansir, and are almost the only monuments of the times of the Khaleefehs now remaining in Egypt. Two of these, called Báb en-Nasr (or the Gate of Victory), and Báb el-Futooh (or the Gate of Conquests), are in the north wall, and between six and seven hundred feet apart. They are each about seventy feet high, and eighty feet or more in width. The former has two square towers, the latter two round fronted towers, and this gate is particularly handsome, but it cannot be viewed to advantage, as there are houses almost close before it. The third of the gates alluded to is that called Báb Zuweyleh.[1] Though in the very heart of the metropolis, it marks the southern limit of the original city. It has two massive round-fronted towers, from each of which rises a lofty and elegant mád'neh, presenting a grand and picturesque effect. The mád'nehs belong to the great mosque of El-Mu-eiyad, which is immediately within the gate, on the left of a person entering. They were built with the mosque, in the year of the Flight 819 (A.D. 1416–17). Before this gate criminals are generally executed. Among the other gates, that called Báb el-Adawee, in the centre of the north wall, may be mentioned as one of solid construction, but not otherwise remarkable; also the Báb el-Hadeed, which was built with the third wall.

In my next letter I must describe the interior of the metropolis.

---

[1] Originally called Zaweeleh. This was the name of the Arab Tribe

LETTER X

MY DEAR FRIEND,

I HAVE already attempted to describe to you my impressions on my first entry into Cairo. My ideas of it, for a considerable time, were very confused; it seemed to me, for the most part, a labyrinth of ruined and half-ruined houses, of the most singular construction; and in appearance so old, that I was surprised at being informed that, only a few years ago, it presented a far less unhappy aspect.[†]

Cairo[‡] is dignified with the name of Umm-ed-Dunya (the Mother of the World) and other sounding appellations. Though it has much declined since the discovery of the passage to India by the Cape of Good Hope, and more especially of late years, it is still one of the most considerable cities in the East. It is altogether an Arabian city; and the very finest specimens of Arabian architecture are found within its walls. The private houses are in general moderately large; the lower part of stone, and the superstructure of brick; but some are little better than huts.

The streets are unpaved, and very narrow, generally from five to ten feet wide. Some are even less than *four* feet in width; but there are others as much as forty or fifty feet wide, though not for any great length. I must describe the streets under their different appellations.

A shárë', or great thoroughfare-street, is generally somewhat irregular both in its direction and width. In most parts the width is scarcely more than sufficient for two loaded camels to proceed at a time; and hence much inconvenience is often occasioned to the passenger, though carriages are very rarely encountered. All burdens are borne by camels, if too heavy for asses; and vast numbers of the former, as well as many of the latter, are employed in supplying the inhabitants of Cairo with the water of the Nile, which is conveyed

---

[†]Lane in his *Modern Egyptians*, chap. IX, 213, informs us that Cairo had suffered severely from the French invasion, "not through direct oppression, but in consequence of the panic which this event occasioned;" and that "learning was in a much more flourishing state before the entrance of the French army than it has been in later years."

[‡]This letter is almost entirely copied from Lane, *Description*, chap. X, 76–83, with occasional omissions. Sophia sometimes adds certain personal remarks of her own as when she indicates a preference for black face veils. She also systematically replaces Lane's "Musr" with the more familiar name, "Cairo."

in skins, the camel carrying a pair of skin bags, and the ass a goat-skin, tied round at the neck. The great thoroughfare-streets being often half obstructed by these animals, and generally crowded with passengers, some on foot, and others riding, present striking scenes of bustle and confusion, particularly when two long trains of camels happen to meet each other where there is barely room enough for them to pass, which is often the case. Asses are in very general use, and most convenient for riding through such streets as those of Cairo, and are always to be procured for hire. They are preferred to horses even by some men of the wealthier classes of the Egyptians. Their paces are quick and easy; and the kind of saddle with which they are furnished is a very comfortable seat: it is a broad, party-coloured pack-saddle. A servant generally runs with the donkey; and exerts himself, by almost incessant bawling, to clear the way for his master. The horseman proceeds with less comfort, and less speed,—seldom beyond the rate of a slow walk; and though preceded by a servant, and sometimes by two servants to clear his way, he is often obliged to turn back: it is, therefore, not often that a numerous cavalcade is seen in the more frequented streets; and there are some streets so contracted that a person on horseback cannot pass through them. It is not uncommon for individuals of the higher and middle classes in Cairo to exchange salutations in the street, though unacquainted with each other. Thus the Muslim salutation was often given to my brother, a fact which I mention merely to show the fallacy of the opinion that the natives of the East can easily detect, even by a glance, a European in Oriental disguise.

A stranger, with lofty ideas of Eastern magnificence, must be surprised at the number of meanly-dressed persons whom he meets in the streets of Cairo. Blue is the prevailing colour; as the principal article of dress, both of the men and women of the lower orders, is a full shirt of cotton or linen, dyed with indigo, which is the production of the country. The blue shirts of the men, particularly of the servants, often conceal vests of silk and cloth. Some persons are so poor as not even to possess a ragged turban; their only head-dress being a close-fitting cap of white, or brown felt, or an old turboosh;[1] and many are without shoes. Christians and Jews are distinguished by a black, or blue, or light-brown turban. The costumes of the women, and especially of the ladies, are the most remarkable in the eyes of the European stranger. The elegant dress which they wear at home is concealed whenever they appear in public by a very full silk gown (called tób), and a large black silk covering (called habarah) enveloping almost the whole person; or, instead of the latter, in the case of unmarried ladies, a *white* silk covering: the face veil (burko') is of white muslin; it is narrow, and reaches from the eyes nearly to the feet. Thus encumbered, it is with some difficulty that the ladies shuffle along in their slippers; but they are seldom seen in the crowded streets on

---

[1]The red cloth skull-cap, round which the turban is wound.

foot: well-trained donkeys are hired for their convenience, and are furnished, for this purpose, with a high and broad saddle, covered with a carpet, upon which the lady sits astride, attended by a servant on each side. A long train of ladies, and female slaves attired in the same manner, one behind another, a whole hareem, is often seen thus mounted; and passengers of all ranks make way for them with the utmost respect. The women of the inferior classes wear a black face veil, which I think much more becoming than the white. It is sometimes adorned with gold coins and beads; or they draw a part of the head veil before the face, leaving only one eye visible.

Numbers of blind persons are seen in the streets of Cairo; and many more with a bandage over one eye; but I seldom see a *woman* with diseased eyes.

Shops, which (I have before remarked) are merely small recesses, and most of which are poorly stocked, generally occupy the front part of the ground-floor of each house in a great street; and the houses, with few exceptions, are two or three stories high. Their fronts, above the ground-floor, projecting about two feet, and the windows of wooden lattice-work projecting still further, render the streets gloomy, but shady and cool. On either side of the great streets are by-streets and quarters.

A darb, or by-street, differs from a shárë' in being narrower, and not so long. In most cases, the darb is about six or eight feet wide, is a thoroughfare, and has, at each end, a gateway, with a large wooden door, which is always closed at night. Some darbs consist only of private houses; others contain shops.

A hárah, or quarter, is a particular district consisting of one or more streets or lanes. In general, a small quarter contains only private houses, and has but one entrance, with a wooden gate, which, like that of a darb, is closed at night.

The sooks, or markets, are short streets, or short portions of streets, having shops on either side. In some of them, all the shops are occupied by persons of the same trade. Many sooks are covered over-head by matting, extended upon rafters, resembling those I observed at Alexandria, and some have a roof of wood. Most of the great thoroughfare-streets, and many by-streets, consist wholly, or for the most part, of a succession of sooks.

Many of the kháns of Cairo are similar to the sooks just described; but in general, a khán consists of shops or magazines surrounding a square or oblong court.

Khán El-Khaleelee, which is situated in the centre of that part which constituted the original city, a little to the east of the main street, and occupies the site of the cemetery of the Fawátim (the Khaleefehs[1] of Egypt), particularly deserves to be mentioned, being one of the chief marts of Cairo. It consists of a series of short lanes, with several turnings, and has four entrances

---

[1]The bones of the Khaleefehs were thrown on the mounds of rubbish outside the city.

from different quarters. The shops in this khán are mostly occupied by Turks, who deal in ready-made clothes and other articles of dress, together with arms of various kinds, the small prayer-carpets used by the Muslims, and other commodities. Public auctions and held there (as in many other markets in Cairo) twice in the week, on Monday and Thursday, on which occasions the khán is so crowded, that, in some parts, it is difficult for a passenger to push his way through. The sale begins early in the morning, and lasts till the noon-prayers. Clothes (old as well as new), shawls, arms, pipes, and a variety of other goods, are offered for sale in this manner by brokers, who carry them up and down the market. Several water-carriers, each with a goat-skin of water on his back, and a brass cup for the use of any one who would drink, attend on these occasions. Sherbet of raisins, and bread (in round, flat cakes), with other eatables, are also cried up and down the market; and on every auction day, several real or pretended idiots, with a distressing number of other beggars, frequent the khán.

Another of the principal kháns of Cairo is that called Kamzáwee,[†] which is the principal market of the drapers and silk-mercers.

There are few other kháns in Cairo, or rather few other buildings so designated; but there are numerous buildings called wekálehs, which are of the same description as most of the kháns, a wekáleh generally consisting of magazines surrounding a square court.

The Wekálet el-Gellábeh (or Wekáleh of the slave-merchants), which is near the Khán El-Khaleelee, has lately ceased to be the market for black slaves. It surrounds a spacious square court, in which were generally seen several groups of male and female slaves, besmeared with grease (of which they are very fond), and nearly in a state of nudity,[‡] excepting in winter, when they were better clad, and kept within doors. As there is a thoroughfare through this wekáleh, the slaves were much exposed to public view. The market for black slaves is now at Káid Bey,[††] which is a city of the dead, comprising a few old habitations for the living, between the metropolis and the neighbouring mountain. The slave-merchants were obliged to transfer their unfortunate captives to this cemetery in the desert in consequence of its having been represented to the government that epidemic diseases originated in the slave-market in Cairo. I have not visited them, nor do I intend to do so; for although slavery in the East is seen under the most favourable circumstances, there is something in it so revolting, that I am not disposed to try

---

[†]The name is misspelled. In Lane, *Description*, 81 it is Hhamza'wee, ascribed to Hamza (proper name of a man).
[‡]Sophia changed her brother's less genteel "naked." Lane, *Description*, 81.
[††]Sophia updated the change in the location of the market for black slaves from the time Lane wrote to the year 1842 and added a few comments of her own before resuming her brother's account.

my feelings when I can do no good. But I am told that they appear careless and happy; for their greatest troubles are past, and they know that the slave of the Muslim fares even better than the free servant. Some of the more valuable of the female slaves (as the *white* female slaves, to whom another wekáleh is appropriated) are only shown to those persons who express a desire to become purchasers.

Having now described the streets and markets of Cairo, I may mention some particular quarters, &c. There are some parts which are inhabited exclusively by persons of the same religion or nation. Many quarters are inhabited only by Muslims.[1]

The quarter of the Jews (Hárat el-Yahood) is situated in the western half of that portion of the metropolis which composed the original city. It is very extensive, but closed and dirty. Some of its streets, or rather lanes, are so narrow, that two persons can barely pass each other in them; and in some parts, the soil has risen by the accumulation of rubbish a foot or more above the thresholds of the doors.

The Greeks have two quarters, and the Copts have several, of which some are very extensive. The Franks inhabit not only what is called the quarter of the Franks (Hárat el Ifreng), but are interspersed throughout a considerable district, situated between the canal (which runs through the city) and the Esbekeeyeh, of which latter I shall presently give you a description.

The motley population of the part of the metropolis where most of the Franks reside, gives it the appearance of a quarter in a sea-port town, like Alexandria. Some of the Franks retain their national costume; others adopt partly or wholly the Turkish dress. The chief thoroughfare-street in this part of the town is the market, called the Mooskee, where are a few shops fitted up in the European style, with glass fronts, and occupied by Franks, who deal in various European commodities. The Hárat el-Ifreng is a short street leading out of the Mooskee, on the southern side.

There are several vacant spaces of considerable extent in the interior of the metropolis, some of which, during the season of the inundation (the autumn), become lakes. The principal of these I must here mention.

The great place which bears the name of the Ezbekeeyeh is an irregular tract, the greatest length of which is nearly half a mile, and the greatest breadth about a third of a mile. It is a very favourite resort of mine, as my children are there secure from the many dangers which I fancy surround them in the crowded streets.

On the south are two modern Turkish palaces, with gardens. On the west is a plain wall (part of the wall of the metropolis), and another Turkish palace, occupying the site of the mansion of the famous Memlook Bey El-Elfee, which became the residence of Napoleon, and of Kleber, who was

---

[1] About three-fourths of the population of Cairo are native Muslims.

assassinated in the adjacent garden. On the north side is a Christian quarter, presenting a long row of lofty but neglected houses. During the season of the inundation, the Nile enters this extensive tract by a canal, and the place is partially inundated; the water remains three or four months, after which the ground is sown. It was formerly, during the season of the inundation, one extensive lake, but is now converted into something like a garden, with an agreeable mixture of trees and water. I am told that the place has a much more pleasing appearance when entirely clothed with green, than it had when it was a lake; and so I should imagine, for the water is very turbid.

The Birket el-Feel (or Lake of the Elephant) also receives the water of the Nile, during the season of the inundation. Only a small part of it is open to the public.

There are two small lakes in the western part of the metropolis, and several others in its vicinity. There are also several cemeteries in the eastern part of the town,[1] and many large gardens. These gardens are chiefly stocked with palm-trees, acacias, sycamores, oranges, limes, pomegranates, &c. Little arrangement is displayed in them. They have generally one or more sákiyehs, which raise the water for their irrigation from wells.

The Canal[2] (El-Khaleeg) which traverses the metropolis is no ornament to it. In most parts of its course through the town, it is closely hemmed in on each side by the backs of houses; therefore it cannot be seen, excepting in a few places, by the passengers in the streets. Most of the bridges over it are moreover lined with shops on both sides, so that a person passing over cannot see that he is crossing the canal. The water of the Nile is admitted into the canal in August, and the entrance is closed by a dam of earth not long after the river has begun to subside; consequently, after three or four months, only stagnant puddles remain in it. While it continues open, boats enter it from the Nile, and pass through the whole length of the metropolis.

Of the public buildings of Cairo, the most interesting certainly are the mosques, the more remarkable of which I have described to you.[†] They are extremely picturesque, and exquisite taste is displayed in the variety and elegance of their mád'nehs or menarets: but the beauty of these and other parts is, in my opinion, much injured by the prevalent fashion of daubing the alternate courses of stone with whitewash and dark-red ochre. The central part of a great mosque is, in general, a square court, which is surrounded by porticoes, the columns of which are, in few cases, uniform; for they are mostly

---

[1] The principal cemeteries are without the town.

[2] This canal is the ancient Ammis Trajanus.

[†] She had not described the mosques in previous letters but would do so in a subsequent one (XII), which like this one does not bear an exact date, merely the same name of the month and year. The order of presentation may have been changed when it was sent for publication.

the spoils of ancient temples, as are also the rich marble slabs, &c., which
have been employed to decorate the pavements and the lower portions of the
inner faces of the walls in many of the mosques.

The domes are beautiful in form, and, in some instances, in their decorations. The pulpits, also, deserve to be mentioned for their elegant forms, and
their curious intricate panel-work. The pulpit is placed with its back against
the wall in which is the niche; is surmounted by a small cupola, and has a
flight of steps leading directly (never tortuously nor sideways) up to the little platform which is the station of the preacher. The congregation range
themselves in parallel rows upon the matted or carpeted pavement, all facing that side of the mosque in which is the niche. These few general remarks
will enable you better to understand the accounts of particular mosques, or
to supply some deficiencies in my descriptions.

Many of these buildings are doubtless monuments of sincere piety; but
not a few have certainly originated in ways far from creditable to their
founders. I passed by one, a handsome building, respecting which I was told
the following anecdote. The founder, on the first occasion of opening his
mosque for the ceremonials of the Fridays prayers, invited the chief 'Ulama
to attend the service, and each of these congratulated him before the congregation, by reciting some tradition of the Prophet, or by some other words of
an apposite nature, excepting one. This man the founder addressed, asking
wherefore he was silent. "Hast thou nothing to say," he asked, "befitting this
occasion?" The man thus invited readily answered, "Yes. If thou hast built
this mosque with money lawfully acquired, and with a good intention, know
that God halth built for thee a mansion in Paradise, and great will be thy
felicity. But if thou raised this temple by means of wealth unlawfully
obtained, by money exacted from the poor by oppression and tyranny, know
that there is prepared for thee a place in hell, and evil will be the transit
thither." The latter was the case; and within a few hours after he had thus
spoken, the only one among the company of 'Ulama who had dared to utter
the language of truth on this occasion—to do which, indeed, required no little courage—suddenly died, a victim, as was well known, of poison.[†]

[†]This anecdote does not appear in Lane.

LETTER XI

MY DEAR FRIEND,

BEING extremely anxious to see the interiors of the principal
mosques, I was much vexed at finding that it had become very difficult for a
Christian to obtain access to them.[†] My brother might, perhaps, have taken
us without risk, as he is generally mistaken for a Turk[‡]; but had he done so,
we might have been spoken to in some mosque in the Turkish language, in
which language we could not have replied; whereas, if we were conducted by
a Caireen, no Turkish ladies were likely to address us, and if any Arab ladies
should do so, our Arabic would only induce them to imagine us Turks. At
length an old friend of my brother's offered to take me if I would consent to
ride after him in the streets and follow him in the mosques, and appear to
be, for the time being, the chief lady of his hareem.

It appeared to me that I should commit a breach in etiquette, by con-
senting thus to displace his wife (for he has but *one*); but finding he would
not consent to take me on any other terms, and being bent on gratifying my
curiosity, I agreed to submit to his arrangement, and the more readily
because his wife expressed, with much politeness, the pleasure she anticipated in contributing to my gratification. I had never seen my kind old conductor but once, and then through the hareem blinds, until the morning
arrived for our expedition, when I and my sister-in-law[††] mounted our donkeys, and submitted ourselves to his guidance. He rode first in the procession; I next; then followed my sister-in-law; and lastly, his wife. We endeavoured on several occasions to induce her to take a more distinguished place,
but in vain, and therefore came to the conclusion that she must be infinitely
better acquainted with Eastern manners than ourselves, and that it would be

---

[†]Cf. Lane, *Description*, chap. X, 85, n.1, "It is not safe (or at least was not at the period of my visit to Musr) for an undisguised Christian to *enter* the mosques: he would
be in danger of being mobbed and ill-treated."

[‡]Lane in his author's preface to *Modern Egyptians* dated 1835, xxv, tells us that "from
the dress which I have found most convenient to wear, I am generally mistaken, in
public, for a Turk." He further remarks that "Having made myself acquainted with
all their common religious ceremonies I have been able to escape exciting in
strangers, any suspicion of my being a person who had no right to intrude among
them, whenever it was necessary for me to witness any Muslim rite or festival."

[††]Nefeeseh, who is very rarely mentioned in Sophia's letters.

safer and better not to oppose her. I use the expression safer, because I was fully aware that if we appeared in any respect *un*-eastern, or rather if we did not *look* like Muslims, we should incur the risk of being turned out of any mosque we might enter, and loaded with reproach and insult.

With (I confess) nervous feelings, we stopped at one of the entrances of the mosque of the Hasaneyn, which is generally esteemed the most sacred in Cairo. It was crowded with ladies who were paying their weekly visit to the tomb of El-Hoseyn.

I felt that I had rather have been initiated before entering the *most sacred* mosque, and thought I had been too bold. Never did a submissive wife walk more meekly after her husband than I followed the steps of my governor *pro tempore*. I gained, however, some confidence by remarking the authoritative air he assumed as soon as he had passed the threshold of the mosque; indeed he played his part admirably.

At the threshold all persons remove their shoes, or slippers, the ladies walking, in the mosque, in the yellow morocco socks, or boots, which I have before described to you; and here I must remark on the scrupulous attention which is paid to cleanliness; for the yellow morocco is scarcely injured by a whole day spent in perambulating these Muslim sanctuaries. The men generally carry the shoes in the left hand through the mosque, placed sole to sole, and some ladies carry theirs, but we, like many others, preferred leaving them with our servants, for the walking-dress in itself is so exceedingly cumbrous, and requires so much management, that two hands are scarcely sufficient to preserve its proper arrangement.[†]

The mosque of the Hasaneyn,[‡] which is situated to the north of the Azhar, and not far distant, was founded in the year of the Flight 549 (A.D.

[†]Here ends Sophia's personalized account of entering the mosque. For the description of the interior, she turns to her brother's *Description*, 86, while adding certain insertions of her own and taking care to consider the time span (for example, where Lane says that the mosque was erected "60 years ago," Sophia writes "70."

[‡]By the Hasaneyn are meant Hasan and Huseyn, the grandsons of the Prophet.

[‡]Both Sophia and Lane call the mosque in question "El-Hasaneyn," and both emphasize the fact with an explanatory footnote that it was named after the two grandsons of the Prophet. This designation has never been used to identify the famous mosque in Cairo, where it is always known as the mosque (masgid) or mashhad of al-Husayn. Al-Maqrizi and al-Jabarti refer to it only as al-Husayn, and in common parlance this is the name that was and is still used. The only source that Lane could have taken "El-Hasaneyn" from is *Description de l'Egypte*, where in the section on Cairo written by M. Jomard ("Description abrégée de la ville et la citadelle du Kaire," *Etat Moderne* II(2): 579–786) we meet with the two appellations. In his key to the map of Cairo (EM I: 26), the name "el-Hasaneyn" is repeatedly used in connection with the mosque and its adjacent landmarks, whereas in the text, Jomard more than once uses the correct name "Hoçeyn."

1154–5); but has been more than once rebuilt. The present building was erected about 70 years ago. The fore part consists of a handsome hall, or portico, the roof of which is supported by numerous marble columns, and the pavement covered with carpets. Passing through this hall, I found myself in that holy place under which the head of the martyr El-Hoseyn is said to be buried deep below the pavement. It is a lofty square saloon, surmounted by a dome. Over the spot where the sacred relic is buried, is an oblong monument, covered with green silk, with a worked inscription around it. This is enclosed within a high screen of bronze, of open work; around the upper part of which are suspended several specimens of curious and elegant writing.[†] The whole scene was most imposing. The pavements are exquisite; some of virgin-marble, pure and bright with cleanliness, some delicately inlaid: and the whole appearance is so striking, that I am persuaded if a stranger were to visit the shrine of El-Hoseyn *alone*, he would never believe that El-Islam is on the wane.

All the visitors whom I saw passed round the tomb, walking from left to right, touching each corner of the screen with the right hand, and then applying that hand to their lips and forehead, reciting at the same time, but inaudibly, the Fát'hah (or opening chapter of the Kurán), a ceremony also observed on visiting *other* tombs.[‡] Many were most devoutly praying, and one woman kissed the screen with a fervour of devotion which interested while it grieved me. For myself, however, I can never think of the shrine of El-Hoseyn without being deeply affected by reflecting upon the pathetic history of that amiable man, in whom were combined, in an eminent degree, so many of the highest Christian virtues.

We next bent our steps to El-Gáme el-Azhar (or the splendid mosque[1]), which is situated, as I have said, to the south of the Hasaneyn, and not far distant, midway between the principal street of the city and the gate called Báb El-Ghureiyib. It is the principal mosque of Cairo, and the *University of the East*; and is also the first, with regard to the period of its foundation, of all the mosques of the city; but it has been so often repaired, and so much enlarged, that it is difficult to ascertain exactly how much of the *original* structure we see in the present state of the mosque. It was founded about nine months after the first wall of the city, in the year of the Flight 359 (A.D.

[†]Sophia's interpolation from here till the end of the paragraph.
[‡]Here ends Lane's account, based on a visit that, as he admits, "was rather a hurried one; for I was fearful of exciting suspicion by gazing too long: but I was afterwards enabled to gratify my curiosity more fully when the visiting of other mosques had given me confidence in my present mind" (Lane, *Description*, 86). Sophia replaces the above with remarks of her own about al-Husayn.
[1]Some travellers have strangely misinterpreted the name of this building, calling it the "mosque of flowers."

969–70). Though occupying a space about three hundred feet square, it makes but little show externally; for it is so surrounded by houses, that only its entrances and mád'nehs can be seen from the streets. It has two grand gates, and four minor entrances. Each of the two former has two doors, and a school-room above, open at the front and back. Every one takes off his shoes before he passes the threshold of the gate, although if he enter the mosque by the principal gate, he has to cross a spacious court before he arrives at the place of prayer. This custom is observed in every mosque. The principal gate is in the centre of the front of the mosque: it is the nearest to the main street of the city. Immediately within this gate are two small mosques; one on either hand. Passing between these, we enter the great court of the Azhar, which is paved with stone, and surrounded by porticoes. The principal portico is that which is opposite this entrance: those on the other three sides of the court are divided into a number of riwáks or apartments for the accommodation of the numerous students who resort to this celebrated university from various and remote countries of Africa, Asia, and Europe, as well as from different parts of Egypt.

These persons, being mostly in indigent circumstances, are supported by the funds of the mosque; each receiving a certain quantity of bread and soup at noon, and in the evening. Many blind paupers are also supported here,[†] and we were much affected by seeing some bent with age, slowly walking through the avenues of columns, knowing from habit every turn and every passage, and looking like the patriarchs of the assembled multitude.[‡] The riwáks are separated from the court, and from each other, by partitions of wood, which unite the columns or pillars. Those on the side in which is the principal entrance are very small, there being only one row of columns on this side; but those on the right and left are spacious halls, containing several rows of columns. There are also some above the ground-floor. Each riwák is for the natives of a particular country, or of a particular province in Egypt; the Egyptian students being of course more numerous than those of any other nation.

In going the round of these apartments, after passing successively among natives of different divisions of Egypt, we find ourselves in the company of people of Mekkeh and El-Medeeneh; then in the midst of Syrians; in another minute among Muslims of central Africa; next amidst Maghár-'beh (or native of northern Africa, west of Egypt); then, with European and Asiatic Turks; and quitting these, we are introduced to Persians, and Muslims of India: we may almost fancy ourselves transported through their respective countries. No sight in Cairo interested me more than the interior of the Azhar;[‡‡] and the many and great obstacles which present themselves

[†]Beginning of an interpolation by Sophia.
[‡]End of Sophia's interpolation.
[‡‡]Beginning of an interpolation by Sophia.

when a Christian, and more especially a Christian lady, desires to obtain admission into this celebrated mosque, make me proud of having enjoyed the privilege of walking leisurely through its extensive porticoes, and observing its heterogeneous students engaged in listening to the lectures of their professors.[†]

To the left of the great court is a smaller one, containing the great tank at which the ablution preparatory to prayer is performed by all those who have not done it before entering the mosque. The great portico is closed by partitions of wood between a row of square pillars, or piers, behind the front row of columns. The partition of the central archway has a wide door; and some of the other partitions have smaller doors. The great portico is very spacious; containing eight rows of small marble columns, arranged parallel with the front. That part beyond the fifth row of columns was added by the builder of one of the grand gates, about 70 years ago. The walls are whitewashed: the niche and pulpit are very plain; and simplicity is the prevailing character of the whole of the interior of the great portico. The pavement is covered with mats; and a few small carpets are seen here and there.

A person of rank or wealth is generally accompanied by a servant bearing a seggádeh (or small prayer carpet, about the size of a hearth-rug), upon which he prays. During the noon-prayers of the congregation on Friday, the worshippers are very numerous; and, arranged in parallel rows, they sit upon the matting.

Different scenes at other times are presented in the great portico of the Azhar. We saw many lecturers addressing their circles of attentive listeners, or reading to them commentaries on the Kurán.[‡] In most cases these lecturers were leaning against a pillar, and I understand that in general each has his respective column, where his pupils regularly attend him, sitting in the form of a circle on the matted floor. Some persons take their meals in the Azhar,[††] and many houseless paupers pass the night there, for this mosque is left open at all hours. Such customs are not altogether in accordance with the sanctity of the place; but peculiarly illustrative of the simplicity of Eastern manners.

We next visited the fine mosque of Mohamad Bey, founded in the year of the Flight 1187 (A.D. 1773–4), adjacent to the Azhar. This is remarkable as a very noble structure, of the old style, erected at a late period.

The great mosque of that impious impostor the Khaleefeh *El-Hákim* (who professed to be a prophet, and afterwards to be God incarnate) derives an interest from the name it bears, and from its antiquity. It is situated immediately within that part of the northern wall of the city which connects the

[†]End of Sophia's interpolation.
[‡]Beginning of an interpolation by Sophia.
[††]End of Sophia's interpolation.

Báb en-Nasr and Báb el-Futooh. This mosque was completed in the reign of El-Hákim, in the year of the Flight 403 (A.D. 1012–13); but was founded by his predecessor. It is now in a state of ruin, and no longer used as a place of worship. It occupies a space about 400 feet square, and consists of arcades surrounding a square court.†

---

†Sophia ends this letter, which is copied (with a few omissions and some interpolations), from Lane, *Description,* 84–86, without including the rest of the monuments Lane mentions

LETTER XII

November, 1842

My Dear Friend,

I WILL continue the subject I left incomplete in my last. Several of the finest mosques in Cairo front the main street of the city. In proceeding along this street from north to south, the first mosque that particularly attracts notice is the Barkookeeyeh, on the right side.[†]

This is a collegiate mosque, and was founded in the year of the Flight 786 (A.D. 1384–5). It has a fine dome, and a lofty and elegant mád'neh; and the interior is particularly handsome, though in a lamentable state of decay.

A little beyond this, on the same side of the street, are the tomb, mosque, and hospital of the Sultán Kalá-oon, composing one united building. The tomb and the mosque form the front part; the former is to the right of the latter; and a passage, which is the general entrance, leads between them to the hospital (Máristán).[1] These three united buildings were founded in the year of the Flight 683 (A.D. 1284–5). The tomb has a very large mád'neh, and is a noble edifice; its front is coloured red and white, in squares: the interior is very magnificent. The mosque is not remarkable. The hospital contains two small oblong courts, surrounded by small cells, in which mad persons are confined and chained; men in one court, and women in the other. Though these wretched beings are provided for by the funds of the establishment, it is the custom to take them food, and they ask for it in a manner which is most affecting. But here I must make one consolatory remark: the poor creatures have certainly more than enough to eat, for none seemed hungry, and I observed that one of the men threw down a piece of bread which was given to him.

Judging by my own anxiety to ascertain the real state of the poor lunatics in the Máristán, I cannot describe to you their condition too minutely. Our ears were assailed by the most discordant yells as soon as we entered the passage leading to the cells. We were first conducted into the court appropriated to men, one of our servants attending us with the provisions. It is surrounded by small cells, in which they are separately confined, and each cell has a small grated window, through which the poor prisoner's chain is fastened to the

---

[†]Sophia continues her verbatim account from Lane where she left off in her previous letter but this time, she gives a lengthy interpolation in which she describes her own experience when she visited the 'Maristan.'

[1]Vulgarly pronounced Muristan.

exterior. Here seemed exhibited every description of insanity. In many cells were those who suffered from melancholy madness; in *one only* I saw a cheerful maniac, and he was amusing some visitors exceedingly by his jocose remarks. Almost all stretched out their arms as far as they could reach, asking for bread, and one poor soul especially interested me by the melancholy tone of his supplication. Their outstretched arms rendered it frequently dangerous to pass their cells, for there is a railing in the midst of the court, surrounding an oblong space, which I imagine has been a tank, but which is now filled with stones; and this railing so confines the space appropriated to visitors, that one of our party was cautioned by the superintendent when she was not aware she was in arms' length of the lunatics.

I trust that the mildness and gentleness of manner we observed in the keepers were not assumed for the time, and I think they were not, for the lunatics did not appear to fear them. The raving maniacs were strongly chained, and wearing each a collar and hand-cuffs. One poor creature endeavoured, by constantly shaking his chain, to attract pity and attention. They look unlike human beings, and the manner of their confinement, and the barren wretchedness of their cells, contributed to render the scene more like a menagerie than anything else. It is true that this climate lessens the requirements of every grade in society, so that the poor generally sleep upon the bare ground, or upon thin mats; but it is perfectly barbarous to keep these wretched maniacs without anything but the naked floor on which to rest themselves, weary, as they must be, by constant excitement.

I turned sick at heart from these abodes of wretchedness, and was led towards the court of the women. Little did I expect that scenes infinitely more sad awaited me. No *man* being permitted to enter the part of the building appropriated to the women, the person who had hitherto attended us gave the provision we had brought into the hand of the chief of the female keepers. The maniacs sit within the doors of open cells surrounding their court, and there is no appearance of their being confined. I shrunk as I passed the two first, expecting they would rush out; but being assured that they were chained, I proceeded to look into the cells, one by one. The first lunatic I remarked particularly, was an old and apparently blind woman, who was an object of peculiar interest, from the expression of settled sadness in her countenance. Nothing seemed to move her. A screaming raving maniac was confined in a cell nearly opposite to hers; but either from habit, or the contemplation of her own real and imagined sorrows, the confusion seemed by her perfectly unheeded. The cell next to hers presented to my view a young girl, about sixteen or seventeen years of age, in a perfect state of nudity; she sat in a crouching attitude, in statue-like stillness, and in the gloom of her prison she looked like stone. The next poor creature was also young, but older than the preceding, and she merely raised her jet-black eyes and looked at us through her dishevelled hair, not wildly, but calmly and vacantly. She, too, had no article of clothing. I was ill-prepared for the sight of such misery, and I hastily passed the poor squalid, emaciated, raving maniacs, all without any covering; and was leaving the court, when I heard a voice exclaiming, in a melancholy tone of supplication, "Stay, O my mistress, give me five paras for tobacco before you go." I turned, and the entreaty was repeated by a nice-looking old woman, who was very grateful when I assured her she should have what she required. She was clothed, and sitting almost behind the entrance of her cell, and seemed on the look-out for presents. The woman who was the superintendent gave her the trifle for me, and I hope she was permitted to spend it as she desired. She and the first I saw were the only two who were not perfect pictures of misery. If insanity, the most severe of human woes, calls for our tenderest sympathy, the condition of these wretched lunatics in Cairo cries aloud for our deepest commiseration. How their situation can be mended, I know not: the government alone can interfere, and the government does not.

We were informed that the establishment was endowed with remarkable liberality. It is, and always has been, a hospital for the sick, as well as a place of confinement for the insane; and originally, for the entertainment of those patients who were troubled with restlessness, a band of musicians and a number of storytellers were in constant attendance.

The friend who conducted us related some anecdotes of the poor maniacs, to which I listened with interest. The first, I am told, has been related by some European traveller, in a work descriptive of the Egyptians; but as I do not know by whom, and you may not have read or heard it, I will give you that as well as the others.

A butcher, who had been confined some time in the Máristán, conceived an excessive hatred for a Delee (a Turkish trooper), one of his fellow-prisoners. He received his provision of food from his family, and he induced his wife one day, on the occasion of her taking him his dinner, to conceal, in the basket of food, the instruments he had used in his trade, viz., a cleaver, a knife, and a pair of hooks. I must here observe, that those lunatics who do not appear dangerous have lighter chains than others, and the chains of the person in question were of this description. When he had taken his meal, he proceeded to liberate himself; and as the cells communicated by the back, he soon reached that of his nearest neighbour, who, delighted to see him free, exclaimed, "How is this? Who cut your chains?" "I did," replied the first, "and here are my implements." "Excellent," rejoined the other, "cut mine too." "Certainly," said he; and he proceeded to liberate not only one, but two, three, and four of his fellow-prisoners. Now follows the tragical part of the story. No keepers were present—the man who possessed the cleaver attacked the door Delee, chained and unarmed as he was; slaughtered him; and after dividing his body, hung it on the hooks within the window of the cell, and believed himself to be—what he was—a butcher.

In a few minutes the liberated lunatics became uproarious; and one of them growing alarmed, forced open the door by which the keepers usually entered, found one of them, and gave the alarm. The keeper instantly proceeded to the cell, and seeing the body of the murdered man, exclaimed, "What, have you succeeded in killing that Delee? he was the plague of my life." "I have," answered the delinquent; "and here he hangs for sale." "Most excellent," replied the keeper, "but do not let him hang here; it will disgrace us: let us bury him." "Where?" asked the maniac, still holding his cleaver in his hand. "Here in the cell," replied the other, "and then the fact can never be discovered." In an instant he threw down his cleaver, and began to dig busily with his hands. In the mean time, the keeper entered by the back of the cell, and throwing a collar over his neck, instantly chained him and so finished his tragedy.

Some time since, the brother of the person who gave the following anecdote, on the occasion of his visiting the Máristán, was accosted by one of the maniacs by name and greeted with the usual salutations, followed by a melancholy entreaty that he would deliver him from that place. On examining him particularly, he found him to be an old friend; and he was distressed by his entreaties to procure for him his liberation, and perplexed what to do. The lunatic assured him he was not insane, and at length the visitor resolved on applying for his release. Accordingly, he addressed himself to the head keeper on the subject, stated that he was much surprised by the conversation of the patient, and concluded by requesting his liberation. The keeper answered that he did appear sane at that time, but that perhaps in an hour he might be raving.

The visitor, by no means satisfied by the reply of the keeper, and overcome by the rational arguments of the lunatic, urged his request, and at length he consented, saving, "Well, you can try him." This being arranged, in a short time the two friends set out together; and, engaged in conversation, they passed along the street, when suddenly the maniac seized the other by the throat, exclaiming, "Help, O Muslims! here is a madman escaped from the Máristán." He wisely suffered himself to be dragged back in no gentle manner to the very cell whence he had released the poor lunatic; and the latter, on entering, called loudly for a collar and chain for a maniac he had found in the street, escaped from the Máristán. The keeper immediately brought the collar and chain; and while pretending to obey his orders, slipped it over his neck, and secured him in his former quarters, I need not say, to the satisfaction of his would-be deliverer.

Our conductor also related, that some years ago, a maniac, having escaped from his cell in the Máristán, when the keepers had retired for the night, ascended the lofty mád'neh of the adjoining sepulchral mosque, the tomb of the Sultán Kala'oon. Finding there, in the gallery, a Muëddin, chanting one of the night-calls, uttering, with the utmost power of his voice, the exclamation

"Yá Rabb!" (O Lord!) he seized him by the neck. The terrified Muëddin cried out, "I seek God's protection from the accursed devil! God is most great!"—"I am not a devil," said the madman, "to be destroyed by the words, 'God is most great!'" (Here I should tell you that these words are commonly believed to have the effect here ascribed to them, that of destroying a devil.) "Then what art thou?" said the Muëddin. "I am madman," answered the other, "escaped from the Máristán." "O welcome!" rejoined the Muëddin: "praise be to God for thy safety! come, sit down, and amuse me with thy conversation." So the madman thus began: "Why do you call out so loud, 'O Lord!' Do you not know that God can hear you as well if you speak low?" "True," said the other, "but I call that men also may hear." "Sing," rejoined the lunatic; "*that* will please me." And upon this, the other commenced a kind of chant, with the ridiculous nature of which he so astonished some servants of the Máristán, who, as usual, were sitting up in a coffee-shop below, that they suspected some strange event had happened, and hastily coming up, secured the madman.

After what I have told you of the miserable creatures at present confined in the Máristán, I am very happy to add, that their condition will, I believe, in a few weeks, be greatly ameliorated. They are, I have since heard, to be removed to an hospital, where they will be under the superintendence of a celebrated French surgeon, Clot Bey. [†]

I now return to the subject of the mosques. [‡]

Proceeding still southwards along the main street, we arrived at a fine mosque, called the Ashrafeeyeh, on the right. It was built by the Sultán El-Ashraf Barsabáy, consequently between the years 825–41 (A.D. 1421 et *seq*.). Frequently criminals are hanged against one of the grated windows of this mosque; as the street before it is generally very much crowded with passengers.

Still proceeding along the main street, through that part of it called the Ghóreeyeh (which is a large bázár, or market), we arrive at the two fine mosques of the Sultán El-Ghóree, facing each other, one on each side of the

---

[†]He was invited by Muhammad 'Ali to come to Egypt and establish a medical school and a school for nurses in 1832.

[‡]Here end Sophia's own observations and she resumes her copying from Lane, *Description*, 87–89. She leaves out his description of the 'Private Houses' and his interesting comment: "I resided at Musr, at different times, a little more than a year and a quarter. As my pursuits required that I should not be remarked in public as a European, I separated myself as much as possible from the Franks, and lived in a part of the town (near the Ba'b el-Hhadee'd) somewhat remote from the Frank quarters. Speaking the language of the country, and conforming with the manners of my Moos'lim neighbours, renouncing knives and forks (which, till I saw the really delicate mode of eating with the fingers, as practised in the East, I was rather averse from doing), and abstaining from wine and swine's flesh (both, indeed, loathsome to me), I was treated with respect and affability by all the natives with whom I had any intercourse" (Lane, *Description*, 90).

street, and having a roof of wood extending from one to the other. They were both completed in the year of the Flight 909 (A.D. 1503–4). That on the left, El-Ghóree designed as his tomb; but he was not buried in it.

Arriving at the southernmost part of the main street, we have on our right the great mosque of the Sultán El-Mu-eiyad, which was founded in the year of the Flight 819 (A.D. 1416–17). It surrounds a spacious square court, and contains the remains of its royal founder, and of some of his family. It has a noble dome, and a fine lofty entrance-porch at the right extremity of the front. Its two great mád'nehs, which rise from the towers of the gate called Báb-Zuweyleh (the southern gate of that portion of the metropolis which constituted the old city), I have already mentioned.

Of the mosques in the *suburban* districts of the metropolis, the most remarkable are those of the Sultán Hasan and of Ibn-Tooloon, or, as the name is commonly pronounced, Teyloon.

The great mosque of the Sultán Hasan, which is situated near the citadel, and is the most lofty of the edifices of Cairo, was founded in the year of the Flight 757 (A.D. 1356). It is a very noble pile; but it has some irregularities which are displeasing to the eye; as, for instance, the disparity of its two mád'nehs. The great mád'neh is nearly three hundred feet in height measured from the ground. At the right extremity of the north-east side of the mosque is a very fine lofty entrance-porch. From this, a zigzag passage conducts us to a square hypæthral hall, or court, in the centre of which is a tank, and near this, a reservoir with spouts, for the performance of ablution; each crowned with a cupola. On each of the four sides of the court is a hall with an arched roof and open front. That opposite the entrance is the largest, and is the principal place of worship. Its arched roof is about seventy feet in width. It is constructed of brick and plastered (as are the other three arches), and numerous small glass lamps, and two lanterns of bronze, are suspended from it. The lower part of the end wall is lined with coloured marbles. Beyond it is a square saloon, over which is the great dome, and in the centre of this saloon is the tomb of the royal founder. Most of the decorations of this mosque are very elaborate and elegant, but the building, in many parts, needs repair.

The great mosque of Ibn-Tooloon (or, as it is more commonly called, Gámë' Teyloon), situated in the southern part of the metropolis, is a very interesting building. It was founded in the year of the Flight 263 (A.D. 876–7), and was the principal mosque of the city El-Katáë, a city nearly a century older than El-Káhireh. The space which it occupies is about 400 feet square. It is constructed of brick, covered with plaster, and consists of arcades surrounding a square court; in the centre of which is a tank for ablution, under a square stone building, surmounted by a dome. The arches in this mosque are slightly pointed: this is very remarkable, as it proves, as the mosque was constructed A.D. 876–7, and has never been rebuilt, that the

Eastern pointed arch is more ancient than the Gothic. This remark I borrow from my brother's manuscript notes.[†] A great mád'neh, with winding stairs round its exterior, stands on the north-west side of the mosque; with which it is only connected by an arched gateway. The whole of this great mosque is in a sad state of decay; and not even kept decently clean, excepting where the mats are spread. It is the most ancient Arabian building, excepting the Nilometer of Er-Ródah (which is about 12 years older), now existing in Egypt: for the mosque of 'Amr, though founded more than two centuries before, has often been rebuilt.

In the neighbourhood of the mosque above described is a large ruined castle or palace, called Kal'at el-Kebsh (or the castle of the Ram[1]), occupying, and partly surrounding, an extensive rocky eminence. It was built in the middle of the seventh century after the Flight (or the thirteenth of our era). Its interior is occupied by modern buildings.[2]

The mosques of the seyyideh[‡] Zeynab, the seyyideh Sekkeeneh, and the seyyideh Nefeeseh (the first and second situated in the southern part of the metropolis, and the third in a small southern suburb without the gates) are highly venerated, but not very remarkable buildings.[3] There are many other mosques in Cairo well worthy of examination; but those which I have mentioned are the most distinguished.

I have been surprised at my having visited the most sacred of the mosques of Cairo without exciting the smallest suspicion of my being a Christian. A few days ago a party of Englishmen were refused admission into the Hasaneyn. They were conducted by a janissary of the Páshá, and he was exceedingly enraged against the officers of the mosque. They seized him, however, and drew him into the mosque, and closing the doors and windows, detained him, shutting out his party; but the interpreter of the Englishmen, being a Muslim, obtained admission by a back door, and liberated the prisoner.[††]

There are, in Cairo, many public buildings, besides the mosques, which attract attention. Among these are several Tekeeyehs, or convents for Darweeshes and others, mostly built by Turkish Páshás, for the benefit of their countrymen. Some of these are very handsome structures.

[†]It is interesting that Sophia should give credit to her brother for this "remark" only.

[1]Kebsh not only signifies a *ram*, but is also the name of the mountain sheep (both male and female which is found in the deserts adjacent to Egypt.

[2]A few years ago, much remained of its principal gateway, which, I am told, had a noble appearance, being very lofty, and of a simple style of architecture.

[‡]Meaning 'lady,' or in this context 'saint.'

[3]The seyyideh Zeyneb was the daughter of Imám 'Alee, the cousin and son-in-law of the Prophet; Sekeeneh was the daughter of Hoseyn, the son of 'Alee; and Nefeeseh was the great-daughter of Hasan, the son of 'Alee.

[††]An interpolation by Sophia.

Many of the Sebeels (or public fountains) are also remarkable buildings. The general style of a large sebeel may be thus described. The principal part of the front is of a semicircular form, with three windows of brass grating. Within each window is a trough of water; and when any one would drink, he puts his hand through one of the lowest apertures of the grating, and dips in the trough a brass mug, which is chained to one of the bars. Above the windows is a wide coping of wood. Over this part of the building is a public schoolroom, with an open front, formed of pillars and arches; and at the top is another wide coping of wood. Some of these buildings are partly constructed of alternate courses of black and white marble.

Hóds, or watering-places for beasts of burden, are also very numerous in Cairo. The trough is of stone, and generally in an arched recess, over which is a public schoolroom.

There are, as my brother has remarked, about sixty or seventy Hammáms, or public baths, in Cairo. Some are exclusively for men, some only for women: others, for men in the morning, and for women in the afternoon. When the bath is appropriated to women, a piece of white cotton is hung over the door. The apartments are paved with marble, have fountains and tanks, and are surmounted by cupolas, pierced with small round holes for the admission of light.

The last of the buildings I shall mention are the Kahwehs, or coffee-shops, of which Cairo contains above a thousand. Only coffee is supplied at these; the persons who frequent them taking their own pipes and tobacco.

LETTER XIII

December, 1842

MY DEAR FRIEND,

FROM the city, you must now accompany me, in imagination, to the citadel. If you could do so in reality, you would be amply repaid for the trouble of ascending its steep acclivities; not by the sight of any remarkable object within its walls, but by gazing on one of the most striking and interesting views in the Eastern world. The citadel (El-Kal'ah) is situated at the south-eastern extremity of the metropolis, upon an extensive, flat-topped, rocky eminence, about 250 feet above the level of the plain, and near the point of Mount Mukattam, which completely commands it. It was founded by Saláh-ed-Deen (the famous Saladin), in the year of the Flight 572 (A.D. 1176–7); but not finished till 604; since which latter period it has been the usual residence of the sultáns and governors of Egypt. Before it is a spacious square, called the Rumeyleh, where a market is held, and where conjurers, musicians, and storytellers are often seen, each surrounded by a ring of idlers.

The Báb el-'Azab is the principal gate of the citadel. Within this is a steep and narrow road, partly cut through the rock; so steep, that in some parts steps are cut to render the ascent and descent less difficult than it would otherwise be for the horses and camels, &c. This confined road was the chief scene of the massacre of the Memlooks in the year 1811. I may perhaps have something to say, on a future occasion, respecting that tragedy.

A great part of the interior of the citadel is obstructed by ruins and rubbish, and there are many dwelling-houses and some shops within it. The most remarkable monument that it contains is a great mosque, built by the Sultán Ibn-Kala'-oon, in the early part of the eighth century after the Flight (or the fourteenth of our era). It is in a ruinous state, and no longer used as a place of worship. It consists of porticoes, surrounding a square court.

On the north-west of this mosque, stood, about twelve or thirteen years ago,[†] a noble ruin—an old palace, commonly called Kasr Yoosuf, or Deewán

---

†Although Sophia copies, almost verbatim, Lane's observations of the interior of the citadel, yet in her interpolations she is careful to update what she sees. In his description, Lane starts with the Old Palace and then moves on to the mosque "which lies to the south-east of the former building" (Lane, *Description*, 91–92), whereas Sophia begins with the ruins of the mosque, which she views, and then continues: "on the north-west of this mosque, stood about twelve or thirteen years ago, a noble ruin—an old palace . . . ," taking into consideration that she is copying what Lane had seen

Yoosuf, and believed to have been the palace of Yoosuf Saláh-ed-Deen; but erroneously. European travellers adopted the same opinion, and called it "Joseph's Hall." My brother informs me, on the authority of El-Makreezee, that this noble structure was built by the prince before-mentioned.[1] Huge ancient columns of granite were employed in its construction; their capitals of various kinds, and ill-wrought, but the shafts very fine. It had a large dome, which had fallen some time before the ruin was taken down. On entering it was observed, in the centre of the south-eastern side, a niche, marking the direction of Mekkeh, like that of a mosque, which in other respects this building did not much resemble. Both within and without are remains of Arabic inscriptions, in large letters of wood; but of which many had fallen long before its demolition.

A little to the west of the site of the old palace were the remains of a very massive building, called "the house of Yoosuf Saláh-ed-Deen," partly on the brow, and partly on the declivity of the hill. From this spot, on the edge of the hill, we have a most remarkable view of the metropolis and its environs. Its numerous mád'nehs and domes, its flat-topped houses, with the sloping sheds which serve as ventilators, and a few palms and other trees among the houses, give it an appearance quite unlike that of any European city. Beyond the metropolis we see the Nile, intersecting a verdant plain; with the towns of Boolák, Masr Ateekah, and El-Geezeh; on the south, the aqueduct, and the mounds of rubbish which occupy the site of El-Fustát, and in the distance, all the pyramids of Memphis, and the palm groves on the site of that city. On the north of the metropolis are seen the plains of Heliopolis and Goshen.[†] No one with a spark of feeling can look unmoved on such a prospect: the physical sight has enough to charm it; but the deepest interest is felt while, in gazing on this scene, the mind's eye runs rapidly over the historic pages of the Word of God. The oppression and the deliverance of the tribes of Israel, and the miracles which marked that deliverance, all these events are overwhelmingly present to the memory, while looking on the scenes they have consecrated—their subsequent prosperity, disobedience, and punishment, all passes in melancholy review. O! that the power of Almighty God may be present with those who labour for their restoration, and "may they at length," as Mr. Wilberforce beautifully expresses his petition on their behalf, "may

---

between 1825 and 1828 during his first visit to Egypt; the palace had by the time of Sophia's visit been destroyed, for Lane in a footnote (Lane, *Description*, 92, n.1) wrote: "This noble ruin has been pulled down since I left Musr," i.e., shortly after 1828.

[1] The Sultán Ibn-Kala'-oon.

[†] Where Lane simply ends the description of the view with a simple sentence: "The world can hardly boast a more interesting view" (p. 92), Sophia typically inserts an evangelical note.

they at length acknowledge their long-neglected Saviour." Well have they been described as "tribes of the wandering foot and weary breast." Often "houseless, homeless, and proscribed," they endure every indignity and become inured to every hardship; but the eye of God is still upon them, and his ear is open to their prayers. How true it is that hitherto "they *will* not turn to Him that they might receive mercy," but they are not forsaken; and while we hear with thankfulness of the zeal of many from among their own people in the cause of Christianity, we trust that the day is not far off when, rather than

"Weep for those who wept by Babel's stream.

Whose shrines are desolate, whose land a dream,"

we shall rejoice in the prospect of that blessed time when the Lord God shall "give unto them beauty for ashes, the oil of joy for mourning, and the garment of praise for the spirit of heaviness;" when all nations of earth shall "rejoice with Jerusalem, and be delighted with the abundance of her glory."

Adjacent to the Kasr Yoosuf is a very large mosque, not yet completed; a costly structure, with a profusion of alabaster columns; but of a mixed style of architecture, which I cannot much admire, though the effect of the building, when it is finished, will certainly be grand. I need hardly add, that the founder of this sumptuous edifice is Mohammad 'Alee, by whose name it is to be called.[†]

The famous well of Yoosuf Saláh-ed-Deen, so called because it was excavated in the reign of that Sultán, is near the southern angle of the old great mosque. It is entirely cut in the calcareous rock, and consists of two rectangular shafts, one below the other; with a winding stairway round each to the bottom. In descending the first shaft my heart and limbs failed me, and I contended myself with seeing as much as I could through the large apertures between the stairs and the well. Our guide bore a most picturesque aspect; she was a young girl, and if I might judge by her beautiful dark eyes, her countenance must have been lovely. She held a lighted taper in each hand, and stepped backwards before us, down the dark and (in my opinion) dangerous descent. Accustomed to the winding way, she continued fearlessly through the gloom, while her light and graceful figure receded slowly, and the glimmer of her tapers shone on the damp rock on either side, and made the darkness seem intense.[‡]

[†]Sophia's interpolation, as the construction of the Muhammad 'Ali mosque had not yet started when Lane wrote.

[‡]Lane does not mention any guide when he deals with the well. Sophia obviously describes a personal experience when she, accompanied probably by Mrs Lieder, descended the well, guided by this young girl. According to the customs of the time, women could not have had a male guide, and presumably one of the female servants or slaves who provided water for the palace would have guided the ladies.

The upper shaft is about 155 feet deep, and the lower about 125; therefore the whole depth of the well is about 280 feet. The water, which is rather brackish, is raised by a sákiyeh at the top of each shaft.

There are several large edifices in the modern Turkish style, worthy in this country of being called palaces, in the southern quarter of the citadel, and in the quarter of the Janisaries, which did not form a part of the *old* citadel, and which lies to the east of the latter. Some of the walls, together with many houses, on the northern slope of the hill, were overthrown by the explosion of a magazine of powder, in the year 1824. On the western slope of the hill is an arsenal, with a cannon-foundry, &c.[†]

Mount Mukattam overlooks both the town and citadel of Cairo, and is composed of a yellowish calcareous rock, abounding with testaceous fossils: it is entirely destitute of verdure. Upon its flat summit, a strong fort has been erected, with a steep causeway, upon high narrow arches ascending to it. On each side of this causeway, the rock has been extensively quarried. On the western side of the mountain are many ancient sepulchral grottoes; but they are difficult of access, and I do not propose visiting them. My brother has seen them, and he could find no traces of hieroglyphics, or other decorations, in any of them.

On the north of the metropolis are many gardens, and, in the season of the inundation, many lakes, in one of which (Birket er Ratlee) abundance of lotus plants are seen in blossom in the month of September. In the same tract is a ruined mosque, which was founded by Ez-Záhir Beyburs, in the year of the Flight 665 (A.D. 1266–7). The French converted it into a fort.

Opposite the Báb en-Nasr is a large cemetery, occupying a desert tract; and here is the tomb of the lamented Burckhardt.[‡]

The great Eastern cemetery, in the sandy waste between the metropolis and the mountain, contains the tombs of many of the Memlook Sultáns. Some of these mausolea (which have been erroneously regarded by some travellers as the tombs of the Khaleefehs) are very noble buildings; particularly those of the Sultan Barkook,[1] and Káid-Bey,[2] or Káitbey. None of the tombs of the Khaleefehs of Egypt now exist: Khán el-Khaleelee (as I have mentioned in a former letter) occupies their site. The central part of this cemetery contains several alms-houses, and is commonly called Káid-Bey. Here, and for some distance towards the citadel, the tombs are closely crowded together, and

---

[†]End of Chapter XI of Lane's *Description*. Sophia continues straight on with Chapter XII.

[‡]Johann Ludwig (aka John Lewis) Burckhardt (1784–1817), the Swiss traveler and orientalist.

[1]Built by his son and successor Fárag, in the beginning of the ninth century after the Flight, or the fifteenth of our era.

[2]Built about a century after the former.

the whole cemetery, being intersected by roads, like streets in a town, may justly be called a Necropolis, or City of the Dead. All the tract is desert; and few persons are to be met here, excepting on the Friday morning, when it is the custom of the Muslims to visit the tombs of their relations and friends. Numerous groups of women are then seen repairing to the cemetery; each bearing a palm-branch, to lay upon the tomb she is about to visit.

On the south of the metropolis is another great cemetery, called El-Karáfeh, still more extensive, but not containing such grand mausolea. This, also, is in a desert plain. Many of its tombs are very beautiful: one kind is particularly elegant, consisting of an oblong monument, generally of marble, canopied by a cupola, or by a pyramidal roof, supported by marble columns. In the southern part of this cemetery is the tomb of the celebrated Imám Esh-Sháfe'ee, the founder of one of the four orthodox sects of El-Islám, that sect to which the people of Cairo chiefly belong. This Imám died in the year of the Flight 204 (A.D. 819–20). The present mosque which covers his tomb is a plain whitewashed building, with a dome cased with lead. This mosque has been twice rebuilt, the present being the third building, and about two centuries and a half old. A little to the north of it is a low building, which is the burial-place of the present Páshá's family. Between this cemetery and the mountain are many ancient mummy-pits choked with rubbish. They evidently show that this tract was the Necropolis of Egyptian Babylon.

Along the western side of the metropolis are several lakes and gardens.[†] The most remarkable of the latter are those of Ibraheem Páshá; but these I might more properly call plantations. I have mentioned them in a former letter. A great portion of the tract they occupy was, a few years ago, covered by extensive mounds of rubbish, which, though not so large nor so lofty as those on the east and south, concealed much of the town from the view of persons approaching it in this direction. All the camels, asses, &c., that die in the metropolis are cast upon the surrounding hills of rubbish, where hungry dogs and vultures feed on them.

On the bank of the river, between Boolák and Masr el-'Ateekah, are several palaces, or mansions, among which is one belonging to Ibraheem Páshá, besides a large square building called Kasr El-'Eynee (which is an establishment for the education of youths destined for the service of the government[‡]), and a small convent of Darweeshes. A little to the south of these buildings is the entrance of the khaleeg, or canal of Cairo; and just above this commences the aqueduct by which the water of the Nile is conveyed to the Citadel. A large hexagonal building, about sixty or seventy feet high, contains the sákiyehs which raise the water to the channel of the aqueduct. The whole

---

[†]Here begins Sophia's updating to account for the change that had taken place after Lane's description of the "extensive mounds of rubbish."

[‡]In Lane's version, the "youths are destined for the army, &c." (Lane, *Description*, 94)..

length of the aqueduct is about two miles. It is built of stone; and consists of a series of narrow arches, very gradually decreasing in height, as the ground has a slight ascent, imperceptible to the eye. The water, towards the end of its course, enters a subterranean channel, and is raised from a well in the Citadel. This aqueduct was built (in the place of a former one of wood) in the early part of the tenth century after the Flight (or the sixteenth of our era). To the south of the aqueduct lies the town of Masr el-'Ateekah, the principal houses of which face the river, and the island of Er-Ródah.

This island (the name of which signifies the Island of the Garden) is about a mile and three-quarters in length, and a third of a mile in breadth. The branch of the river on its eastern side is very narrow; and when the Nile is at its lowest point, the bed of this narrow branch becomes nearly dry. The island contains several pleasure-houses and gardens,[†] and the palm, the orange, the lime, the citron, the pomegranate, the vine, the sycamore (which affords a deep and broad shade), and the banana, form a luxuriant variety. The banana is especially beautiful; its long leaves spreading and drooping from the summit of the stem, like the branches of the palm-tree. On this verdant island we find also the henna-tree, so much esteemed by the women of this country for the dye afforded by its leaves, and so justly valued by persons of all countries for the delicious perfume which its flowers exhale. But the great charm of Er-Ródah is a garden belonging to Ibraheem Páshá, under the able superintendence of Mr. Traill, who has rendered it the most attractive thing of its kind in the neighbourhood of Cairo.

Masr el-'Ateekah, though more than a mile in length, is a small straggling town, lying along the bank of the Nile, and occupying a part of the site of El-Fustát.[‡] Many of the vessels from Upper Egypt unload here; and a constant intercourse is kept up, by means of numerous ferry-boats, between this town and El-Geezeh. Behind the town are extensive low mounds of rubbish, covering the rest of the site of El-Fustát. In this desolate tract are situated the Mosque of 'Amr, the Kasr esh-Shema, and several Christian convents.

The mosque of 'Amr has been so often repaired and rebuilt, that almost every part of it may now be regarded as modern: yet there is something very imposing in the associations connected with this building, where the conqueror of Egypt, surrounded by "companions of the Prophet," so often prayed.

The building occupies a space about 350 feet square; its plan is a square court, surrounded by porticos, and its whole appearance very simple and

---

[†]Sophia updates Lane's account. He had mentioned the "remains of a massive Roman wall," and most important of all the Nilometer, which was completed in A.D. 861–62 "on the site of one more ancient." He also mentioned other remains (Lane, *Description*, 95), which Sophia ignores.

[‡]Lane mentions that it "contains about 4,000 inhabitants" (Lane, *Description*, 95).

plain. The exterior is formed by high bare walls of brick. The portico at the end of the court towards Mekkeh has six rows of columns; that on the left side, four rows; that on the right, three; and on the entrance side only one row. The columns are of veined marble; some, being too small, have an additional plinth, or an inverted capital, at the base. The capitals are of many different kinds, having been taken, as also the columns, from various ancient buildings.

The Kasr esh-Shema is an old Roman fortress, which was the stronghold of Egyptian Babylon, and the headquarters of the Greek army, which the Arabs, under 'Amr, contended with and vanquished. It is said that this building was, in ancient times, illuminated with candles on the first night of every month; and hence it derived the name it now bears, which, signifies " the pavilion of the candles." The area which it occupies extends about a thousand feet from north to south and six or seven hundred feet from east to west. Its walls are very lofty, constructed of brick with several courses of stone, and strengthened by round towers. The interior is crowded with houses and shops, occupied by Christians, and it contains several churches; among which is that of St. Sergius, where a small grotto, somewhat resembling an oven, is shown as the retreat of the Holy Family. The Egyptian Babylon was situated on a rocky eminence, on the south-east of the Kasr esh-Shema. El-Makreezee and other Arab historians prove that this was the Masr[†] which 'Amr besieged and took. There was another fortress here, besides the Kasr esh-Shema, called the Kasr Babelyoon (or the pavilion of Babylon.) This, I am told, was the spacious square building since called Istabl 'Antar (or the stable of Antar,) which in later times became a convent, and is now converted into a powder-magazine. To the west of the hill of Babylon, and close to the Nile, is the small village of Atar en-Nebee; so called from a stone, bearing the impression of the Prophet's foot, preserved in a small mosque, which rises, with a picturesque effect, from the verge of the river.

El-Geezeh, which is opposite to Masr el-Ateekah, is a small poor town, surrounded, excepting on the side towards the river, by a mean wall, which would scarcely avail to defend it from a party of Bedawees. It has been supposed to occupy a part of the site of Memphis; but this conjecture is known to be erroneous.

I must mention also a few places north of the metropolis. A fine straight road, bordered by mulberry-trees, sycamores, and acacias, leads to Shubra, the favourite country residence of the Páshá, rather more than three miles from Cairo. The palace of Shubra is situated by the Nile. Its exterior is picturesque, especially as viewed from the river, and it has an extensive garden laid out with much taste.

[†]Sophia generally replaces Lane's "Musr" (the common Arabic name) for the capital with the English name, Cairo. Here she retains Lane's appellation but alters the spelling.

About six miles distant from the northern gates of the metropolis, towards the north-northeast, is the site of Heliopolis, the City of the Sun, called by the Egyptians, "On;" and by the Arabs, "Eyn-Shems," or, "the fountain of the sun;" though, to bear this signification, the name should, I am told, be written "Eyn esh-Shems," which may also be interpreted, "the rays, or light of the sun." The route from Cairo to the site of Heliopolis lies along the desert; but near the limits of the cultivable soil. This part of the desert is a sandy flat, strewed with pebbles, and with petrified wood, pudding-stone, red sandstone, &c. A small mountain of red sandstone, called "El-Gebel el-Ahmar" (or "the red mountain"), lies at a short distance to the right, or east.‡ On approaching within a mile of the site of Heliopolis, the traveller passes by the village of El-Matareeyeh, where are pointed out an old sycamore, under the shade of which (according to tradition), the Holy Family reposed, and a well which afforded them drink. The balsam-tree was formerly cultivated in the neighbouring fields: it thrived nowhere else in Egypt; and it was believed that it flourished in this part because it was watered from the neighbouring well. The name given by the Arabs to Heliopolis was perhaps derived from this well. In a space above half a mile square, surrounded by walls of crude brick, which now appear like ridges of earth, were situated the sacred edifices of Heliopolis. The only remaining monument appearing above the soil is a fine obelisk, standing in the midst of the enclosure. The Arabs call it "the obelisk of Pharaoh." It is formed of a single block of red granite, about sixty-two feet in height, and six feet square at the lower part. The soil has risen four or five feet above its base; for, in the season of the inundation, the water of the Nile enters the enclosure by a branch of the canal of Cairo. Upon each of its sides is sculptured the same hieroglyphic inscription, bearing the name of Osirtesen the First, who reigned not very long after the age when the pyramids were constructed. There are a few other monuments of his time: the obelisk of the Feiyoo'm is one of them. 'Abd El-Lateef, in speaking of Eyn-Shems, says that he saw there (about the end of the twelfth century of the Christian era) the remains of several colossal statues, and *two* great obelisks, one of which had fallen, and was broken in two pieces. These statues, and the broken obelisk, probably now lie beneath the accumulated soil.

Such are the poor remains of Heliopolis, that celebrated seat of learning, where Eudoxus and Plato studied thirteen years, and where Herodotus derived much of his information respecting Egypt. In the time of Strabo, the

---

‡Here Sophia omits two sentences from the rest of the recital that is faithfully copied from Lane, they are as follows: "On the left of the route is a large settlement of courtesans, composing a complete village. Passengers generally attract several of these girls from their huts; and are often much annoyed by their importunity." (Lane, *Description*, p. 96).

city was altogether deserted; but the famous temple of the sun still remained, though much injured by Cambyses. The bull Mnevis was worshipped at Heliopolis, as Apis was at Memphis. It is probable that the "land of Goshen" was immediately adjacent to the province of Heliopolis, on the north-north-east.

Thirteen miles from Cairo, in the same direction as Heliopolis, is the village of El-Khánkeh, once a large town, and long the camp of the regular troops. El-Khánkeh is two miles to the north of the Lake of the Pilgrims, which is so called because the pilgrims collect and encamp by it before they proceed in a body to Mekkeh. This lake is more than two miles in length, from west to east, and a mile in breadth. It is filled by the canal of Cairo during the season of the inundation.

LETTER XIV

December, 1842

MY DEAR FRIEND,

YOU must bear with me if I recur to the subject of the haunted house, for our disturbances came to a sort of climax which I think as curious as it was exciting, and so strikingly characteristic, that I must describe to you the particulars of the case.

Ramadán ended about a month ago, and with it ended the comparative quiet of our nights. To describe to you all the various noises by which we have been disturbed is impossible. Very frequently the door of the room in which we were sitting late in the evening, within two or three hours of midnight, was violently knocked at many short intervals: at other times, it seemed as if something very heavy fell upon the pavement close under one of the windows of the same room, or of one adjoining, and as these rooms were on the top of the house, we imagined at first that some stones or other things had been thrown by a neighbour, but we could find nothing outside after the noises I have mentioned. The usual noises continued during the greater part of the night, and were generally like a heavy trampling, like the walking of a person in large clogs, varied by knocking at the doors of many of the apartments, and at the large water-jars[†] which are placed in recesses in the galleries. Our maids have come and gone like shadows ever since our residence here, excepting during Ramadán, and *sauve qui peut* seems to have been their maxim; for they believe that one touch of an 'efreet[‡] would render them demoniacs.

A few evenings since, a maid, who had only passed two days in the house, rushed to our usual sitting room, whence she had just removed our supper, exclaiming that a tall figure in white had stood with arms outspread at the entrance of the upper gallery to prevent her passing. We all immediately returned with her, and as you will anticipate, found nothing. This white figure our servants call a saint, and they assert that the house is haunted by a saint and an 'efreet. One man assures us that this same saint, who is, to use his expression, "of dazzling whiteness," applied himself, one night, to the bucket of the well in the court, and, having drawn up water, performed his ablutions and said his prayers. Frightening servant maids is rather inconsistent, I ween, with such conduct. Certainly the servants do not complain without reason, and it is particularly grievous, because there is

---

[†]Earthenware jars for cooling water.
[‡]'Demon.'

not, throughout the whole healthful part of the city, one comfortable house vacant.

During Ramadán, the Muslims believe that 'efreets are imprisoned, and thus our servants accounted for our freedom from annoyance during that month. We on the other hand believed we had bolted and barred out the offender, by having discovered his place of ingress, and were much disappointed at finding our precautions useless.

A few days since, our doorkeeper (a new servant), complained that he not only could not sleep, but that he *never had* slept since his arrival more than a few minutes at a time, and that he never could sleep consistently with his duty, unless the 'efreet should be destroyed. He added, that he came up every night into the upper gallery leading to our sleeping rooms, and there he found the figure I have mentioned, walking round and round the gallery; and concluded with an anxious request that my brother would consent to his firing at the phantom, saying that devils have always been destroyed by the discharge of fire-arms. My brother consented to the proposal, provided the servant used neither ball nor small shot. Two days and nights passed, and we found on the third, that the doorkeeper was waiting to ascertain whether the spectre were a saint or a devil, and had therefore resolved to question him on the ensuing night before he fired.

The night came, and it was one of unusual darkness. We had really forgotten our man's intention, although we were talking over the subject of the disturbances until nearly midnight, and speculating upon the cause, in the room where my children were happily sleeping, when we were started by a tremendous discharge, which was succeeded by the deep hoarse voice of the door keeper, exclaiming "There he lies, the accursed!" and a sound as of a creature struggling and gasping for breath. In the next moment, the man loudly called his fellow servant, crying, "Come up, the accursed is struck down before me!"—and this was followed by such mysterious sounds that we believed either a man had been shot, and was in his last agonies, or that our man had accidentally shot himself.

My brother went round the gallery, while I and my sister-in-law stood like children trembling hand in hand, and my boys mercifully slept (as young ones do sleep), sweetly and soundly through all the confusion and distress. It appeared that the man used not only ball-cartridge, but put two charges of powder, with two balls, into his pistol. I will describe the event, however, in his own words. "the 'efreet passed me in the gallery and repassed me, when I thus addressed it. 'Shall we quit this house, or will you do so?' 'You shall quit it,' he answered; and passing me again, he threw dust into my right eye. This proved he was a devil," continued the man; "and I wrapped my cloak around me, and watched the spectre as it receded. It stopped in that corner, and I observed attentively its appearance. It was tall and perfectly white. I stooped, and before it moved again, discharged my pistol, which I had before concealed, and the accursed was struck down before me, and here are the remains." So saying, he picked up a small burnt mass, which my brother showed us afterwards, resembling more the sole of a shoe than anything else, but perforated by fire in several places, and literally burnt to a cinder. This, the man asserted (agreeably with a popular opinion), was always the relic when a devil was destroyed, and it lay on the ground under a part of the wall where the bullets had entered.

The noise which succeeded the report, and which filled me with horror, is, and must ever remain, a mystery. On the following morning we closely examined the spot, and found nothing that could throw light on the subject. The burnt remains do not help us to a conclusion; one thing, however, I cannot but believe—that some one who had personated the evil one suffered some injury, and that the darkness favoured his escape. It is truly very ridiculous in these people to believe that the remains of a devil resemble the sole of an old shoe. It reminds me of the condensed spirits of whom we read in the "Thousand and One Nights," who were (so say tradition) bottled up, hermetically sealed, and thrown into the sea, by order of Suleyman the son of Da-ood.

I need scarcely say that the servant was reprimanded for disobeying his orders with regard to charging the pistol. With this one exception, he has proved ever obedient, most respectful, and excellent in every point. I really believe the man was so worn out by want of sleep, and exasperated by finding the same figure nightly pacing round the galleries, and preventing his rest, that he became desperate.

You will remember the story, in the "Thousand and One Nights," of the revenge threatened by an 'Efreet on a merchant, for having unconsciously slain his son by throwing a date-stone, which occasioned a mortal wound. The fear of unknowingly injuring an 'Efreet and incurring his resentment is as strong as ever in the minds of these people. They always say "Destoor" (permission) when about to step down from any elevated place, or when they see another person going to do so. A poor little boy fell on his face the other day near our house, and hurt himself certainly, but before he cried, he exclaimed, "Destoor!" I suppose concluding that if he had fallen on an 'Efreet unwittingly, the asking permission after the fact might cancel the offence; and having done so he was satisfied, and cried heartily.

LETTER XV

Cairo, February, 1843

My Dear Friend,

YOU know how much I desired to obtain access to respectable
hareems, as well those of the highest as those of the middle classes; and now
that my hope has been realized, I find that I did not desire what would dis-
appoint my expectations. Indeed I have felt exceedingly interested in
observing the manners of the ladies of this country; in some cases I have been
amused by their familiarity, and in many fascinated by the natural grace of
their deportment. I am aware that by description I cannot do them justice,
but I will endeavour to give you faithful pictures of those hareems I have
already seen; and first I must tell you that I am indebted exceedingly to the
kindness of Mrs. Lieder, the lady of our excellent resident missionary, who
has gained the confidence of the most distinguished hareems in this country,
and has given me some introductions I particularly desired without any
reserve, and in the most ready and friendly manner. Among the ladies to
whom she has introduced me are those of Habeeb Eféndee, the late governor
of Cairo; and in relating to you the particulars of my first visit to them, I give
you an account of my initiation into the mysteries of the high hareems.

I had been some time in Cairo before I dared to mount the "high ass;" for
their appearance is really formidable. I adopted the plan followed by many
ladies here, that of a prayer-carpet spread on a common saddle; but in visiting
the *high hareems*, it became necessary to ride the *high* ass; and I found it
infinitely more agreeable than my usual donkey's equipment. Certainly I was
obliged constantly to stoop my head under the gateways, and came nearly
in contact with some projecting first-floor windows; therefore I found it
necessary to be on the alert; but setting aside these objections, there is no
comparison to be made between the "high ass" and the ordinary donkeys—
the former is so decidedly preferable.

When we arrived at the house of Habeeb Efendee, and had passed the
outer entrance, I found that the hareem apartments, as in other houses of the
great in this country, are not confined to the first and upper floors, but form
a separate and complete house, distinct from that of the men. Having passed
a spacious hall, paved with marble, we were met at the door of the first apartment by the elder daughter of Habeeb Efendee, who gave me the usual
Eastern salutation, touching her lips and forehead with her right hand, and
then insisted on removing my riding-dress herself, although surrounded by
slaves. This was a mark of extraordinary condescension, as you will presently

see. In the houses of the middle classes, the ladies generally honour their vis-itors by disrobing them of their riding-dress; but in the high hareems this office is generally performed by slaves, and only by a member of the family when a guest is especially distinguished.

In visiting those who are considered the noble of the land. I resume, under my Eastern riding costume, my English dress; thus avoiding the necessity of subjecting myself to any humiliation. In the Turkish in-door costume, the manner of my salutations must have been more submissive than I should have liked; while, as an Englishwoman, I am entertained by the most distinguished, not only as an equal, but generally as a superior. I have never given more than the usual salutation, excepting in the case of addressing elderly ladies, when my inclination leads me to distinguish them by respectfully bending, and lowering my right hand before I touch my lips and forehead, when I am pre-sented, and when I leave them. On receiving sweetmeats, coffee, sherbet, or any refreshment, and on returning the cup, plate, &c., which contain them, I give always the customary salutation to the chief lady of the hareem, whose situation on the divan points her out as the superior of the party.

At home, and when visiting ladies of the middle class, I wear the Turkish dress, which is delightfully comfortable, being admirably adapted to the cli-mate of this country. I have never gone out but in the Eastern riding-dress, which I have already described to you.

When the lady I have mentioned had removed my surtout apparel, a slave in attendance received them in an exquisite pink kerchief of cashmere, richly embroidered with gold. The kerchiefs of this kind, in the hareems of the wealthy, are generally very elegant, but that was the most perfect specimen I have seen of correct and tasteful embroidery. The riding-dress was imme-diately taken into another room, according to a usual custom, which is observed for the purpose of creating a short delay, giving an opportunity to offer some additional refreshment when the guest has proposed to take her leave. My new acquaintance then conducted me to the divan, and placed me next to the seat of honour, which was reserved for her mother, the first cousin of the late Sultan Mahmoud, who soon entered the room, and gave me a cor-dial welcome, assigning to me the most distinguished seat on her right hand, the same to which her daughter had conducted me, while the grand-mother of Abbas Pasha sat on her left. She was soon followed by her second daughter, who greeted me with much politeness, and in a very elegant manner assured me that I was welcome. She was more richly attired than her sister; therefore I will describe to you her dress.

She wore on her head a dark handkerchief twisted round a tarboosh, with a very splendid sprig of diamonds attached to the right side, and extending partly over her forehead. The sprig was composed of very large brilliants, dis-posed in the form of three lutes, in the centre, from each of which a branch extended, forming an oval shape, at least five inches in length. High on the left side of her head she wore a knot or slide of diamonds, through which was drawn a bunch of ringlets, which, from their position, appeared to be artificial; her tarboosh had the usual blue silk tassel, but this was divided and hanging on either side. Her long vest and trowsers were of a dark flowered India fabric; she wore round her waist a large and rich cashmere shawl; and her neck was decorated with many strings of very large pearls, confined at intervals by gold beads. She was in one respect strangely disfigured; her eyebrows being painted with kohl, and united by the black pigment in a very broad and most unbecoming manner. Many women of all classes here assume this disguise: some apply the kohl to the eyebrows as well as to the eyes, with great delicacy; but the lady in question had her eyebrows so remarkable, that her other features were deprived of their natural expression and effect.

A number of white slaves formed a large semicircle before us, received from others, who waited in the ante-chamber, silver trays, containing glass dishes of sweetmeats. There were three spoons in each dish, and two pieces of sweetmeat in each spoon. These were immediately succeeded by coffee, which was also brought on silver trays; the small china cups beings, as usual, in stands, shaped like egg-cups; but these were not, as in ordinary houses, simply of silver filagree, or plain, but decorated with diamonds. They were certainly elegant, but more costly than beautiful. The coffee is never handed on the tray, but gracefully presented by the attendant, holding the little stand between the thumb and finger of the right hand. After these refreshments a short time elapsed, when two slaves brought in sherbet on silver waiters, in exceedingly elegant cut-glass cups, with saucers and covers. Each tray was covered with a round pink richly-embroidered cover, which the slave removed as she approached us. To receive our cups, of the contents of which, accordingly to custom, we drank about two-thirds, another slave approached, with a large white embroidered kerchief, ostensibly for the purpose of wiping the mouth; but any lady would be thought quite a novice who did more than touch it with her lips.

In the course of conversation, I expressed my admiration of the Turkish language, and, to my surprise, the elder of the young ladies gave me a general invitation, and proposed to become my instructress: addressing herself to Mrs. Lieder with the most affectionate familiarity, she said, "O my sister, persuade your friend to come to me frequently, that I may teach her Turkish; in doing which, I shall learn her language, and we can read and write together." I thanked her for her very polite offer, but made no promise that I would become her pupil; foreseeing that it would lead to a very considerable waste of time. In all the hareems I have visited, Arabic is understood and spoken; so I do not expect any advantage from a knowledge of Turkish, unless I could devote to its study considerable attention.

The perfect good humour and cheerfulness which pervaded this family-circle is well worthy of remark, and much engaged my thoughts during the morning of my visit. All that I observed of the manners of the Eastern women, at Habeeb Eféndee's and elsewhere, leads me to consider the perfect contrast which the customs of Eastern life present to the whole construction of European society. If you have read Mr. Urquhart's 'Spirit of the East,' you have felt interested in his view of the life of the hareem, and have thought that the Eastern "home" which he represents in such a pleasing manner possesses considerable attractions. Believe me, there is much to fascinate and much to interest the mind in observing peculiarities in these people which have no parallel in the West; and I could furnish a letter on contrasts nearly as curious as Mr. Urquhart's.

How extraordinary it seems that girls, until they are given away in marriage, see only persons of their own sex, with the exception of a few very near male relations, and then receive as their future lord and master one with whom no previous acquaintance has been possible! This is so revolting to the mind of an Englishwoman, that the mere consideration of such a system (which indeed, I am told, is beyond what the rigour of the law requires) is intolerable; therefore I must observe, and admire all that is admirable, and endeavour to forget what is so objectionable in the state of Eastern society.

Before our departure it was proposed that I should see their house; and the elder daughter threw her arm round my neck, and thus led me through a magnificent room which was surrounded by divans; the elevated portion of the floor was covered with India matting, and in the middle of the depressed portion was the most tasteful fountain I have seen in Egypt, exquisitely inlaid with black, red, and white marble. The ceiling was a beautiful specimen of highly-wrought arabesque work, and the walls as usual white-washed, and perfectly plain, with the exception of the lower portions, which, to the height of about six feet, were cased with Dutch tiles.

I was conducted up stairs in the same manner; and I could not help feeling exceedingly amused at my situation; and considering that these ladies are of the royal family of Turkey, you will see that I was most remarkably honoured.

When we approached the bath, we entered the reclining room, which was furnished with divans, and presented a most comfortable appearance; but the heat and vapour were so extremely oppressive in the region of the bath, that we merely looked into it, and gladly returned to the cool gallery. I am not surprised that you are curious on the subject of the bath and the Eastern manner of using it; and I hope to devote a future letter to a description of the operation (for such indeed it may be styled), and the place in which that operation is performed.

On our reaching the stairs, the second daughter of Habeeb Eféndee took her sister's place; and with her arm round my neck, we descended the stairs, and re-entered the room where I had received so kind a reception. When we rose to take our leave, the elder daughter received my riding-dress from a slave, and was about to attire me, when her sister said, "You took them off;

it is for me to put them on." The elder lady partly consented, retaining the habarah, and thus they dressed me together. Then, after giving me the usual salutation, they each cordially pressed my hand, and kissed my cheek. We then descended into the court, attended by the ladies, and a crowd of white slaves. Having crossed the court, we arrived at the great gate, through which I had before passed, which was only closed by a large mat, suspended before it, forming the curtain of the hareem. This mat was raised by black eunuchs, who poured from a passage without, and immediately after the ladies bade us farewell, and returned, followed by their slaves. The principal eunuch ascended first the mounting platform, and placed me on the donkey, while two others arranged my feet in the stirrups; our own servants being kept in the background.

A few days after this visit, I received a second invitation from this hareem, with the polite assurance that they intended making a festival and fantasia for my amusement.

LETTER XVI

March, 1843

My Dear Friend,

I DOUBT whether I shall be bold enough to attempt anything like a description of the present political state of this country; but I shall here offer you a sketch of its past history, from the period of its conquest by the Arabs, which, I hope, will interest. For this purpose, I shall draw freely from my brother's manuscript notes.

In the 20th year of the Flight (A.D. 640–41), Egypt was conquered by the Arabs; and since that period, it has continued to be subject to Muslim rulers. It has been governed by Arab viceroys, and by Turkish independent princes; by Arab khaleefehs; by a dynasty of Kurds; by Turkish and by Circassian Sultáns, who, in their youth, were Memlooks (or slaves): it has been annexed to the great Turkish empire, and governed by Turkish pashas, in conjunction with Memlooks; has become a prey to the Memlooks alone; been conquered by the French; wrested from them by the English, and restored to the Turks: it has been a scene of sanguinary contention between the Turks and Memlooks; and is now again solely under a Turkish ruler. Of these various revolutions I shall give a short account.

During the space of nearly two centuries and a half the authority of the khaleefehs was maintained in Egypt by viceroys whom they appointed, and who were frequently changed. The first of these viceroys was 'Amr Ibn-el-'A's, the conqueror of the country. The history of their times, transmitted to us by Arab writers, contains, as far as it relates to Egypt, little that is worthy of mention. On the occasion of the overthrow of the dynasty of the Ummaweeyeh (or khaleefehs of the race of Umeiyeh), the seat of whose empire was Damascus, there ensued no change in the form of government to which Egypt had been subject; but the town of El-'Askar was then founded, and became the residence of the successive viceroys appointed by the new dynasty of the 'Abbaseeyeh (or khaleefehs descended from El-'Abbás, an uncle of the Prophet), who changed the seat of the Arabian empire to Baghdád.

At the close of the period above mentioned, the empire of the Khaleefehs had begun to decline: those princes had no longer sufficient power to overawe their lieutenants in distant provinces. The viceroy of the greater part of Northern Africa had already set the example of rebellion against the successor of the Prophet, and had secured his independence; and now, at the close of the year of the Flight 269 (A.D. 883), the governor of Egypt, actuated by motives of self-defence, rather than ambition, threw off his allegiance to his sovereign, the Khaleefeh El-Moatamid, and rendered himself absolute master not only of Egypt, but also of Syria, after having governed the former country as viceroy during the space of fifteen years. This prince was Ahmad Ibn-Tooloon (commonly called Ibn Teyloon), the founder of the noble city of El-Katáë (which he made the seat of his government), and of the grand mosque which is called by his name, and which remains a proud monument of his reign. He was the son of a Turkish slave, who had been promoted to a high office in the court of Baghdád. Though he became the independent sovereign of Egypt, the Khaleefeh continued to be acknowledged, in that country, as the head of the religion; and, as such, was still named in the public Friday-prayers in the mosques. Four independent princes of the same family succeeded Ibn Tooloon; and thus, during rather more than twenty-two years, the khaleefehs of Baghdád remained deprived of one of the finest provinces of their wide empire. The dynasty of the Benee-Tooloon was overthrown in the year of the Flight 292 (A.D. 905) by Mohammad Ibn-Suleymán, who, at the head of a numerous army, set fire to El-Katáë, plundered El-Fustát, and re-established the supereme authority of the khaleefehs in Egypt.

At the expiration of about thirty years after that period, the great Arabian Empire began to be dismembered on every side. In the year 323 (A.D. 935) a Ta'ta'r, or Turk, named Mohammad El-Ikhsheed (or El-Akhsheed), succeeded, for the second time, to the government of Egypt, and soon after acquired the sole dominion of that country and of Syria. The latter was wrested from him; but it again became subject to his authority. This prince was the founder of the dynasty of Ikhsheedeeyeh (or Akhsheedeeyeh), the second and third of whom were his sons; the fourth was a black eunuch, surnamed Káfoor, whom he had purchased and emancipated. On the death of this eunuch, a dispute arose respecting the succession; and though a grandson of the founder of the dynasty was proclaimed, and acknowledged by many, still the general voice seemed to be against him. This was in the year of the Flight 358 (A.D. 968–9). Of this crisis advantage was taken by El-Mo'ezz, the fourth of the Fawátim (or khaleefehs of the race of Fátimeh), who ruled over the greater part of Northern Africa. The Fawátim had succeeded the dynasty of Beni-l-Aghlab, founded by Ibráheem Ibn El-Aghlab, who, having been appointed governor of Africa Proper by the Khaleefeh Hároon Er-Rasheed, rendered himself an absolute prince. Immediately upon hearing of the distracted state of affairs in Egypt, El-Mo'ezz sent thither a numerous army, and secured to himself, without the least opposition, the possession of that country. The city of El-Káhireh, or Cairo, which his general Góhar founded, became the residence of El-Mo'ezz and his successors. The title of "khaleefeh," as applied to a Muslim sovereign, signifies the legitimate successor of the Prophet, and, consequently, the head of the Muslim religion: the Fawátim, therefore, by assuming that title, excluded the princes of the race of El-'Abbás from the honour of being prayed for in the mosques of

Egypt, considering that as their own prerogative. The period of their sway was most eventful: it was most remarkable for the horrid impiety and tyranny of El-Hákim, the seven years' famine in the reign of El-Mustansir (a wise and prudent prince, who reigned sixty years), and the burning of El-Fustát, under El-'A'did, the last of the Fawátim. This dynasty, which consisted of eleven khaleefehs (besides the three predecessors of El-Mo'ezz), lasted until the year of the Flight 567 (A.D. 1171).

The Fawátim were succeeded by the Eiyoobeeyeh, or sultáns of the race of Eiyoob, who were a Kurd family. The first of these was the renowned Saláh-ed-Deen (the Saladin of European historians). He had been sent by Noor-ed-Deen, Sultán of Syria, with an army commanded by his uncle Sherkooh, to assist El-'A'did, the last of the Fawátim, against the crusaders, who had taken the town of Bilbeys, and laid siege to El-Káhireh; El-Fustát having been burned (as before mentioned) to prevent its falling into their hands: the invaders, however, accepted a sum of money to raise the siege, and evacuated the country before the arrival of the troops which Sherkooh and Saláh-ed-Deen accompanied. These two chiefs were most honourably received by El-'A'did, who, soon after their arrival, appointed the former of them his prime-minister; but Sherkooh died only two months and five days after his promotion; and the office he had enjoyed during that short period was conferred upon Saláh-ed-Deen, who requited his benefactor with ingratitude. In the year above mentioned (567), while El-'A'did was suffering from a fatal illness, Saláh-ed-Deen, urged by his former sovereign (the Sultán of Syria), ordered that the Khaleefeh of Baghdád should be prayed for in the mosques of El-Káhireh, to the exclusion of El-'A'did, who died that year, ignorant of this act of his minister. Immediately after his death, Saláh-ed-Deen caused himself to be proclaimed Sultán of Egypt. The title of Khaleefeh he did not presume to take, not being descended from any branch of the family of the Prophet: he therefore continued to acknowledge the Khaleefeh of Baghdád as the head of the religion. To secure his independence he had to contend with many difficulties; but his energetic mind, and personal bravery, aided by the possession of vast treasures amassed by the Fawátim, enabled him to overcome every obstacle. Soon after his assumption of royalty, he had to quell an insurrection raised by the adherents of the family of Fátimeh. The Sultán of Syria, while meditating the invasion of Egypt, died in that same year; and Saláh-ed-Deen subsequently added Syria to his former dominions; whence resulted his frequent conflicts with the crusaders, which spread his fame over Europe. The apprehension of insurrections or invasions induced him to build the Citadel and third wall of El-Káhireh; but the wars in which he afterwards engaged were those of conquest rather than defence. There were eight princes of his dynasty, which lasted eighty-one years and a few days: several of them rendered themselves memorable by their exploits against the crusaders. Syria was under princes of the same family, descendants of Saláh-ed-Deen.

To the dynasty of the Eiyoobeeyeh succeeded that of the Turkish or Turkomán Memlook Sultáns, also called the Bahree Memlooks.[1] Nearly a thousand of this class of Memlooks had been purchased by El-Melik Es-Sáleh Negm-ed-Deen, the last but one of the sultans of the race of Eiyoob: they resided in his palace on the island of Er-Ródah; and hence they received the appellation of "the Bahree Memlooks;"[2] the word Bahree, in this case, signifying "of the river." After having been instructed in military exercises, these slaves constituted a formidable body, whose power soon became uncontrollable. A very beautiful female slave, called Sheger-ed-Durr (or the tree of pearls), of the same race as these Memlooks, was the favourite wife of Negm-ed-Deen. This prince died at El-Mansoorah, whither he had gone to protect his kingdom from the crusaders, who, under Louis IX., had taken Damietta. Toorán Sháh succeeded his father Negm-ed-Deen on the throne of Egypt,[3] but reigned only seventy days: he was put to death by the Memlooks, to whom he had rendered himself obnoxious; as he had also to Sheger-ed-Durr, who was an instigator of his death. Under this sultán, the French invaders of Egypt suffered a signal defeat, and Louis himself was taken prisoner. Sheger-ed-Durr caused herself to be proclaimed queen of Egypt, with the concurrence, and through the influence, of the Memlooks; and thus commenced, with a female, the dynasty of the Bahreeyeh, in the year of the Flight 648 (A.D. 1250), but this queen was soon obliged to abdicate, and one of the Bahree Memlooks, 'Ezz-ed-Deen Eybek Et-Turkamánee, was raised to the throne, with the surname of El-Melik El-Mo'ezz. Sheger-ed-Durr became his wife; but being slighted by him on account of her age, she caused him to be put to death, after he had reigned nearly seven years. His successor, who was his son by another wife, delivered this infamous woman, Sheger-ed-Durr, into the hands of his mother, who, together with her female slaves, beat her to death with their wooden clogs, or pattens; her body was stripped naked, and thrown outside the walls of the citadel, whence, after some days, it was taken, and buried in a tomb which had been constructed for her by her own order. Syria, as well as Egypt, was under the government of the sultáns of this dynasty; it was several times wrested from them, but promptly regained. The dynasty of the Bahreeyeh consisted of the queen above-mentioned, and twenty-four sultáns; and lasted, according to El-Makreezee, one hundred and thirty-six years, seven months, and nine days. Several of these Memlook sultáns (as El-Melik Ez-Zahir Beybars, Kala-oon, Mohammad Ibn-Kala-oon, and some

---

[1] The term Memlook is generally restricted to a white slave, particularly a military slave.

[2] El-Makreezee.

[3] D'Herbelot and some other European writers have fallen into an error in saying that Sheger-ed-Durr was the mother of Toorán Sháh. She bore to Negm-ed-Deen one son, who died in infancy.

others) are celebrated for their conquests, and for the noble mosques and other public edifices which they founded. Few of them died a natural death: many were deposed, or banished, or imprisoned; and a still greater number were victims of assassination. It is remarkable that the first of their dynasty was a woman, and the last a boy only six years of age.

The Bahree Sultáns increased the number of the Memlooks in Egypt by the purchases of Circassian slaves, who, in process of time, acquired the ascendancy. During the short reign of the child El-Melik Es-Sáleh Hajjee, the last of the Bakreeyeh, a chief of the Circassian Memlooks, named Barkook, was regent. In the year of the Flight 784 (A.D. 1382) the latter usurped the throne, and with him commenced the dynasty of Circassian Memlooks, also called the Burjee Memlooks, which name was given to them because the Sultán Kalaoon had purchased a considerable number of this tribe of slaves (three thousand seven hundred), and placed them, as garrisons, in the towers of the citadel:[1] the word burg signifies a tower. Syria continued subject to the Burjee sultáns. This dynasty consisted of twenty-three sultáns, and continued one hundred and thirty-eight years and a half. Ez-Yahir-Barkook, El-Mu-eiyad, Káid Bey, and El-Ghórre may be mentioned as the most renowned of these princes: their splendid mosques and mausolea, as well as their military exploits, or private virtues, have kept up the remembrance of their names. Many of the sultáns of this dynasty were deposed, and several voluntarily abdicated; but nearly all of them died a natural death.

The conquest of Egypt by the Turks, under the Sultán Seleem, in the year of the Flight 923 (A.D. 1517), put an end to the dynasty of the Burjee sultáns. El-Ghóree, the last but one of those princes, was defeated in a dreadful engagement with the army of Seleem, near Aleppo, and was rode over by his own troops. His successor, Toomán Bey, offered an ineffectual opposition to the invading army of Turks in the neighbourhood of his capital: he was hanged (or, according to some authors, crucified) at the Báb Zuweyleh, one of the gates of Cairo. A different form of government, in which the Memlooks were allowed to share, was now established. Egypt was divided into four and twenty provinces; each of which was placed under the military jurisdiction of a Memlook Bey; and the twenty-four beys were subject to the authority of a Turkish páshá, a general governor, appointed by the sultán. Other members of the new administration were seven Turkish chiefs, the generals of seven military corps, called in Turkish Ojáklees, and by the Egyptians Ogaklees, or Wugaklees: these composed the páshá's council. One of the beys was styled Sheykh el-Beled, or Governor of the Metropolis; and this chief enjoyed a higher rank than any of the other beys, among whom, consequently, there were seldom wanting some whose ambition rendered them his secret or avowed enemies. By means of intrigue, or by the sword,

---

[1] El-Makreezee.

or the poisoned cup, the office of Sheykh el-Beled was generally obtained. The Memlooks who thus shared, with the Turkish páshás, the government of Egypt, were commonly called collectively El-Ghuzz, that being the proper name of the tribe to which most of them belonged.[1] They disdained marrying Egyptian women, preferring females of their own or other more northern countries; but few of them had children; for most of the foreign females in Egypt are sterile, or have weak, sickly children, who die in early age. Such being the case, the Memlooks were obliged continually to recruit their numbers with newly purchased slaves from the same countries. Most of them, when first brought to Egypt, were mere boys, unable to wield the sabre; purchased by a bey, or other great officer, they served, for a while, as pages: those who were handsome were sure to be great favourites of their master; and every favourite who (after having been instructed in military exercises) displayed remarkable courage, fidelity, and other good qualities, was emancipated, and promoted to some high office: perhaps he became a káshif, and soon after, a bey. Thus it often happened that several beys owed their advancement to one and the same patron, to whose interests they generally remained devotedly attached. Each bey was constantly intent upon multiplying his Memlooks; and frequent arbitrary exactions from the peasants of the province under his command were the base means which enabled him to accomplish this object. During nearly two centuries after the conquest of Egypt by the Sultán Seleem, the authority of each successive páshá was, with few exceptions, respected by the beys; but the latter, by degrees, obtained the ascendancy; and, after the period above-mentioned, few of the páshás possessed any influence over the Sheykh el-Beled, and the other beys. Egypt thus became subject to a military oligarchy; and the condition of its inhabitants was rendered yet more miserable by frequent sanguinary conflicts between different parties of the Ghuzz. Such was the state of the country when it was invaded by the French; of whose government, in general, the people of Egypt speak in terms of commendation, though they execrate them for particular acts of oppression. After the expulsion of the French, Egypt remained in a very disturbed state, in consequence of the contentions between the beys and the Turkish páshás, until the power of the former was completely annihilated by Mohammad 'Alee, the present ruler.

---

[1]The Egyptians, in speaking of the the times of the Memlooks, who governed Egypt after its conquest by the Turks say "In the days of the Ghuzz such an event happened."

LETTER XVII

MY DEAR FRIEND,

YOU will congratulate us on our having quitted "the haunted house;" and you will do so heartily when I tell you that six families have succeeded each other in it, in as many weeks, since our departure. The sixth family was about to quit immediately when we heard this news; five having been driven out by most obstinate persecutions, not only during the nights, but in broad daylight, of so violent a description, that the windows were all broken in a large upper chamber, our favourite room. The sixth family suffered similar annoyances, and also complained that much of their china was demolished. Like ourselves, no one has been able to obtain quiet rest in that house, or rather I should say, others have been in a worse state than ourselves, for we obtained some relief in consequence of our doorkeeper's achievement. And now I hope I have done with this subject. I have said much upon it, I must be held excusable, as " 'tis passing strange."[†]

Our present house is extremely commodious, and much taste and judgment have been displayed in its construction. The terrace is extensive and very picturesque, and the upper rooms are well situated. Most of the rooms are furnished with glass windows, and the house altogether, being exceedingly well built, is adapted for affording warmth in the winter, and proving a cool summer residence.

With regard to a sojourn in Egypt, it is not an easy matter to give you the *pour et contre*. Of one thing I am convinced, that persons must remain a year in this country, that is, they must go the round of the seasons, or nearly so, before they can fully judge of the comforts it offers. I well remember the extreme annoyance I experienced, for some months after our arrival, from the unusually prolonged heat, of which I complained to you, and from the flies and musquitoes, which were really and constantly distressing; and I could scarcely believe what people told me, namely, that I should soon find myself very well contented with the climate of the country. As to the musquitoes, they interfere so much with enjoyment, that a traveller who visits Egypt only during the great heat may assert, with truth, that he has no comfort by day, nor by night until he enters his curtain.[‡] I confess that I often feared we could not remain here as long as I wished. No sooner, however, did

---

[†]Shakespeare, *Othello*, I iii 160.
[‡]A mosquito-net that covers the bed from top to bottom like a tent

the Nile subside, than my hopes revived; and finding that the most charming temperature imaginable succeeded the heat, I began to understand what travellers mean when they call this a delicious climate. November is a sweet month here—December and January are rather too cold, taking into consideration that there are neither fire-places nor chimneys in any of the houses, excepting in the kitchens. February and March are perfectly delightful, the temperature then being almost as mild as that of summer in England. During April there occur some instances of hot wind, otherwise it is an agreeable month. In May the hot winds are trying, and then follow four months of oppressive heat.

Devoted as I am, justly, to my own dear country and her blessed associations, I can give you my candid opinion, without any fear that I shall be suspected of preferring a residence in the Levant to my English home, and will show you, without reserve, in what consist the fascinations of this part of the East;—in the climate, in the manners of the people, and in the simplicity of their habits, which not only attract my admiration, but render me much less affected by their general poverty than I am by less distress in my own country. It is very certain that if a daily journal were published in Cairo, we should not see paragraphs headed "death by starvation," "distressing case," &c.; but why is it? for there are no houses here for the reception of the poor, as in England. It results from the contented spirit of the poor, if provided simply with bread and water; and, more than all, from the sort of family union which subsists throughout the East, and which literally teaches the poor to "bear each other's burthens." In visiting the middle and higher classes of society, the same family compact is observable, and the mother of the family continues always the mother and the head; her gentle reign lasting with her valued life, and the love and respect of those around her increasing with her years. It is asserted, that when Mohammed was asked what relation had the strongest claim on affection and respect, he replied with warmth, "The mother! the mother! the mother!"

All blood relations in the East take precedence of the wife, who is received into a family as a younger sister. It could scarcely be suffered here, or in Turkey, that a father or mother should quit a house to make way for a son's wife. This you will remember is remarked in Mr. Urquhart's 'Spirit of the East;'[†] and let me ask you, is not this as it should be? I cannot understand how any person with a spark of nature in his breast could allow a beloved parent to resign what a child should be willing to shed his heart's blood to preserve.

[†]Urquhart, *Spirit of the East*, 357–58: "The wife in the East is not the mistress of the household, she is the daughter of her husband's mother. If they were told of a country where the mother has to remove from the family roof to make room for the son's wife, they would consider the tale as a trial of their credulity, or as a satire on human nature."

In obtaining an insight into the habits and manners of the women, I possess considerable advantages; first, from my brother's knowledge of the East, and secondly, from my plan of adhering strictly to habits cherished by the people, which system has secured at once their respect, while it has excited their surprise. We have even gone so far as to adopt their manner of eating;[†] and here I must digress to beg you not to say "How very disgusting!" but read *how* we do it, and then you may confess that it is not unpleasant as you thought. The dishes are prepared in a very delicate manner; for instance, small cucumbers[‡] and other vegetables of a similar kind are scooped out and stuffed with minced meat and rice; minced meat is wrapped in vine-leaves, and so dexterously cooked, that each leaf with its contents continues compact, and is easily taken in the fingers. Fried meat in cakes, and the same in form of sausages, are equally convenient; and all I have mentioned, and a hundred others (for there is great variety in their cookery), may be taken almost as delicately as a slice of cake. For soups, rice prepared in the Eastern manner, and stews, we use spoons; and so do the Turks. One difficulty occasionally presents itself; but not at home. The chief lady of a house, to do her guests honour, presents them with morsels of her own selection, with her own fingers;[††] and in some cases repeats this compliment frequently. It would be a positive affront to refuse these; and I am quite sure that no Englishwoman can so far strain her politeness as to eat as much as her hostess, in her excessive hospitality, desires, though the latter sets her a wonderful example. I have really seen the ladies of this country eat as much as should suffice for three or four moderate meals at one sitting. But to return to my difficulty. I always found it to be the best plan to receive readily, for a time, the morsels which were offered; and when satisfied, to accept perhaps another, and sometimes two or three; at the same time assuring my entertainer, that they were redundant, but that her viands were so extremely well chosen, that I must, after the repast, inquire who has superintended the *cuisine*, and derive from her some information. Thus I removed the impression which was immediately formed, that the dinner was not dressed agreeably with my

---

[†]In this she follows Lane's example, who from the time of his first visit to Egypt in 1825 had, as he remarked, "associated, almost exclusively, with Muslims, of various ranks in society: I have lived as they live, conforming with their general habits; and, in order to make them familiar and unreserved towards me on every subject, have always avowed my agreement with them in opinion whenever my conscience would allow me, and in most other cases refrained from the expression of my dissent, as well as from every action which might give them disgust; abstaining from eating food forbidden by their religion, and drinking wine, &c.; and even from habits merely disagreeable to them; such as the use of knives and forks at meals" (Lane, *Modern Egyptians*, Author's Preface, xv).
[‡]Probably zucchinis.
[††]This habit is still practiced by people from the villages as a mark of hospitality.

taste: and induced only the remark, that " the English eat so much less than the Easterns;" accompanied by regret that so little satisfied me, but followed by an expression of pleasure that the dinner was so agreeable to me.

I have not found the system of Eastern etiquette difficult of adoption; and from the honourable manner in which I have been received, and treated, and always pressed to repeat my visit, I may draw the conclusion fairly, that I have understood how to please the people. It has been a favourite opinion of mine, and one in which I have been educated, that a little quiet observation of the manners and habits of others will always prevent those differences about trifles which so often disturb society, and sometimes separate even friends. Here, I have indeed found the advantage of exercising this observation, and it has proved the means of securing to me invariably polite attention and respect.

I think you would be amused could you see our dinner-arrangements at home. First, a small carpet is spread on the mat; then, a stool cased with mother-of-pearl, &c. is placed upon it, and serves as the support of a round tray of tinned copper, on which is arranged our dinner, with a cake of bread for each person.† A maid then brings a copper ewer and basin, and pours water on the hands of each of our party, and we arrange ourselves round the tray, our Eastern table-napkins spread on our knees. These are larger and longer than English hand-towels, that they may cover both knees when sitting in the Turkish manner. During the meal, the maid holds a water-bottle, or defends us from flies with a fly-whisk. Having no change of plates, knives, or forks, no time is lost at dinner; and it usually occupies twenty minutes. Thus, much valuable time is saved by avoiding works of supererogation. One or two sweet dishes are placed on the tray with those which are savoury; and it is singular to see the women of this country take morsels of sweet and savoury food almost alternately. Immediately after dinner, the ewer and basin are brought round, the stool and carpet are removed with the tray, and the stool is always placed in another room until again required. There is something very sociable in this mode of sitting at table, and it is surprising to see how many persons can sit with comfort round a comparatively small tray. I should advise you and other friends in England to resume the use of small round tables: I have often regretted they are no longer in fashion: for a small family, they are infinitely more comfortable than the large square or oblong tables used in England.

It is true, as you suppose, that I am sometimes amused at my position, and more particularly so, when, on the occasion of any thing heavy being brought into the hareem, one of the men passes through the passage belonging to it.

---

†This method is still practiced by the common people, who use a low, round, wooden table (*tabliya*) or a large tin tray placed on the floor, on which the food is laid in the same manner Sophia describes, and around which they sit cross-legged. The *tabliya* or tray is then removed or placed in a corner of the same room.

Their approach is always announced by their saying audibly, " O Protector! (Ya Sátir) and "Permission!" (Destoor), several times. Excepting on such occasions, no man approaches the hareem but the sakka, or water-carrier; and I often think that any person with a knowledge of Arabic, and none of the habits of the people, would think these sakkas devotees, judging by their constant religious ejaculations. The men are quite as careful in avoiding the hareem, as the ladies are in concealing their faces, and indeed, in many cases, more so. I have been amused particularly by the care of one of our men, who, having lived many years in a Turkish family, is quite a Turkish servant. On one occasion, on returning home from riding with my boys, my donkey fairly threw me off as he entered the court; and when this man raised me up (for my head was on the ground), I supported myself for a moment with my hands against the wall of the house, while I assured my poor children, who were exceedingly frightened, that I was not hurt, forgetting that I was *showing my hands* not only to our own men, but to the men who attended the donkeys! I was immediately recalled to a consciousness of where I was, and of the impropriety of such an exposure, by the servant I have mentioned, who most respectfully covered my hands with my habarah, and wrapped it around me so scrupulously that the men had not a second time the advantage of seeing a finger.

No person can imagine the strictness of the hareem without adopting its seclusion, nor can a stranger form a just estimate of the degree of liberty enjoyed by the women without mixing in Eastern society. One thing is certain, that if a husband be a tyrant, his wife is his slave; but such cases are extremely rare. I do not pretend to defend the system of marrying blindfold, as it were; nor do I look for those happy marriages which are most frequently found in England; but I am pleased to find the Eastern women contented, and, without a single exception among my acquaintances, so cheerful, that I naturally conclude they are treated with consideration. The middle classes are at liberty to pay visits, and to go to the bath, when they please; but their fathers and husbands object to their shopping; therefore female brokers[†] are in the frequent habit of attending the hareems. The higher orders are more closely guarded, yet as this very circumstance is a mark of distinction, the women congratulate each other on this subject; and it is not uncommon for a husband to give his wife a pet name, expressive of her hidden charms, such as "the concealed jewel."

There lives opposite to us a good old woman, a devotee, who is a sort of Deborah to the quarter, and who passes judgment from her projecting window on all cases which are proposed for her opinion, much to our edification.

[†]Female brokers still to a certain extent ply their trade among women, not so much because of any restrictions, but due to the fact that they accept payment by installment (with interest, of course). They are known as 'dallala.' In Sophia's time, the female brokers would also act as marriage brokers, as they had access into many houses.

One occurred a few days since, which will show you that the system I have described is not confined to any particular grade in society. A young man in the neighbourhood had been betrothed to a very young girl, upon the recommendation of his fellow-servant, without sending any of his own female relations to ascertain if her appearance were agreeable, or the reverse. Becoming anxious on this subject, two days after the betrothal, he sent a female friend, who asserted that this bride had but one eye, that she was pitiable in appearance, and unfit to become his wife. The person who had recommended her was a married man, and the bridegroom accused him of culpable negligence, in not having ascertained whether she had two eyes or not, as he might have sent his wife to pay her a visit; while, on his own part, he had taken no such precaution, and, being the most interested, was certainly the most to blame. Such was the state of the case when referred to Deborah. After hearing it patiently, she said to the young man, "My son, why did you consent to be betrothed to a girl who was not known to your mother and to the women of your house?" "They have been, since my betrothal, to see her," he answered, in a very melancholy tone of voice, "but she sat in a dark room, and they could not tell whether she had two eyes or not; and, in truth, O my mother, I have brought her many articles of dress, and I have paid four hundred piastres as her dowry, the savings of many months." "Has she learnt any trade," asked the old woman, "that so much was required as her dowry?" "No," replied the bridegroom; "but she is of a higher family than mine, possessing houses, and lands, and property." "Property belongs to God," replied she; and so saying, she retired from the conference. We have since heard that, although the family of the girl is *too respectable* to permit that her betrothed husband should see her face even in her mother's presence, he has put the houses, and lands, and property in the scale, and found her defect too light to be worthy of consideration.

LETTER XVIII

April, 1843

My Dear Friend,

It is indeed, true, that slavery cannot be presented to the mind but with a revolting aspect; yet I do assure you that slavery in the East is not what you imagine it to be. Here, perhaps, the slave is more in the power of the master than in the West, and there are some monsters, at whose names humanity shudders, who dreadfully abuse the power they legally claim; but, generally speaking, an Eastern slave is exceedingly indulged, and many who have been cruelly torn from their parents at an early age, find and acknowledge fathers and mothers in those to whom they are sold. They are generally extremely well dressed, well fed, and allowed to indulge in a degree of familiarity which would astonish you. If they conduct themselves well, they are frequently married by their masters to persons of respectability, and the ceremony of the marriage of a slave in the high hareems is conducted with extreme magnificence. It is not unusual for a grandee to give away in marriage several female slaves, and sometime concubines, on the same day, to husbands of his own selection. In some instances, the slaves are distressed at being thus disposed of, and would rather remain in their old home, but generally a marriage of this kind is a subject for extraordinary rejoicing; and accustomed as the women are to submit to the will of others in the affair of matrimony, from the highest to the lowest in the East, the fact of their superiors choosing for them their husbands rather recommends itself to their approval, and excites their gratitude. On the day of their marriage they are dressed in the most costly manner; while in the hareems to which they belong, Cashmere shawls, sometimes cloth of gold, are laid that they may walk over them. Singing and dancing women are engaged for the occasion, and several girls bearing censers, and others sprinkling perfumes, attend each bride. You have heard and read of the Arab dancing, which is far from delicate, but the dancing in the Turkish hareems is not in any respect objectionable. The girls throw themselves about extravagantly, but frequently gracefully; and turn heels over head with amusing dexterity. It is not a pleasing exhibition, but not a disgusting one.

I cannot admire the singing, the women choose generally such exceedingly high keys that it resembles screaming rather than singing. I sometimes think that with the support of a tolerable accompaniment the songs might be agreeable, but the instruments of the country are anything but musical, and interfere considerably with the purposes of harmony. The voices of the singers are remarkably fine, and would be perfection under European culture; and the performers are usually enthusiastic in their love for their art, but still more so are their hearers. The vocalists are for the most part respectable.

When the slave of a grandee is given away in marriage, the man chosen as her husband is almost always somewhat of a dependant; and the lady generally treats him as if he were somewhat of a dependant with respect to herself.

I have been exceedingly amused lately, by reading in the "Sketches of Persia," the account which is given by some natives of that country (including persons occupying high offices under government, therefore the noble of the land), of the liberty and power of their women; and I am disposed to think with them, that women, in many respects, have the ascendency among the higher orders throughout the East. We imagine in England that the husband in these regions is really lord and master, and he is in some cases; but you will scarcely believe that the master of a house may be excluded for many days from his own hareem, by his wife's or wives' causing a pair of slippers to be placed outside the door, which signifies that there are visitors within. It is true that the husband sometimes becomes tired of frequent exclusion, and forbids, as indeed he has a right to do, the constant admission of visitors; but in so doing, he draws down on his head much discomfort. He has his remedy, certainly; but how sad is the system of divorce! Who can defend it? Where a wife has become a mother, the husband is seldom willing to divorce her; but where this is not the case, the affair is far too easily managed.

Among the lower orders, some of the husbands are sad tyrants. The fact is, that the men foolishly marry such little young creatures, they are more like their children than their wives, and their inexperience unjustly provokes their husbands. While on this subject, it occurs to me to tell you that Deborah has a most refractory grand-daughter, who is certainly the plague of her life. This child is in the habit of reviling the neighbours' servants; and a few days since she used abusive language to a man who was sitting in his master's doorway. The doorkeeper was exceedingly provoked, and at once retorted, "When I have a little more money, I will marry you, and punish you every day." This manner of revenge is something really new to us Europeans.

Last week, a little bride was paraded through the streets in our neighbourhood, whose age could scarcely have exceeded ten years. Thinking the procession, and the whole affair, an exceedingly good joke, she was impatient of control; and instead of walking under the canopy, and submitting to march between two of her female friends, preceded by a woman fanning her, she insisted upon walking backwards before the former, and fanning them herself. This will give you some idea of the mere children who are married here.

The employments of the hareem chiefly consist in embroidery, on an oblong frame, supported by four legs; but they extend to superintending the kitchen, and indeed the female slaves and servants generally; and often ladies of the highest distinction cook those dishes which are particularly preferred.

The sherbets are generally made by the ladies; and this is the case in one
hareem I visit, where the ladies, in point of rank, are the highest of Eastern
haut ton. The violet sherbet is prepared by them in the following manner:-
The flowers are brought to them on large silver trays, and slaves commence
by picking off the outer leaves; the ladies then put the centres of the violets
into small mortars, and pound them until they have thoroughly expressed
the juice, with which, and fine sugar, they form round cakes of conserve,
resembling, when hardened, loaf-sugar dyed green. This produces a bright
green sherbet, prettier than the blue or pink, and exceedingly delicate. I do
not know of what the blue is composed, but am told that it is a particular
preparation of violets; the pink is of roses; the yellow of oranges, apricots, &c.
It would be tedious were I to describe the variety of sherbets; but those I have
mentioned will give you an idea of these cooling summer drinks. About four
table-spoonfuls of syrup in three-quarters or a pint of water form a most
agreeable beverage.

You will be surprised to hear that the daughter of the Pasha, in whose
presence the ladies who attend her never raise their eyes, superintends the
washing and polishing of the marble pavements in her palaces. She stands on
such occasions barefooted on a small square carpet; holding in her hand a silver rod: about twenty slaves surround her; ten throw the water, while others
follow them wiping the marble, and lastly polishing it with smooth stones.

It is very grievous that the women in general are merely instructed in hand-
iwork. But I must not speak slightingly of their embroidery; for it is
extremely beautiful—as superior as it is unlike to any fancy-work practised in
England. Taste of a very remarkable kind is displayed in its execution; and
similar, in many respects, to that exhibited in the most elaborate decorations
of Arabian architecture; but its singular beauty is in some measure produced,
where colours are employed, by the plan of often taking the colours at random.

The embroidery which is done in the hareems is very superior to any
other, and frequently interspersed with precious stones, generally diamonds,
pearls, emeralds, and rubies. The rich large brocade trowsers often are richly
ornamented with jewels, and are stiff with decoration; but the Saltah (a small
jacket) for chasteness and elegance is that which I most admire of all the
embroidered articles of dress. For winter wear, it is of velvet, or fine cloth,
lined with silk. Saltahs of rich silk are worn during the autumn and spring;
and, during the summer, dresses of European muslin are almost universally
adopted, and are the only kind of apparel suited to the intense heat of an
Egyptian summer.

Few of the ladies can read and write even their own language. I know, however, some exceptions. In one family, the daughters have been extremely well
instructed by their brother, whose education was completed in Europe. In
their library are to be found the works of the first Italian poets and the best
literature of Turkey; and these they not only read, but understood.

LETTER XIX

Cairo, June, 1843

MY DEAR FRIEND,

THERE has been an alarm of plague in Cairo, and several of the great hareems have been in quarantine. The apprehension has been induced by the fearful murrain which has raged during nine months, as a similar misfortune has proved in former years the forerunner of a severe pestilence.

I mentioned to you some time since that such a calamity was dreaded; and it has in some measure arrived. At El-Mansoorah,[†] the cases of plague have not been few; and while on this subject I must tell you an extraordinary fact, which will show you that it is even possible to extract sweet from one of the bitterest of human draughts. Some Russians have been at El-Mansoorah for the purpose of studying the disease. As a means of discovering whether it be contagious or not, they have employed persons to wear the shirts of the dead, and paid them five piastres a day for so doing. This was a considerable salary, being equal to a shilling per day! Now when the poor of this country consider half a piastre per day a sufficient allowance for each person, and maintain themselves well, in their own opinion, on this trifling sum, you can conceive how charmed they might be with the liberal offers of these Russian gentlemen, were it not for the risk they incurred. Risk, however, they did not imagine. The poor flocked to the physicians from all parts of the town, and *entreated* to be permitted to wear the plague-shirts. One old man urged his request, saying, "I am a poor old man, with a family to maintain; do not refuse me; by your life, let me wear a shirt." The women crowded round the house where their imagined benefactors had taken up their quarters, to bless them for having undertaken to support them, their husbands, and their children: and when the chief of these adventurous gentlemen found the dwelling thus surrounded, he walked forth among them, and, taking off his hat, made a courteous low bow to his dark-eyed visitors; whereupon they made the air resound with the shrill zaghareet,[‡] or cries of joy.

Not one of the shirt-wearers died, although the physicians after a short time (during which they awaited the result of their experiment) had recourse to heating the shirts to 60° Réaumur. Still the poor peasants lived, and

---

[†]al-Mansura, in Lower Egypt, on the right bank of the Damietta branch of the Nile. It marks the spot where the Crusaders were finally overcome (al-Mansura means 'the victorious').

[‡]A trilling sound made with the tip of the tongue against the teeth.

throve on their good fare; but one of the physicians died. How he took the disorder is of course a subject for controversy, but that the shirt-wearers escaped, is a great triumph to the non-contagionists of Cairo; and from all we can learn, the best informed are of this party.

In the house of a merchant in Cairo, a slave has lately died of plague, and according to custom, a soldier was placed at the door to enforce strict quarantine. The merchant did not relish this restraint, and desired the comfort of going in and out at pleasure. Accordingly, he attacked the cupidity of his temporary gaoler, and coaxingly addressed him, saying, "Thou knowest, O my brother, that I am a merchant, and therefore have much business to transact in the markets, where my presence is necessary. Let me go, I beseech thee, and I will hire another to take my place. Consider my case in thy generosity, " he added, putting into his hand a piece of nine piastres; and the soldier found his pity so sensibly touched, that further remonstrance was unnecessary: the merchant passed, and the substitute was accepted—a new way of keeping quarantine!

Long since I told you that I feared the plague might induce us, this year, to go to Upper Egypt; but the accounts have never been such as to show us the necessity; indeed, on the contrary, though constantly making the most anxious inquiries, we did not hear that there had been many cases of plague in the city, until the time of danger had passed.

It is a singular and sad fact, that during our few month's sojourn here this country has been visited by three of its peculiar plagues—murrain, boils and blains (or common pestilence), and locusts. The first has destroyed cattle to an almost incredible amount of value; the second has not been so severe as it usually is; but the locusts are still fearfully eating the fruits of the ground. In the gardens of Ibraheem Pasha and others, the peasants are employed to drive them away by throwing stones, screaming, beating drums, &c.

My assertion with regard to the small daily pay that contents these poor people will show you how much it is in the power of a person of moderate income to dispense comfort to a considerable number of poor grateful fellow-creatures; and could you but see the blind, lame, old people who solicit alms in the streets of Cairo, you would yearn to supply their simple wants.

Those who are above distress are, with the exception of a very small proportion, such as we should number in England among the poor; but, in many respects, they husband their little property in a very strange manner: though they never waste a morsel of food, they are sometimes extravagant with trifles, simply from want of management. A short time since we received from a shop a little parcel about a span long, round which was wound forty-seven feet of string, so that the paper was only here and there visible; and this was not, as you might suppose, on account of the value of its contents, which cost but a few pence.

The climate produces a great degree of lassitude, and the people will often use anything within their reach (if their own property) rather than make the smallest exertion; and yet, as I have remarked to you some time since, no people can work harder or more willingly when called on to do so. I do exceedingly like the Arabs, and quite delight in my rides in remarking the grace and politeness which cast a charm on their manners. It is very interesting to see two peasants meet; there appears so much kindly feeling among them, many good-humoured inquiries ensue, and they part with mutual blessings.

While riding out, a few days since, I was surprised by witnessing the extreme display which is exhibited during the wedding festivities of a mere peasant. When I arrived within a few doors of the house of the bridegroom, I passed under a number of flags of red and green silk, suspended to cords extending across the street; above these were hung seven immense chandeliers, composed of variegated lamps; and awnings of green and white canvas were stretched from roof to roof, and afforded an agreeable shade. Here the bride was paraded, covered with a red Cashmere shawl, numerously attended, and preceded by her fanner, beneath a rose-coloured canopy.

A stranger might imagine that the feast which concludes this display is the result of extreme hospitality, but this is not the case; I was surprised at hearing of the system on which it is conducted. A peasant, for instance, will often buy two sheep, two hundredweight of flour, and butter in proportion; these things forming always the chief articles of a feast prepared for the lower orders in Egypt. He will then add different kinds of fruit according to the season, and abundance of tobacco and coffee; and for the amusement of his visitors, he engages singers, and sometimes dancing-girls. To effect this, he will borrow money, and his next step will be to invite all his relations, and all his friends and acquaintance. These feel obliged to accept the invitation; and no one joins the party without a present in his hand: therefore, at the conclusion of the feast, the bridegroom is often rather a gainer by the festivities than otherwise. In every instance his friends enable him to repay those from whom he has borrowed.[†] Real hospitality has no part in the affair whatever. Ostentation alone actuates the bridegroom in making his preparations.

On the morning after his marriage he is generally accompanied by his friends into the country, or to a garden, where they feast together, and are usually entertained by dancing and songs. The expense of this *fête champêtre*, in like manner, seldom falls heavily upon the bridegroom.

[†]A similar custom is still practiced among the "lower orders," when relatives and guests of the bride and groom give presents of money known as *nuqta*, meaning 'a drop.' The parents, who receive the gifts, keep careful note of the amount each guest has paid so as to repay it (adding slightly more) when the givers have a celebration of their own.

The Egyptians have an especial passion for gardens and water. Even stagnant water, if sweet, they consider a luxury: running water, however dirty,
they hold to be extremely luxurious; and when, during the inundation, the
canal of Cairo is full, all the houses on its banks are occupied by persons who
sit in their leisure hours smoking by its muddy waters: but the height of
their enjoyment consists in sitting by a fountain—this they esteem Paradise.

How much I wish we had the comfort of occasional showers in Egypt:
however, one of my boys amuses me often by supplying this desideratum by
watering their garden from an upper projecting window; employing for its
purpose a large watering-pot with an ample rose, whence many a refreshing
shower falls before the lower windows, washing the thick dust from a
mulberry-tree and really giving an agreeable idea of coolness.

This same mulberry-tree was an object of great admiration to a man who
described our present house to us before we saw it: he said, after stating the
accommodation which the house afforded, "And there is a *tree* in the court!"
Having forgotten what sort of tree it was, he blessed the Prophet (as these people do when they want to brush up their memory), and then said, "It is a vine."

This sultry day I can write no more; and if able to forget the heat, the poor
little sparrows would remind me that it is indeed oppressive, for they are
flying in and out of our windows with their beaks wide open. They do not
seem calculated to bear this intense heat; and they congregate round their
food and water on the terrace, looking so pitiable during a hot wind, that we
should like to transport them to England. There, however, I am afraid they
would not tenant the houses so fearlessly of harm as they do in Egypt. Here
is no wanton cruelty: a great deal of apathy with regard to suffering is apparent in the character of the people; but I do not think the Arabs, in general,
ever inflict an intentional injury.

LETTER XX

July, 1843

My Dear Friend,

SINCE I remarked to you the general cheerfulness which reigns in the hareems I had then seen, I have visited one belonging to a Turkish grandee, which offers a sad exception, and touchingly exhibits a picture of family love and blighted happiness. The old and beloved master of this hareem is under a cloud; he is suffering the displeasure of the Pasha, and is confined in the state prison. I received a most kind welcome from the ladies of his family. I remarked with regret the depression which weighed down the spirits of all who composed it, and I was shocked to hear from the chief lady that she also was a prisoner, having orders not to quit her house.

She was attired in a kind of morning-dress, of white, embroidered with black; but wore a splendid kind of crown.[1] This was composed of diamonds, set in gold, forming flowers, &c.,—the whole being a convex shape, circular, and about six inches in diameter. It was worn upon the crown of the head, attached to the cap round which the head-kerchief was wound, and had a very rich appearance, the diamonds being so near together, that the interstices only served, like the red gold in which the stones were set, to heighten their brilliancy. At a little distance, the crown seemed like one heap of diamonds.

When this lady referred to her heart's trouble, tears rolled down her cheeks; and I do not think there was one lady or slave present whose eyes were not suffused with tears; one especially interested me, for she was quite unlike any Eastern I have seen, having the complexion and the auburn hair and eyes of the pretty Irish. She manifested by the expression of her countenance more distress than her companions. I imagined she was one of her master's wives; for she was attended by her nurse carrying her child (an exquisite little cherub) and several slaves. She did not, however, sit on the divan by "Hánum," or the chief lady.

The mothers here exceedingly fear the evil or envious eye; and it is quite necessary, when an infant or young child appears, to exclaim, "Máshálláh,"[†] and to refrain from remarking its appearance; it is also important to invoke for it the protection and blessing of God; and having done so by repeating the expressive phrases used on such occasions in Eastern countries by Christians as well as Muslims, the parents are happy that their children have been introduced to the notice of those who put their trust in God.

---

[1] In Arabic a "Kurs."
[†] 'What God wills.'

125

The apartments of this hareem are situated in a large garden; and the interior decorations are like those of most Turkish palaces in this country. The walls are painted in compartments, and adorned with ill-executed landscapes, representing villas and pleasure-grounds.

I once told you that in all the hareems I had seen, the chief lady was the only wife: I can no longer make such a boast; but look and wonder, as an Englishwoman, how harmony can exist where the affection of the husband is shared by—I do not like to say how many wives.[†]

Hareem-gardens are never agreeable places of resort in or near a town; for the walls are so high that there is no free circulation of air, and the trellises for the support of vines over the walks are really roofs, necessary certainly at noon-day under a nearly vertical sun, but excluding the only refreshing morning and evening air.

I was surprised, during my second visit to the hareem of Habeeb Effendi, to find the ladies (whom I had not seen for a long time on account of the late plague) immersed in politics, and painfully anxious on account of the difference of opinion which has arisen between the Emperor of Russia and their cousin the Sultán. They earnestly inquired whether England would espouse the cause of Turkey, and were in some measure comforted by a reference to the friendship which England had so warmly manifested for the young Sultán, and the active measures which our government had adopted for the re-establishment of his rule in Syria. I find the feeling very strong in favour of England in the hareems; and I conclude that I hear general opinions echoed there.[‡] I judge not only from the remarks I hear, but from the honourable manner in which I am treated; and the reception, entertainment, and farewell I experience are in every respect highly flattering.

I told you of the great politeness that was shown me on the occasion of my first visit to the royal ladies I have just mentioned. On my second visit to

---

[†]Urquhart, makes an interesting comment on this subject: "All the convictions of our habits and laws stand in hostile array against the country where the principle of polygamy is admitted into the laws of the state. But yet, while we reproach Islamism with polygamy, Islamism may reproach us with practical polygamy, which unsanctioned by law, and reproved by custom, adds degradation of the mind to dissoluteness of morals" (*Spirit of the East*, II: 387). Also: "Some may be startled by the mere mention of the word polygamy; but polygamy is not denounced by the inspired writings—the patriarchs practised it" (389).

[‡]Urquhart pertinently remarks: "What an influence over Turkey does not the joint character of Christian, Protestant, and Englishman afford? As Christian, you are the depository of their differences amongst themselves; as Protestant, you are an object of interest, by an affinity of religious simplicity and worship, and even of dogma; while distinct from the Greek and the Romish Churches, idolatrous and sacriligious through their forms, in the eyes of the Turks: as Englishman, you are the depository of all their political and national hopes and alarms" (*Spirit of the East*, 345–46).

them I was almost perplexed by the honour with which they distinguished me; for the chief lady resigned her own place, and seated herself below me. I was obliged to comply with her desire; but did so with much reluctance.

I saw nothing that I need describe, in the way of dress or ornament, on this occasion, excepting the girdle of the elder daughter. This was a broad band, of some dull material of a pale grey colour, embroidered with small white beads, which composed an Arabic sentence, and having a most splendid diamond clasp, in the form of two shells, somewhat wider than the belt. There was another visitor present, who by her title and appearance I saw to be a lady of very high rank; and if the Turks, as some people say, admire fat women, she must be considered a prodigious beauty. I have seldom, if ever, seen a larger person.

One of the most beautiful women I have seen in Egypt is the wife of a celebrated poet. I love to look on a pretty face, and hers is especially sweet. Her manners, too, are charming; her welcome on my introduction was particularly cordial, and her request that I would pay her a long visit was made with evident sincerity of kindness. With the exception of her diamond crown, her dress was simple, and her whole demeanour free from affectation; I should imagine her character is a source of cheerful contentment to her husband and her children. You will forgive my national pride and prejudice when I say she reminded me of an Englishwoman.

The house of this lady's family is of the old Arab description, and is situated on the margin of a lake in the outskirts of the city, surrounded by excellent and very picturesque houses, having, on the ground-floors, courts roofed with trellises, supported by pillars, and other fanciful wood-work, and covered with jasmines and vines. In these the male inhabitants spend their pastime or idle hours, looking on the water. The upper floors are furnished with meshrebeeyehs[†] (the projecting windows I have described to you) overlooking the lake.

From visits I turn to visitors; to tell you that a most unwelcome guest made his appearance yesterday. Between the blind and glass of a window in the room where we usually sit, I discovered a large snake, more than a yard and a half long. It was outside the window; but directly it saw me through the glass, it raised its head, and protruded its black forked tongue. It was of a light brown colour, and down the centre of its back its scales were of a bright yellowish hue. It was in such a situation that it was scarcely possible to catch it, and indeed my brother was the only man in the house who would attempt to do so; for our servants were so overcome by superstitious dread, that they would not approach the intruder, and one of the men dared not even look at it: we were therefore unwilling he should touch it, and persuaded him to send for a snake-charmer.

[†]Meaning literally 'the place one drinks from,' as pottery water jars were placed there for cooling.

There was considerable difficulty in finding, at such a moment, a man of this profession, although Cairo abounds with them. At length a poor old man arrived, who was nearly blind, and mistook a towel (which was pressed between the sashes to prevent the creature entering) for the object of my dread. He addressed it with much courtesy, saying "O Blessed!" several times, which expressed an invitation: to this, however, the snake turned a deaf ear; and twining itself dexterously through the trellis blind, it curled into a window in the court, and was entirely lost. We certainly would rather it had been found, although assured it could only be, from our description, a harmless house-snake.

You have doubtless read many accounts of the feats of Eastern snake-charmers, and wondered at their skill. Very lately, a friend of ours witnessed an instance of the fascination, or rather attraction, possessed by one of these people. He was in the house of an acquaintance when the charmer arrived, who, after a little whistling, and other absurd preliminaries, invoked the snake thus: "I conjure thee, by our Lord Suleymán" (that is, Solomon, the son of David), "who ruled over mankind and the Ján" (or Genii); "if thou be obedient, come to me; and if thou be disobedient, do not hurt me!" After a short pause, a snake descended from a crevice in the wall of the room, and approached the man, who secured it. No other snake appearing, it was decided that the house was cleared, and our friend requested the snake-charmer to accompany him to his own house. He did so, and invoked the snakes in the same words. The invocation was attended by the same result: a snake descended, and in the same manner resigned itself to the serpent-charmer.

With regard to the serpent still in our house, let us say, with the Muslims, we are thankful it is not a scorpion. Their philosophy is a lesson to us.

Several poor neighbours have lately been stung by scorpions: we sent them some carbonate of ammonia to apply to the wounds, and it was the means of producing the happiest results.

Cairo, with its many ruined houses, affords innumerable nests for noxious reptiles; and the progress of its decay has lately been so rapid, that at last a proclamation has been issued by the Pasha for extensive alterations and repairs throughout the city. The houses are to be whitewashed within and without; those who inhabit ruined houses are to repair or sell them; and uninhabited dwellings are to be pulled down for the purpose of forming squares and gardens; meshrebeeyehs are forbidden, and mastabahs are to be removed. Cairo, therefore, will no longer be an Arab city, and will no longer possess those peculiarities which render it so picturesque and attractive. The deep shade in the narrow streets, increased by the projecting windows—the picturesque tradesman, sitting with one friend or more before his shop, enjoying the space afforded by his mastabah—these will be no more; and while I cannot but acknowledge the great necessity for repairing the city, and removing the ruins which threaten the destruction of passengers, I should have liked those features retained which are essentially characteristic—which help, as it were, to group the people, and form such admirable accessories to pictures.

I must add to this letter an account of a shameful and very ridiculous imposition which was practised upon us a fortnight ago. A poor old man who had for some time filled the situation of doorkeeper to our quarter, had long been ill, and had been assisted by several gentlemen in procuring some necessary comforts. One day my brother received a letter from the Sheykh of the quarter, telling him that poor Mohammad the doorkeeper had received mercy at the sixth hour of the preceding night, and expressing a hope that he would give them the price of his shroud. My brother, accordingly, sent one of his servants to the house of Mohammad, where he found his body laid out, a washer of the dead attending, and his wife apparently in great distress on account of her loss. She returned the most grateful acknowledgments for the bounty which was sent to aid in enabling her to bury her poor husband; and after a while the affair passed from our recollection (we never having seen the poor man), or if remembered, it was only to inquire who would supply his place.

The old woman removed to another house a few days after; and a maid-servant of ours, on passing by chance her new dwelling, was surprised to the last degree to see the late doorkeeper sitting within its threshold. "What," exclaimed she, "my uncle[†] Mohammad alive, and well!" "Praise be to God," he answered, "I am well, and have lived on the bounty of your master, the Efendee; but, by your life, my daughter, do not tell him that I am alive." The old man, I should here tell you, is no relation of the maid's; this being one of the usual modes of address among the lower orders. The maid promised his existence should continue a secret; but she found on her return home it was impossible to keep her word, and the quarrel which ensued between her and the servant who conveyed the money for the shroud (both believing their own eyes) was as violent as that between Hároon Er-Rasheed and his wife Zubeydeh, or rather that between their two emissaries, on the subject of Abu-l-Hasan the wag.

[†]A courtesy designation added to the name of an elderly man.

Letter XXI

My Dear Friend,

In describing to you the honourable reception and elegant entertainment I experienced in the Pasha's hareem, I cannot be too minute.

The chief residence of his ladies is the Kasr ed-Dubárah, a fine house situated on the west of Cairo, on the eastern bank of the Nile, and justly their favourite retreat. After riding through the plantations of Ibraheem Pasha, which almost surround the palace, we arrived at the great gates of the Kasr, through which we entered a long road within the high walls covered with trellis closely interwoven with vines. At the end of this we dismounted, and walked on a beautiful pavement of marble through several paths, until we arrived at the curtain of the hareem. This being raised, we were immediately received by a young wife of Mohammad 'Alee, who addressed my friend Mrs. Lieder in the most affectionate terms, and gave us both a most cordial welcome. In a moment a crowd of ladies assembled round us, vying with each other in paying us polite attention; and having disrobed me, they followed us (the wife of the viceroy with us leading the way) to the grand saloon.

This is a very splendid room, paved with marble, as indeed are all the passages, and, I imagine, all the apartments on the ground-floor; but as several are entirely covered with matting, I cannot assert this to be the case. The pavement in the saloon is simply white marble, the purest and best laid I have seen in the East. The ceiling (which is divided into four distinct oblong compartments) is painted admirably in stripes of dark and light blue, radiating from gilded centres, from each of which hang splendid chandeliers containing innumerable wax-lights. The corners and cornices are richly decorated. The pavement under the two centre compartments is not matted, but the two ends, to the right and left on entering, are covered with fine matting, and fitted with crimson divans.

The windows are furnished with white muslin curtains edged with coloured fringe, some pink and some blue. All the looking-glasses (of which there are perhaps six in the saloon) are furnished with festoons and curtains of pink and blue gauze. There is one table with a cover of pink crape embroidered in stripes of gold, and having upon it a large glass case of stuffed birds. On either side of the door are fanciful stands for large square glass lanterns, composed of pillars, round which are twined artificial flowers. The windows are European in form, and the hareem blinds are composed of tasteful iron-work[†]; I can scarcely say filigree, the pattern is too bold. The entire interior decorations are in light and summer taste, and the saloon charmingly cool.

We crossed to an apartment on the opposite side, where the same lady placed us on the divan and seated herself by our side. This room is entirely covered with matting, and furnished with most luxurious divans, extending round three sides, not raised (as is usual) on a frame about a foot or more in height, but entirely of cotton, forming mattresses two feet in thickness, placed on the ground. These are covered with very gay chintz, as are also the cushions which incline against the walls; and at the right and left upper corners are distinct square cushions, covered with white muslin embroidered with black braid, and each having back cushions to correspond. Above all these there is a row of small cushions, covered with white muslin and embroidered with black, corresponding in pattern with the corner seats. The curtains resemble those in the saloon.

Here we received coffee, which was handed to us by the chief lady of the household, the treasurer, a particularly lady-like person, to whom it was handed by a lady who bore it on a silver salver, attended by several others; one carrying the little coffee-pot in a silver vessel, suspended by chains, and also used as a censer, containing burning charcoal. The whole group was most picturesque, and many of the ladies were fair, young, and beautiful.

The lady of the Páshá then proposed our returning to the saloon, that she might conduct us to the widow of Toosoon Páshá, and to the daughter of Mohammad 'Alee Páshá, who were sitting at the upper corner. I found the former lady seated on a cushion on the ground, next to the right-hand corner, and the daughter of the Viceroy took the seat of honour, which was also a cushion placed on the ground. Numerous ladies and slaves were in attendance; all standing in a line before the edge of the mat.

We were soon joined by another wife of the Páshá, the mother of Mohammad 'Alee Bey (a boy about nine years of age); her designation is "The lady, the mother of Mohammad 'Alee Bey."

It would be a breach of etiquette, and contrary to hareem laws, were I to describe *particularly* the persons of the wives of the Páshá, or any lady after distinguishing her by her name or her situation in a family; but I may in *general* terms express my admiration of the two ladies I have seen, and I think they are the *only* wives of the viceroy. Both are young—the one is a dignified and handsome person, and the other especially gentle and very lovely.

Soon after noon, dinner was announced; and the widow of Toosoon Páshá led the way to a room adjoining the saloon, where a most elegant dinner was arranged, on a very large round silver tray, placed on a stool, and surrounded

---

[†]Not blinds as we know them, but grills for security. This can still be seen in old houses, especially windows on the ground floor.

by cushions. The passages we passed were occupied by innumerable black female slaves, and some eunuchs, dressed in all the variety of gay Eastern costume, and forming a curious contrast and a most picturesque back-ground to the ladies and white slaves who surrounded and accompanied us. On either side of the door several ladies, each with an embroidered napkin hung on her right arm, held silver ewers and basins that we might wash our hands before advancing to the table.

No one was admitted to the table but the widow of Toosoon Páshá, the daughter of Mohammad 'Alee Páshá, the mother of Mohammad 'Alee Bey, with ourselves, and a lady of great importance in the East, the foster-mother of 'Abbás Páshá.[1] The place of the younger wife was vacant.

The tray was covered with small silver dishes filled with various creams, jellies, &c., and most tastefully garnished with exquisite flowers. In the centre was a fore-quarter of lamb, on piláv. I was truly glad, on this occasion especially, that my home-habits had been Eastern; had the case been otherwise, a joint of meat to be eaten without knife or fork would have been a formidable object; for, under any circumstances, I should not have anticipated that the widow of Toosoon Páshá, who is also the mother of Abbás Páshá, and who, being the eldest, was the most honoured at table, would have distinguished me as she did, by passing to me, with her own fingers, almost every morsel that I ate during dinner. The mother of Mohammad 'Alee Bey in the same manner distinguished Mrs. Lieder.

The lamb was succeeded by stew; the stew by vegetables; the vegetables by savoury cream, &c., composing an innumerable variety; and each was removed, and its place filled, when perhaps only tasted. Sweet dishes, most delicately prepared, succeeded these in rapid succession; and, with one exception, all were in silver dishes. Ladies attended close to our divan with fly-whisks; behind them about thirty formed a semicircle of gaily-dressed, and, in many cases, beautiful women and girls; and those near the door held large silver trays, on which the black slaves who stood without placed the dishes, that the table might be constantly replenished.

Black female slaves in the houses of the great are not permitted to enter an apartment where are visitors; but black eunuchs, when favourites with their masters, are constantly to be found in the very centre of a high hareem.

In presenting the morsels to me, the widow of Toosoon Páshá constantly said, "In the name of God;" and these words are always said by the Muslims before eating or drinking. "Praise be to God" is the grace after either.

There is one particularly agreeable custom observed after dinner in the East; each person is at liberty to leave the table when satisfied. To a European it is really a relief to do so, the dishes are so numerous, varied, and rich.

---

[1] 'Abbás Páshá is the reputed successor to the Páshálik.

There is much grace in the manners of the ladies of the East even in the most trifling actions: it was pretty to observe the elegance with which the silver ewers and basins were held for us when we left the tray. We were succeeded at the table by the highest ladies of the household; and I imagine others, according to their rank, dined after these, until all had taken their meal.

We returned to the saloon, where we were met by the younger wife of the Páshá, who had been prevented joining us at table by indisposition. She gave me a most kind general invitation to the Kasr ed-Dubárah, and a particular one to a festival which is to take place on the occasion of a grand marriage some time before I quit this country. The fantasia, she assured me, is to be the most splendid that can be prepared or arranged; and I shall soon be permitted to tell you the name of the bride. This she told me; but I must not mention it until the day is fixed for the marriage. It is an Egyptian state-secret!

There are many extremely beautiful women in the hareem of the Páshá, and many handsome young girls; some not more than ten years of age. The Turkish ladies, and the Circassians, and Georgians, are generally extremely fair; and I must particularly mention one who was remarkably beautiful, and more splendidly dressed than any of her companions. She did not enter the saloon until we heard dinner announced; and her appearance was something very attractive. Her yelek and shintiyan (or long vest and trousers) were of rich plum-coloured silk, and the quiet colour of her dress exhibited with brilliant effect a profusion of costly diamond ornaments. Her head-dress was tastefully arranged, and the richer sprays of diamonds were lavishly interspersed in a dark crape headkerchief.

I cannot take a better opportunity of describing the Eastern dress, as worn by the Turkish ladies, than while the hareem of the Páshá is fresh in my recollection. The tarboosh (or red cap) is trimmed with a very large and full tassel of dark blue silk, which is separated and spread over the crown, and those ladies who wear rich ornaments almost always display their most costly jewels on the back of the head, either in the form of a kurs, which I have described to you, or a spray, very much resembling in form a *fleur de lis*, but broader and shorter; this is placed at the division of the tassel, which latter is often so broad when spread, as to extend an inch beyond the head on either side in a front view. The headkerchief is wound round the head, partly over the forehead, and the fringed ends are arranged on one side; the front hair is cut short, and combed towards the eyebrows, and this is extremely unbecoming, disfiguring even a beautiful face, excepting in cases where the hair curls naturally, and parts on the forehead. The long hair is disposed in numerous small plaits, and looped up on either side over the headkerchief. In many cases, the hair of the younger ladies, and white slaves, is dishevelled, and hanging loosely on the shoulders; but this I have only observed in the Turkish hareems: many in the Kasr ed-Dubárah wear their long hair flowing on their shoulders, and, in some instances, their attractions are considerably heightened by this simplicity; but no *coiffure*, however studied, or simple, is so pretty as that worn by the Arab ladies, whose long hair hanging down the back is arranged in many small plaits often lengthened by silk braid, and generally adorned with hundreds of small gold ornaments, resembling oval spangles, which harmonize better with the Eastern costume than any other fashion.

To return to the Turkish ladies: they wear the yelek considerably longer than their height; the back part resting on the ground, and forming a graceful train; and in walking over a mat or carpet, they hold the skirts in front over the arm. The shirt is of silk gauze, fine muslin, or a very beautiful thin crape, with glossy stripes, which is made of raw silk in the hareems, and is cream colour: the sleeves of this are not confined at the wrist. The shintiyán are extremely full, and generally of a different material from the yelek: the former being of rich brocade, large patterned muslin, or chintz, or sometimes of plain satin, or gros de Naples. The yelek, on the contrary, is made of material with a delicate pattern, generally a small stripe, whether of satin, Indian silk, or muslin.

Those ladies who are not perfectly idle, and who have not slaves as train-bearers, tuck their skirts through their girdles; and thus, I think, the dress is very gracefully worn. Ladies of distinction always wear Cashmere shawls round the waist, generally red; and those in Kasr ed-Dubárah had a narrow edge of gold, with gold cords and tassels at the corners. There, the mezz were different from any I had before seen; being of embroidered cloth, of various colours; and the daughter of the Páshá, and others, had their long sleeves buttoned at the wrist. The sleeves are always so made that they can be buttoned if their length prove inconvenient; but as the great ladies of the land do not occupy themselves in any way, but spend their time on their divans, they can scarcely find these hanging draperies incommodious.

This description of dress leads me back to the lady whose appearance so especially attracted my admiration. After I requested that my riding-dress might be brought, I observe several ladies crossing the saloon, among whom she walked, bearing it towards me, and looking like a queen in person and in dress. She dressed me with much grace, and then with her companions stepped back into the doorway to receive and give the parting salutation. One circumstance I have omitted, namely, the crimson embroidered curtains, which hang before all the doorways in the palace; for the doors stand open, a closed door being never permitted in the hareems. Much taste is displayed in the embroidery of these curtains; indeed, the perfection of taste is to be found in the decorations of the Kasr ed-Dubárah.

LETTER XXII

December, 1843

MY DEAR FRIEND,

I CANNOT better give you an idea of the order and discipline observed in the hareems of the great and wealthy than by comparing each to a petty state, with its rulers and its officers. The person occupying the place of highest rank, next to the master, is the chief lady, who is often called, properly or improperly, Hánum, or, correctly, Khánum. This title, which literally signifies 'My Lord,' (for Turkish ladies, whom we in England generally look upon as persons treated with little respect, are honoured with male titles) by right belongs first only to those ladies of the Sultán whom we call sultanas; that is, to any of the near female relations of the sovereign, and to any of his ladies who has borne a prince or princess; secondly, to the wives of the grand vezeer; but it is sometimes given by courtesy to the wives of grandees in general, and sometimes to ladies of inferior grades. The male title Efendim (literally 'My Master') is also given to the same ladies.

The chief lady of the hareem is the mother of the master; or, if his mother be not living, his sister, or sisters, take precedence; and next to them ranks his favourite wife. The question of priority among the wives of one man is more easily arranged than you, with European notions respecting the rights of women, could imagine possible. It is generally settled thus: the first wife, if she become a mother, retains her rank above any wife subsequently taken; but if not, she yields to another more fortunate, and consequently, more beloved and honoured. The other wives take their stations according to the preference of their husbands.

Each wife, among the higher classes, has her separate apartments, and distinct attendants; for *even Eastern* wives might manifest jealousy under circumstances of constant intercourse with each other. In the cases of the great, it is not unusual for each wife to occupy a separate mansion; but whether in one large house, or several smaller ones, the hareem of the grandee occupies the whole, or nearly the whole, of the abode, which is generally enclosed by garden walls as lofty as the houses in the immediate neighborhood. Without

---

†Urquhart notes: "Among the Turks, from time immemorial, this peculiarity is to be found . . . that there is no distinction of gender, that men and women are addressed in precisely the same forms of speech and manner, nor is there even distinction in the terms or pronouns" (*Spirit of the East*, 403–4). This is a linguistic feature of the Turkish language.

the aid of scaling ladders, or the more effectual mean of admission—intrigue, the hareem of the Turkish grandee is well secured from illicit visitors. At the outer door is stationed a bowáb, or door-keeper, and the second is guarded by eunuchs. Beyond the second is suspended the hareem curtain which I have before described; and in the first of the inner apartments are the black female slaves who undertake the menial offices of the hareem. After passing the outer apartments white slaves are found carrying silver sprinkling bottles of scented water, small silver censers suspended by chains, coffee, pipes, sherbet, and sweetmeats; each set of coffee-cups or sherbet-cups being placed on a small tray, and often concealed beneath a round splendidly embroidered cover, bordered with deep and heavy gold fringe. Among the white slaves may be observed several who are considered superior to their companions, walking about as though superintending their arrangements; and among the former, especially, I have found the most lovely girls in the hareems, many of them fully justifying my preconceived ideas of the celebrated Georgian and Circassian women. Excepting in two cases, cheerfulness has appeared to me to reign among these fair prisoners; entirely excluded as they are from intercourse with any persons of the other sex, except their master and his very near relations. If any other man attempted to pass beyond the first entrance, his temerity would in all probability be punished with death the moment his purpose should be discovered.

The houses of the grandees, separate from their hareems, are generally accessible; and the liberty of ingress is sometimes not a little abused. Last month Mohammad 'Alee was residing in his palace at Shubra, and two Europeans resorted thither for the purpose of seeing the gardens. They wore the Frank dress, with the exception of their having adopted the tarboosh, a shawl round the waist, and red shoes. After perambulating the gardens, they entered the palace, and meeting with no opposition, they examined one apartment after another, and at length entered the bedroom of the Páshá, where sat his highness, nearly undressed! Although taken by surprise, his Turkish coolness did not forsake him: calling for his dragoman, he said, "Enquire of those gentlemen where they bought their tarbooshes." The Europeans replied, "They were purchased in Constantinople;" "and there," rejoined the Páshá, "I suppose they learned their manners. Tell them so." Judging from this retort that their presence was not agreeable, the Franks saluted the viceroy, and withdrew.

This reminds me of another late occurrence, in which, however, was exihibited only a want of knowledge of Turkish etiquette; no absence of gentlemanly mind. An European gentleman who lately visited Egypt was introduced, among others in this city, to a grandee, and was accompanied to his residence by a friend of my brother, and Mons. L——, both of whom, during many years, have resided in this country, and visited in the best Eastern society. After they had partaken of the usual refreshment of pipes and coffee, sherbet was brought, and handed first to the stranger. He looked at it for a moment, and then at the gaily embroidered napkin hung over the arm of the slave who presented it; and following the impulse given, I conclude by his preconceptions of Eastern habits of cleanliness, dipped his fingers in the sweet beverage, and wiped them on the napkin. Mons. L———, with the perfect delicacy which characterises French politeness, followed his example, dipped his fingers in the sherbet, and wiped them on the napkin. I wonder whether their host understood his motive for such strange doings. My brother's friend sat at a little distance from his companions, and confessed that he drank his sherbet.

To return to the organization of the great hareems; the Hánum generally has four principal attendants, two of whom are elderly, and act simply as companions: the third is the treasurer, and the fourth, the sub-treasurer. The next in rank are those who hand pipes and coffee, sherbet and sweetmeats; and each of these has her own set of subordinates. Lastly rank the cooks and house-slaves, who are mostly negresses. The hareem is a little world of women, in which many have passed their infancy and their childhood; the scene of their joys and sorrows, their pleasures and their cares; beyond which, they have no idea of a wider theatre of action; and from which they anticipate no change but to the hareem of their husbands.

The ideas entertained by many in Europe of the immorality of the hareem are, I believe, erroneous. True it is, that the chief ladies have much power which they might abuse; but the slaves of these ladies are subject to the strictest surveillance; and the discipline which is exercised over the younger women in the Eastern hareem can only be compared to that which is established in the convent. A deviation from the strictest rules of modesty is followed by severe punishment, and often by the death of the delinquent. The very framework of Eastern society is so opposed to the opinions of Europeans, that I will venture to prophecy it must be the work of several generations to root up prejudice before the mind of the Eastern can be prepared for the reception of our ideas of civilization. That Christianity is the only medium through which happiness may be attained by any people is most certain; therefore as the Easterns are very far from being Christians, except in the mere dogmas of their faith (inasmuch as they acknowledge the Messiah, though denying his divine nature, and his atonement for sin), so they are very far from being really happy.

The prejudice existing among the Turkish women against the pure doctrines of Christianity is evident from occasional, or rather, I should say, from frequent remarks made in my presence, and to my friends. One lady, who gave me a general and warm invitation to her hareem, and treated me really affectionately, so far betrayed her opinions, that she exclaimed to me, and to my friend, "What a pity that you are Christians!" Alas! such feeling are too general for our minds to be blinded to the fact of their existence; and so long as martyrdom awaits the convert to our blessed faith, little or no progress will be made by those benevolent men, whose devotion of happiness and of life to our Saviour's cause will secure for them the favour of their God, however unsatisfactory may be results of their labours.

Of those female slaves who, after the age of childhood, have been brought from countries where they have enjoyed almost unbounded liberty, few, perhaps, become reconciled to confinement within the narrow and limited precincts of the hareem. Some, by their personal charms rendered favourites of the master, doubtless delight in the luxurious prison. Others, who have, in addition to his favour and affection, a stronger tie to their foreign home—that of their having borne him a child, would receive their emancipation, if accompanied by a dismissal and a marriage to some other person, with earnest prayers for the retraction of the intended boon. Brought up, in general, with Muslim feelings, they become the most affectionate of mothers. Their maternal tenderness is often most especially manifested by their dread of the evil eye; a superstition which obliges me, in my intercourse with Muslim mothers, to observe the utmost caution in making any remarks upon children.

In one instance, I was unfortunate, in one respect, in a remark of this kind; but fortunate in another respect, inasmuch as one of my own children was the subject. I occasioned much distress to an Arab lady who was passing the day with me (when, in the course of conversation, the effects of climate on the constitution of the young were discussed) by observing that my eldest boy had not suffered as the rest of our party had done from the heat; adding thankfully, that I considered him strong. In an instant she vociferated, "Bless the Prophet! bless the Prophet!"[†] and repeated this for some time, while she coloured deeply, and exhibited the most extraordinary agitation. I confess I was at first confounded; for although I perceived that in her enthusiasm she feared that I had endangered my dear boy's welfare by expressing my opinion of his health, and that she earnestly desired I should avert any calamity by doing as she directed at the moment, I was not at all disposed to *bless the Prophet*; but I endeavoured to quiet her apprehensions by repeating in Eastern phraseology "Praise be to God for the health of my family," and "If it please God may it continue." Finding me calmly and gravely endeavouring to convince her that the English do not fear expressing their satisfaction in the welfare of those they love, she became more tranquil, but I do not think she felt reassured. By saying "O God, bless our Lord Mohammad!" the effect of the evil eye is believed to be prevented; and it is not a little singular, that my friend feared the effect of my own admiring eye, upon my own child.

It is very difficult for a stranger, like myself, to avoid making mistakes in various other ways. For example, I heard footsteps on the stairs leading to our

---

[†]Meaning, avert evil that the devil might inflict, by mentioning the name of God and the Prophet.

terrace a few days since, and beckoned a maid, who was passing, that she might inquire for me who was gone up stairs, when, to my astonishment, she ran from me immediately; and though I called her by name, and induced her to look round, she saw me again beckoning with my hand, and continued her flight. Annoyed at what appeared to be perverseness, I clapped my hands, and she at once returned. "Why did you run away when I beckoned you?" said I. "Because," replied she, "you made a signal to me to go away." That is, I turned towards her the back of my hand. Had I reversed the position, or beckoned with the palm downwards, she would have understood that I wanted her; as it was, she supposed that she was to run away as fast as possible.

I do not remember that I mentioned to you the uncouth dresses that are worn here at this season of the year by the ladies of the higher classes. When I pay an unexpected visit to such persons, I generally find most of them in quilted jackets of a description as little becoming as can be imagined, or enveloped in any warm covering that they have at hand. Their rooms are warmed by means of the brazier, which produces a close and suffocating smell, such as I cannot easily endure; and, indeed, I seldom feel much occasion for a fire. The weather is now really delightful; but it has not been so uniformly since the commencement of winter. As in the cases of most travellers, our residence here has been marked by peculiarities. The extraordinary inundation of last year, and the heavy rain of this, are events which have had no precedents on record during the lives of the present generation. After wishing for occasional showers during eight months in vain, not a drop of rain falling, we had on the thirtieth of October a tremendous storm of rain, attended with thunder and lightning, and one almost continuous peal of thunder lasted two hours, rattling and rolling in a most awful manner, while the rain fell in torrents; but on the first of last month, the rain was still more copious: it poured through the roofs and ceilings; and we and our servants during the storm were seeking dry corners in which to deposit cushions, mattrasses, and other furniture; and were running hither and thither to remove them as the water gained upon us. Our house is extremely well-built for Cairo, and yet, in the upper rooms, pretty smart showers fell through the ceilings for some time after the storm abated, and only one room in the house escaped the general flooding, Our poor neighbours suffered severely, and fearful has been the illness which has ensued; indeed, the inhabitants are still feeling lamentably the effects of that tremendous storm. Many houses have fallen in consequence of it; and others have been greatly injured. The roofs, in many instances, are seldom plastered with anything better than mud, but simply composed of planks and strong beams, on which coarse matting is laid; and often over all only rubbish is strewed to preserve the matting from being blown away: therefore the showers which penetrate these roofs sometimes become showers of mud, to the destruction of furniture. Rain, however, seldom falls in this part excepting in the cooler season, when a few showers occur, and those are generally light.

LETTER XXIII

January, 1844

MY DEAR FRIEND,

I WAS presented yesterday to Nezleh Hánum, by my friend Mrs. Lieder. My reception was remarkably flattering, and perhaps unusually so, because it took place in her bed-room. I was not aware that she was suffering from severe indisposition when I called at the Kasr ed-Dubárah, and would not have intruded when I was informed that this was the case; but when she heard that I had arrived, she expressed her desire to see me as soon as her two physicians, then in attendance, should have quitted her chamber. Her highness is the eldest daughter of the Páshá, and therefore holds the highest rank among the ladies of Egypt. I have before said that she is the widow of the Deftardár Mohammad Bey.†

While we were sitting in one of the rooms opening into the saloon, the curtain before our door was suddenly closed; for the physicians were passing. In a few minutes the curtain was withdrawn, and I was conducted to the presence of her highness. She was supported by pillows, and evidently suffering much from cough, and oppression of the chest. She received me with much affability, and at once requested me to sit by her side on a raised divan, which I imagine is her bed. Low divans surrounded the room, and the pavement was covered with a Turkey carpet. It had in no respect the character of a bed-room, but rather that of a luxuriously furnished Turkish winter sitting-room. It opens into a noble saloon, over that which I formerly described to you. I found the youngest son of the Páshá, Mohammad 'Alee Bey, sitting on a cushion at the feet of his sister, Nezleh Hánum, and finding me to be unacquainted with Turkish, he politely conversed with me in French. He is nine years of age, and in a few months will be considered beyond the hareem age. His mother, and other ladies, sat on my left hand. Thus I saw, on the one hand, a lady about fifty years of age—the daughter of the Páshá, and on the other, a very lovely young woman, step-mother to her highness, the wife of her father, and the mother of her little brother.

Her highness, in features, and especially in her eyes, bears a strong resemblance to her father, having a countenance full of intelligence, and capable of the most varied expression; generally quick and searching in glance; but

---

†Al-Jabarti describes the double wedding of Ismail Pasha, son of Mohammad Ali Pasha, and his sister Nezleh Hanem, who married Deftardar Muhammad Bey on 27 Ramadan 1228 (23 September 1813).

140

often beaming upon me with the sweetest smile imaginable. She directed one of the Páshá's favourites, the mother of two of his children, to wait upon me.¹ This lady received the coffee from another at the entrance of the chamber, and handed it to me in an exquisite gold zarf, richly set with rows of large and small diamonds, arranged spirally, and ornamented between the rows with most delicate enamel. Yesterday was the fourth day of the Great 'Eed, or Great Beirám (the latter of the two principal annual festivals of the Muslims),† a day appropriated to visits of ceremony to her highness by those ladies who have access to her; the three preceding days having been spent by them in visiting the tombs of relations and friends. While I was sitting with her, many ladies came in to pay their respects to her; but in consequence of her illness, they were simply dressed, with the exception of one lady, who was most splendidly attired. She had on the back of her head a profusion of diamonds, and wore a long orange-coloured Cashmere jubbeh, richly embroidered, and forming, as she walked, a glittering train of gold. She only kissed the border of her highness's robe, and left the room without speaking; none of her visitors did more than kiss her hand; nor did any one of them speak a single word; neither did Nezleh Hánum take any notice of their salutation, otherwise than by allowing them to take her hand. This etiquette, I am informed, is not only observed during her illness, but at all times. The visitors never raised their eyes;‡ and here I felt peculiarly the advantage of being an Englishwoman, for she kept up with me a lively conversation, and really treated me as an equal. With true Eastern politeness, her highness assured me that our presence made her feel really well; and begged I would consider her house my own; using every persuasion to induce us to prolong our visit. Sherbet was handed to us in deep purple cups, exceedingly elegant, and containing a very delicious beverage. I need only say of the sherbet and coffee covers, and the napkins, that they were as splendid as the most exquisite embroidery could render them; but I must notice her highness's pipes. The mouth-pieces were most tastefully adorned with brilliants, set in rich patterns, and the silk covering of each was elaborately decorated with embroidery. She smoked incessantly; but was the only lady in the room who

---

¹She has lost both her children.

†See Lane, *Modern Egyptians*, 487.

‡We learn from al-Jabarti (obituaries for the year A.H. 1228 [A.D. 1813]) that the lowest of the low were permitted to offer their salutation only by kissing the hem of a robe or the hand. Sophia may have been witnessing here a scene of deliberate affront and humiliation meted out to the remainder of the Mamluk women after their downfall (Muhammad 'Ali's had massacred the Mamluk beys in 1811): they were forced to present their homage on special occasions to ladies of the viceroy's hareem (al-Jabarti, A.H. 1224 [A.D. 1809]). Their simple, unadorned clothes reflect their sorry state, except for one, who—as it were, in defiance—appeared in all her former glory. Nezleh Hanem did not even deign to look at them, and the whole scene took place in ominous silence.

did so. By the way, I have become quite reconciled to sitting among those who smoke, for the scent of the tobacco used by the ladies here is extremely mild, and quite unlike what offends my sex so much in England.

Nezleh Hánum requested me three times to remain when I proposed leaving her, and when at length I urged that I must depart, as it was near sunset, she bade me farewell in the most flattering terms she could employ. On quitting her chamber, I found the lady next in rank to her who handed me the coffee and sherbet, waiting with another cup of sherbet for me to take *en passant*. I mention this because it is always intended as a distinguished mark of honour. Several ladies accompanied us to the door, and the treasurer followed me with the present of an embroidered handkerchief from her highness.

Do not think me egotistical, because I describe thus minutely my reception: I consider it important in a description of manners, especially as the receiving and paying visits is the every-day business of an Eastern lady; and by thus entering into detail, I hope to give an idea of the extreme politeness which characterises those with whom I am acquainted. I may also add, that I think it due to the hareem of the Páshá, and others of distinction, to show the respect they manifest towards the English. Were I a person of rank, there would be nothing remarkable in the honourable attentions I receive; but as a private lady, I confess they are exceedingly beyond my anticipations. On quitting the Kasr, my attention was attracted by one of the most perfect visions of loveliness I have had the gratification of seeing, in the person of a white slave-girl about seventeen years of age. She stood leaning her head against the doorway, while the line of beauty was described to perfection in the grace of her attitude: her complexion was delicately fair; and her hair and eyes were neither of them dark, but of that gentle shade of brown which harmonises so charmingly with a fair complexion. I cannot minutely describe her features; for there is a perfection of beauty which defies description, and such was her's. There was an expression of melancholy on her sweet countenance, and something so impressive in her appearance, that those who have seen her once cannot forget her.

I fear that I shall not soon receive my summons to the wedding in the Páshá's hareem. There seems to be some cause for delay which I do not know; and it is a subject respecting which I cannot, consistently with politeness, ask any questions of those who are able to give me the desired information; but a cousin of the Sultán told me, a few days ago, with the utmost gravity, in allusion to this affair, that there remained *one point* unsettled, namely, the *choice of a bridegroom*! Everything else was arranged. Among the great, in this part of the world, the wishes of a daughter who is to be given away in marriage seem to be very seldom considered. She is nourished and brought up in the expectation of a day when she will be delivered over by her parents to the protection of a husband, a stranger to her both in person and in mind. You may well wonder that such conduct can be tolerated in any land; and may sigh for those helpless women who are disposed of in this manner; but the reform of such a practice, under present circumstances, is impossible; for I am perfectly confirmed in my opinion that the women themselves would shrink with horror at the proposal to make an intended husband personally acquainted with his wife before the marriage.

Marriages among the middle classes in this city are often conducted with much display of a most singular kind. A bridal procession which passed a few days ago through the principal streets in our neighbourhood, was headed by a fool, or buffoon, who mounted on a horse, and attired in the most grotesque manner, with a high pointed cap, and a long false beard, performed a variety of ridiculous antics. Two men upon camels, each beating a pair of kettle-drums, of enormous but unequal dimensions, attached to the saddles, imme-diately followed the fool. Then came a man bearing a cresset, formed of a long pole, having at the top several receptacles for flaming wood, which were covered with embroidered handkerchiefs. This cresset, the proper use of which is to serve as a light at night, was thus used merely for display. Next came a man on tall stilts, and two swordsmen gaily attired in cloth of gold, brandishing drawn swords, and occasionally engaging in a mock fight. The swordsmen were succeeded by two dancing men, and these by vocal and instrumental musicians, singing and playing with the utmost vigour. Then followed five boys, each about five or six years of age, attired in female appar-el of the richest description, heavy with gold, and decorated with a profusion of women's ornaments composed of gold and costly jewels, which dazzled the sight. These boys were being paraded previously to circumcision; and each of them partly covered his face with a folded embroidered handkerchief, to guard against the evil eye. They were followed by four women, whose office had been to summon the female friends to the wedding. Each of these, who, like all who followed them, were on foot, had a rich piece of cloth of gold thrown over her left shoulder, with the edges attached together on her right side. The pieces of cloth were presents which they had received. About thir-ty young girls, all veiled and handsomely dressed, and then about the same number of married ladies (the latter of whom, enveloped in their black silk habarahs, looked, to the eye of a European, as if they were attired rather for a funeral rather than for a wedding) followed next; and then came the bride. She was entirely covered by a rich Cashmere shawl, as usual; but upon that part of it which covered her head-dress and bridal crown were attached such splendid jewelled ornaments as are seldom seen except in the hareems of grandees. Attended by two female relations, one on each side of her, followed by others, and preceded by a woman, who walked backwards, constantly fan-ning her (notwithstanding the coldness of the weather) with a large fan of black ostrich-feathers, she walked under a canopy of yellow gauze, supported by four poles, at the upper ends of which were attached embroidered hand-kerchiefs. Behind this walked a band of musicians. The whole was like one of those scenes described in the Thousand and One Nights; so gay, so brilliant, and so strikingly Eastern. The procession advanced almost as slowly as a tortoise.

While on the subject of processions and marriage, I may mention a late ridiculous occurrence, arising out of a matrimonial case. Four lawyers of our neighbourhood were last week condemned to hard labour, and paraded through the streets on asses, with their faces towards the tails, for illegal conduct in a suit respecting a refractory wife. In illustration of their offence, I may remind you of a case, which I heard referred for judgment to our neighbour Deborah; that a young man who agreed to take as his bride a girl reported to have but one eye, because she was a person of property. He did take her, and expended an extravagant sum upon the wedding festivities; but the affair did not end as he expected. He found his wife to be about thirteen years of age, a little delicate child; but possessing some spirit; for she positively and obstinately refused to acknowledge him as her husband. Having been legally married, he could only divorce her, or cause her to be registered as refractory; and he adopted the latter course; in consequence of which he is not obliged to support the girl, her family doing so until she shall resign herself to him. Cases of this kind are of frequent occurrence, and though it often happens that a woman twenty years of age submits without a murmur to be married to a man of threescore, a girl who has not passed the commencement of her 'teens' very seldom will accept a husband whose chin shows him to be a man.

Letter XXIV

February, 1844

My Dear Friend,

My brother's account of the hareem, and all that he has written respecting the manners and customs of the women of this country, I have found to be not only minutely accurate, but of the utmost value to me in preparing me for the life which I am now leading. His information, however, on these subjects, being derived only from other men, is, of course, imperfect; and he has anxiously desired that I should supply its deficiencies, both by my own personal observation, and by learning as much as possible of the state and morals of the women, and of the manner in which they are treated, from their own mouths.[†]

When my experience with respect to the hareem was much shorter as to time, and more limited as to its objects, than it has now been, I was unwilling to express to you an opinion with which I was forcibly impressed within a few months after my arrival in this country; that a very large proportion of the men, and a few of the women, are frequently, and almost habitually, guilty of the most abominable acts of cruelty and oppression. Though I have seen much that is amiable in the persons with whom I am acquainted here, the opinion above expressed has been so frequently and strongly confirmed that I cannot withstand the conviction of its being correct.

The wives and female slaves, in the houses of the higher orders, are generally, if I may judge from what I have seen and heard, treated by the husband and master with much kindness; and the condition of the slaves seems to be, in one respect, preferable to that of the wives; as the latter are often in constant fear of being divorced; while the sale of a slave who has been long in a family, unless on account of pecuniary distress, is reckoned highly disreputable; and if she have borne a child to her master, and he acknowledge

---

[†]Lane informs us: "Many husbands of the middle classes and some of the higher orders, freely talk of the affairs of the hareem with one who professes to agree with them in their general moral sentiments, if they have not to converse through the medium of an interpreter" (Lane, *Modern Egyptians*, 175). Urquhart says more or less the same: "I feel it only encumbent on me to anticipate the question, how a male traveller can in Turkey know anything of the women. Without seeing or conversing with a single Turkish woman, it is no very difficult thing to form an idea of their state. You must commence by knowing the men; in them, and through them, it is easy to know the women" (*Spirit of the East*, 354).

it to be his own, to sell her is illegal. But among the middle and lower classes, both wives and female slaves are often treated with the utmost brutality: the former are often cruelly beaten; and the latter, not unfrequently, beaten to death!

A neighbour of ours, a few weeks ago, flogged his wife in a most barbarous manner, and turned her out of doors, because his supper was not ready precisely at the time appointed. Two days after, however, he brought her back. The same man, not long since, beat a female slave so severely, that she lingered in great pain for about a week, and then died. This man is a Copt, by profession a Christian! Another man beat one of his female slaves until she threw herself from a window, and thus killed herself on the spot. This man also is of the same profession! Much are they mistaken who say, "What need is there of missionaries here to instruct the Copts, who are a Christian people?" One who knows them well assures me that their moral state is far worse than that of the Muslims; that in the *conduct* of the latter there is much more Christianity than is exhibited in that of the former. But the remarks which I am making apply to both the Muslims and the nominal Christians, but to these are more extensively applicable. How sad that the duty of regarding truth should oblige me to make such a distinction!

The English Institution in this city, the chief object of which is to introduce among the Copts that sound knowledge which is the first requisite to improve their religious and moral condition, I look upon as one of the most useful of all the establishments of the Missionary Society. The accounts of it which have appeared in the publications of that Society have scarcely shown its full importance; for this cannot be duly appreciated by any one who does not know by experience the state of the people whom it is designed to benefit, and the admirable judgment and indefatigable and self-denying zeal with which its objects are pursued. Connected with this Institution is a chapel, sufficiently large and very commodious and comfortable, where I am thankful to have opportunities to join in the service of our Church, and to hear many an excellent sermon. But I must return from this digression, to resume the subject which occasioned it.

Seldom do many days elapse without our hearing the most piteous screams from women and children suffering under the whip or stick; and much trouble do we experience in our endeavours to stop the barbarities practised in our immediate neighbourhood. The answer usually returned to our messages of reproach on these occasions are of the most civil kind, assuring us, with many salutations, that, for our sakes, the offender shall be forgiven. I believe that the cruelty which now seems so common may, in some degree, be attributed to the oppression which its exercisers themselves suffer; for every one who has studied the human mind will agree with me, that, with few exceptions, the oppressed become the hardest of oppressors.

The women generally seem full of kind and tender feeling, although (as I have remarked) there are not a few instances of the reverse, and lately we have been distressed by the conduct of two women, our near neighbours. The one, old Deborah, whom I mentioned to you in a former letter, has so cruelly beaten a little girl who lives with her, on three or four occasions, that we have taken the poor child into our house each time until she has, by her own choice, returned, when her cruel mistress, who is said to be her grandmother, has promised us not to repeat her violence.

The other was a more distressing case. A woman residing in a house adjoining our own had lost seven piastres, and discovering that a little grandson had stolen them, she sent for a man, by profession a *beater*, to chastise him. One of my boys heard this; and finding that by mounting a little ladder he could reach a window commanding the court of this woman's house, he did so, and immediately called to tell me that the report was a true one; that the man had arrived, and was tying the arms and legs of the poor child; but that his grandmother was standing by him. That being the case, I assured my boy that her only object could be to frighten the child by confining his limbs, and that I felt certain she could not suffer him to be hurt. I formed this opinion from my love for the grandmothers of England, whose children's children are the crown and glory of their age.[†] Alas! for my mistake in supposing this Arab possessed the feelings of woman's nature! I hardly left the foot of the ladder, when I was recalled by the screams of my own dear child, who was crying and scolding in an agony of distress; for the man in the court below was beating the limbs, the back, the chest of the poor little boy, as in writhing and rolling on the ground each part fell under the dreadful blows of a ponderous stick, while between each infliction the old woman cried "again!" This brutality could not be suffered, and my brother instantly sent one of our servants with such a threat of vengeance if they did not immediately desist, that the child was at once released, and quiet was restored to our house, but not tranquility to our minds. This same wretched woman periodically laments the loss of her son, the father of this child, and fills the air with her discordant wailings regularly every alternate Monday. She has always been to us a most annoying neighbour, and is the more so now that we know the hypocrisy of her lamentations.

The Muslim ceremonies that have reference to the dead are, however, generally very interesting; and their wailings would always be deeply affecting, were they always sincere, and not confined to stated periods; for they seem to express the most intense, heart-breaking, despairing grief. The art of wailing in the most approved style appears to be an accomplishment that can only be acquired by long practice; and regular professors of it are usually hired on the occasion of the death of a person of the middle or higher classes. These

---

[†]An Arabic proverb says: "Dearer than the child is the child's child."

accompany their lamentations with a tambourine, and occasionally interrupt their screams by plaintive songs. Their performance, and those of the female mourners in general, are such as were practised in most remote ages; such as we see portrayed upon the walls of the ancient Egyptian tombs, and such as are mentioned in many parts of the Holy Scriptures; as in 2 Chron. xxxv. 25; Jerem. ix.18; Amos v. 16; and St. Matt. ix. 23; vividly bringing to mind "the minstrels and the people making a noise" for the death of the daughter of Jairus. As illustrative of the Bible, these and other Eastern customs are to me most especially interesting. "Consider ye," says Jeremiah, exhorting his countrymen to bewail their disobedience, "and call for the mourning women, that they may come: and send for the cunning women, that they may come: and let them make haste, and take up a wailing for us, that our eyes may run down with tears, and our eyelids gush out with waters:" and by the same means the feelings of a mourning Eastern family seem to be most powerfully excited in the present day, for, in general, the most piercing cries and screams that I hear, on account of a death, are those which interrupt the lamentations of the hired mourner, who is "cunning" in her art. The cemeteries in the neighbourhood of Cairo are among the most picturesque of the various scenes which surround us; and in these are many private burial-grounds, each belonging to one family, who, if of sufficient wealth, have within its walls a house of mourning. To this house the females of the family regularly repair at the period of each of the two great annual festivals, as well as on extraordinary ones, to bewail their dead; having previously sent thither such furniture as is necessary for their comfort; and there they remain, on the occasions of the two festivals above mentioned, and immediately after a death, three or more days and nights. Some of the houses of mourning are pretty and cheerful-looking buildings, and enlivened by a few trees and flowers; and I believe that the women often find no small pleasure in visiting them; their life being in general so monotonous. Some women, who have not houses in the burial-ground for their reception, have tents pitched for them when requisite.

Yesterday we spent some hours at the Southern cemetery, which is adjacent to the city, but within the confines of the desert; and were much interested in examining the tombs of the family of Mohammad 'Alee. The tombs in the cemetery exhibit a strange mixture of various tastes and dimensions: some are in perfect repair, substantially and well built; others are of more fragile kinds; though many of the smaller monuments are composed entirely of white marble; but the most picturesque are the most ancient; displaying exquisite taste in their general forms, and more especially in their domes and minarets, and their arabesque decorations; these are of yellow limestone, here and there relieved by columns of white marble. The building containing the tombs of the Páshá's family is surmounted by several domes, but is low, and in no respect deserving of much admiration. How can I tell you of the cheerful appearance of the interior? Two noble saloons are filled with tombs at nearly equal distances: these are cased with white marble, and most gorgeously decorated with gilded and painted carved work. The floors are covered with beautiful carpets, and the scene has at once a complete air of gaiety and comfort. It has little that can lead the mind to the reflection that this is the resting-place of the dead. Such a variety of gay colours, and such varied forms meet the eye, that if the consciousness intrude that it is a sepulchral building, it is soon banished by the speculation as to which tombs may be considered more splendid than those around them. We generally gave the preference to that of the mother of Nezleh Hánum, and of Mohammad Bey Deftardár: the latter, I think, bears the palm.

The tombs are generally about eight feet long, and four high; and on the top of these is placed an oblong slab, about a foot thick: the upright slabs at the head and feet are eight or ten feet high; and on that at the head is a representation of the head-dress of the deceased, carved in stone, and painted. There are four unoccupied tombs in the principal saloon, raised, but not decorated. The embellishments altogether are such as only suit saloons appropriated to festivity. Turkish taste is ill calculated for decorating the abodes of the living, and does not apply at all where quiet and solemn effect is indispensable. It is not so with regard to Arabian taste: the Turkish is gaudy and florid: the Arabian is chaste and elegant, as much in domestic architecture as in the construction and decoration of sepulchres and mosques.

I felt that I could at any time spend a day in the saloons above mentioned, admiring the beauties of the place, with much personal comfort, and without the frequent intrusion of any melancholy reflection.

In a charming house, adjoining the tombs, appropriated to the use of the hareem of the keeper, we paid his ladies a visit, and were welcomed with true Eastern hospitality. The chief lady, who was handsomely attired in scarlet cloth, embroidered with gold, is a kind agreeable person, but woefully mistaken in her manner of training the dispositions of children. Two little babies belonging to the hareem were brought in to show us: the eldest, a boy, could just walk; and as soon as he made his appearance, the chief lady called for a stick, that puss, who was quietly crossing the carpet might be beaten for his amusement. Not being aware that the beating was not to be in earnest, I interceded for the cat; when my acquaintance replied mysteriously, "I like her very much, I will not hurt her." Accordingly, she raised her arm with considerable effort, and let it fall gently. She next desired one of her slaves to kneel, which the girl did most gracefully, and bent her head with an air of mock submission, to receive the kurbáj; and the same farce was performed. Though neither slave nor cat was a sufferer on the occasion, the effect must have been equally bad on the mind of the child. Alas! for the slaves and cats when he is big enough to make them feel!

LETTER XXV

MY DEAR FRIEND,

ALTHOUGH so many have written of the pyramids, and a new description cannot fail to have something of the character of an often repeated tale, I find much that I must say respecting these stupendous monuments, the greatest, perhaps, of the Wonders of the World, which have been objects of our curiosity and astonishment even in the age of childhood, and the sight of which forms an era in one's life. I will, however, as much as possible, avoid troubling you with a repetition of what you have read, or may read, on this subject, in the works of various travellers.

Having arranged that, during our visit, we should spend our days in a sepulchral grotto, and our nights in a tent, we set out on this agreeable excursion with the most pleasing anticipations.† The illusion so general in the East with regard to distance, occasioned by the extraordinary clearness of the atmosphere, is strikingly demonstrated in approaching the pyramids; it is very remarkable that the nearer we approached the objects of our destination, the less grand and imposing did they appear. From their aspect, as I first drew near to them, I should have formed a very inadequate idea of their dimensions. As soon as we had crossed the river they appeared within a mile of us; and after we had proceeded more than a league from el-Geezeh, I could scarcely believe that we were still a full league from the pyramids; for the distance to them from El-Geezeh, by the route which we took, is more than six miles, though it is just five miles in a direct line. When we arrived within a mile of the pyramids, the illusion became greater: the courses of stone were then plainly discernible, and it was easy to calculate that they were not more in number than the courses of brick in a house about fifty or sixty feet high. These presented a scale by which the eye was much deceived in estimating

---

†After introducing her own visit to the pyramids in February 1844, Sophia reverts for the descriptive passages to her brother's notes on his earlier visit in October 1825 (Lane, *Description*, 160), with brief as well as lengthy insertions on her part. It is noteworthy that Sophia does not refer to her brother when she mentions the illusion of distances but uses his first person remarks as her own. Sophia resumes the account of her own experience and adds Lane's account of his second visit to the area in December 1825, which included the story of the missing Mebrookeh, updating it to 1844. She then brings in Lane's ascent of the Great Pyramid (Lane, *Description*, 168–69) and ends her letter with comments of her own.

the altitude of the structure; being unaccustomed to the sight of stones of such enormous magnitude employed in building. But neither of these caus- es would be sufficient to produce such an illusion if there were any neigh- bouring object with which the pyramids might be contrasted. I was fully convinced of this when I arrived at the base of the great pyramid. It was then curious to observe how distant appeared those places where I had thought myself nearly at my journey's end. The clearness of the air would have deceived me then, as before; but I was looking at objects less strange to me; such as palm trees, villages, and the tents of Arabs.

A conspicuous object as we approached the pyramids was an old ruined causeway, most probably a part of that which was built by Kara-Koosh for the convenience of transporting stones from the pyramids to Cairo, when he constructed the citadel, and third wall of that city; and this portion may have been raised on the ruins of that which Herodotus describes, as the more ancient causeway was raised for the purpose of facilitating the conveyance of stones from the quarries on the eastern side of the Nile to the site of the Great Pyramid, to line the passages of that structure, and perhaps to case its exterior.

When we were at least a mile from our journey's end, I remarked to my brother, "The Pyramids do not appear so grand as I expected now we are almost close to them." "Almost close to them!" replied he; "wait a little, and tell me what you think." Accordingly we rode on; the provoking appearance of nearness to the objects of our visit surprising me during our whole approach. At this season it occupies three hours to reach the pyramids from Cairo, and this month, on account of its coolness, is particularly agreeable for such an excursion. A kind friend, Mr. Bonomi, well known for the length of time he has spent in this country, and his extensive acquaintance with its monuments, was staying at the pyramids, and prepared for us a tent, and another comfortable place of abode, an ancient sepulchral grotto in a rock, which latter has served as the foundation of a pyramid, now for the most part destroyed. This excavation we found ample and airy, having three large square apertures, serving us as windows, besides the entrance. Our tent was pitched near it, our carpets spread, and our home in the desert had an air of comfort I had hardly anticipated. There is much that is homeish in carrying one's own carpet: place it where you will, in the boat or in the desert, your eyes rest upon it while thinking, and its familiar patterns afford a sort of wel- come. The habit of placing the seggádeh (a small carpet) on the saddle enables an Eastern lady to take it wherever she may wander. When she is dis- posed to rest, her attendants spread it; and nothing is more refreshing dur- ing a desert excursion than to rest upon it, and take a simple meal of bread and fruit, and a draught of delicious Nile water.

As soon as possible after our arrival, we mounted the rock on which the pyramids are built, and there observed the effect I have described with regard to the objects we had passed on our way. From the brightness of their colour, apparently little changed by the thousands of years that have passed since their erection, the pyramids do not appear venerable: there is an appearance of freshness about them which amazed me: but with regard to their wonderful magnitude, I found that I was no longer disappointed when I had ascended the rocky elevation on which they rest: when I was within a few yards of the base of the Great Pyramid, I was enabled to the full to comprehend its vastness.

We lingered late among the objects of our visit, and were interested in observing the enormous shadows of the two greater pyramids, stretching across the cultivated plain to the river, as the sun was setting. The general view from the rocky eminence on which they are built is the most imposing that can be conceived.

Returning to our grotto, we enjoyed our evening meal with the appetite of desert travellers, and went to rest with our minds impressed by reflections on what we had seen, and by the novelty of our situation.

We were not the only dwellers in tombs during our stay near the pyramids; for a row of sepulchral excavations, which Colonel Vyse and his party occupied in 1837, are now inhabited by a Nubian, who has taken possession of them to afford lodgings (for a small remuneration) to travellers. Also at a short distance from our grotto, an Arab had taken up his abode in a similar but better tomb. Living there as a hermit, he is esteemed a saint by the people of the neighbouring villages, and is supported entirely by casual charity. Very probably he has adopted the life of an anchorite because he is idle, and finds it easier to depend on others than to gain his own bread. It is common to see the Arabs on their way to leave a deposit of bread or other food, and sometimes money, with this recluse, more especially on Friday, when he receives numerous visitors.

My brother, during a long visit to the pyramids in 1825, occupied one of the tombs of which the Nubian has now taken possession. They are excavated in the eastern front of the rocky eminence on which stands the Great Pyramid. At that time a family consisting of a little old man (named 'Alee) his wife (who was not half his equal in age) and a little daughter, occupied a neighbouring grotto; guarding some antiquities deposited there by Caviglia. Besides these, my brother had no nearer neighbours than the inhabitants of a village about a mile distant. The Sheykh 'Alee made himself useful in bringing water from a well which Caviglia had dug in the sandy plain, just at the foot of the slope before the grottoes. He was a poor half-witted creature, but possessed strong feelings, as was exemplified by an occurrence which happened during my brother's stay at the pyramids. One afternoon, his cook had sent old 'Alee's little girl to the neighbouring village to purchase some tobacco. The child not having returned by sunset my brother became uneasy, and dispatched a servant to search for her, and bring her back. 'Alee had also become anxious, and had sent his wife for the same purpose; but when the night had closed in, and he had received no tidings of the

little girl, he became almost frantic: he beat his breast, stamped on the
ground, and continued for sometime incessantly screaming, "Yá Mebrookeh!
yá Mebrookeh!" (the name of the child, signifying blessed.) After my brother
had endeavoured for a little while to pacify him, he set off towards the village. About five minutes more elapsed, and my brother was sitting before
the grotto, wondering that no one had returned, and that not even his two
Bedawee guards had come as usual, when he was alarmed by loud and
piteous cries in the desert plain before him. Leaving a servant in the grotto—for a strange youth was there—my brother ran towards the spot whence
the voice seemed to issue. As it was dark, he could see nothing; but after he
had proceeded some distance, he heard the following words repeated very
rapidly over and over again. "I testify that there is no deity but God, and I
testify that Mohammad is God's apostle;"—and soon he found poor old
'Alee lying on the ground. He told my brother that an 'efreet (or demon)
had seized him by the throat, and thrown sand into his mouth, and that he
was almost suffocated. (It seems that the Arabs are subject to a spasm in the
throat, which they attribute to the above cause.) The two Bedawees, in the
meantime, whom the servant and 'Alee's wife had engaged to assist them in
their search, had found the child, and were, like my brother, drawn to that
spot by the old man's cries. They helped him to walk back, but the poor
creature had been so terrified and distressed, that for several days after he
was quite idiotic.

On the second day after my brother had taken up his quarters at the pyramids, a young Bedawee—the stranger I have mentioned—claimed from
him the rights of hospitality. He remained with him until he quitted his
sepulchral abode, and, being a very clever and witty youth, amused him
exceedingly, every evening while he was smoking his pipe, by reciting stories and verses from the popular romance of 'Aboo-Zeyd[†]: but at the same
time he gave much offence to my brother's Egyptian servants, by his con-
tempt of the felláheen (or peasants). He had deserted from the Páshá's army
of regular troops, as he frankly confessed; and was afraid to enter the villages,
lest he should be recognized, and sent to the camp. When my brother was
leaving the pyramids, he asked this young man what he would now do for
provision, as he dared not enter the villages. He replied, "Who brought you
here? God is bountiful."[‡]

On the occasion of our visit to the pyramids, my brother inquired of our
guards if they knew or remembered poor old 'Alee, to which one of them

[†]The saga of Abu Zayd al-Hilali, a very oral long epic, originated in the Mamluk
period and describes the Bedouin tribes of the extensive desert between Egypt and
Tunisia; Abu Zayd is one of the legendary heroes mentioned.
[‡]The last two sentences are additions by Sophia, not mentioned in Lane, *Description*
(164); she may have heard the rest of the story directly from Lane.

replied that he was his son, and that he had been dead for some years. He then inquired whether Mebrookeh was living—"Yes," answered the man, "she is well and married, and the mother of two children." He went on to assure my brother he remembered his former visits well, and there was something satisfactory in the prospect of being guarded by one man, at least, who, for old acquaintance sake, might be on the alert. This man, though especially remarkable for his honesty, is not distinguished for his social virtues—he has married ten wives, and says he would marry twenty if he could afford to do so; asserting that although he has divorced several, he has only done so because they deserved it, for that they failed in their duty to him, notwithstanding his kindness to them. According to his own account, he was always good to them; he never reviled, but only beat them! The facility of divorce is a prodigious evil; often productive of want and misery. It is sadly common to find wives rejected for some trifling offence; when a kind admonition would have shown them all that had been amiss in their conduct, and would have rendered them valuable helpmates. I grieve to say that wives here are generally divorced merely from caprice.

Our guards, three in number, were remarkably picturesque objects; more like Bedawees than like peasants; belonging to a tribe which, not many years ago, exchanged the life of desert-wanderers for that of agriculturists; and having retained the dress of their fathers, which consists chiefly of a loose shirt, and a kind of blanket, which envelops the body, and gives to the wearer an appearance quite primeval. It was at first amusing, but at last very tiresome, to hear these men calling to each other during the whole night, as though they feared their companions might be asleep: their constant repetition of, "Open your eyes! open your eyes well!" effectually kept us watching also. One guard lay outside the tent, close to my head, and amused himself by singing constantly. I should have been very happy if something more substantial than canvas had separated me from such a lively neighbour. We rose in the morning fatigued, but the invigorating desert-air soon revived us; and we set out on our adventures with becoming energy.

The bed of rock on which the Great Pyramid is situated is about one hundred and fifty feet above the sandy plain which intervenes between it and the cultivated land. It is a soft testaceous lime-stone, abounding particularly with those little petrifactions described by Strabo as found in great quantities around the pyramids, and supposed to be *petrified lentils*, the leavings of the workmen who built the pyramids! These abound in many parts of the chain of mountains by which the valley of the Nile is confined on this side. The stone, when newly cut, is of a whitish colour; but, by exposure to the air, it becomes darker, and assumes a yellowish tint. The level parts and slopes of the rock are covered with sand and pebbles and fragments of stone, among which are found pieces of granite and porphyry, rock crystal, agates, and abundance of petrified shells, &c.

The Great Pyramid is that which is described by Herodotus as the work of a Pharaoh named Cheops, whom Diodorus Siculus calls Chemmis. Diodorus adds, that some attributed this pyramid to a king named Armæus. According to Manetho (a better authority in that case), it was founded by Suphis, the second king of the Fourth Dynasty, which was the second dynasty of the Memphite kings.

Colonel Vyse's most interesting discoveries of the hieroglyphic names of the royal founders of the first and third pyramids afford remarkable confirmations of the truth of the statements of Manetho and others respecting these monuments. The name of the founder of the Great Pyramid in hieroglyphics, according to the pronunciation of different dialects is Shofo, or Khofo: the former nearly agreeing with the Suphis of Manetho, the latter with the Cheops of Herodotus.

The height of the Great Pyramid is not much greater than that of the second: the former having lost several ranges at the top; while the upper part of the latter is nearly entire: but the base of the former is considerably larger; though the difference is not remarkable to the eye, and in the solidity and regularity of its construction, it is vastly superior.

The pleasure which is felt by the modern traveller in surveying the pyramids is not a little increased by the consideration of their venerable antiquity, and the reflection that many philosophers and heroes of ancient times have in like manner stood before them, wrapt in admiration and amazement. The stupendous magnitude of the Great Pyramid is most clearly apparent when the observer places himself near one of its angles. The view of the pyramid from this point, though the best that can be obtained, cannot convey an adequate idea of its size; for a gap in the angle, which appears to be near the summit, is not much more than half-way up. Thus greatly is the eye deceived by this extraordinary object.

Each side of the base of the Great Pyramid is seven hundred and thirty-three feet square, and the perpendicular height is four hundred and fifty-six feet, according to my brother's measurement. It consists of two hundred and three courses, or layers of stone; therefore the average height of a single course is about two feet and a quarter: but the courses vary in height from about *four* feet to *one* foot. The lower courses are higher than the rest; and the lowest is hewn out of the solid rock; as is also part of the second. Opposite the angle from which my brother's view was taken, about twelve feet distant, is a square place, twelve feet in width; and between two and three inches in depth; apparently marking the place of the original corner stone of the pyramid. About the middle of each side of the pyramid, the exterior stones have been much broken by the masses which have been rolled down from above; but at the angles they are more entire, and *there*, consequently, the ascent is not difficult. The upper and lower surfaces of the stones are smoothly cut; but the sides have been left very rough, and in many cases, not square: the interstices being filled up with a coarse cement, of a pinkish colour. This cement is, in some parts, almost as hard as the stone itself; and sometimes very difficult to detach. Among the dust and small fragments of stone which have crumbled away from the sides and yet rest upon the upper surfaces of the steps, or exterior stones, we find a great number of the small petrifactions in the form of lentils, which I have before mentioned.

Dr. Lepsius lately gave, at a meeting of the Egyptian Society in this city, a very interesting account of the mode in which the Great Pyramid, and similar monuments, appear to have been constructed, as suggested by Mr. Wild, an English architect, accompanying the Doctor. The following engraving will explain the description of the system which appears to have been adopted:—

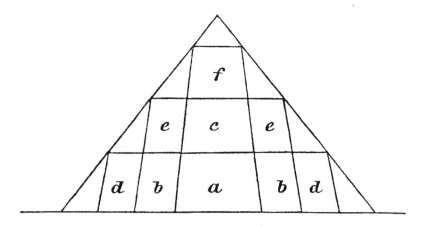

A structure of moderate size, *a*, with its sides slightly inclining inwards, containing, or covering the sepulchral chamber, and with a flat top, was first raised. Then a structure, *bb*, of the same height as the former, with its exterior sides similarly inclined, and its top flat, was raised around. Next, another structure, *c*, was raised on the first. Another circumstructure, *dd*, was raised around that marked *bb*; then another *ee*, around the structure *c*, then another structure, *f*, upon the latter. After this manner, the building probably continued to increase (like the royal tombs at Thebes) as long as the founder reigned. The structure was finished, as Herodotus says, from the top downwards. A small pyramid being constructed on the top, occupying the whole of the highest platform, and the angles formed by the other platforms, and the sides of the structures against which they were built being filled up, the simple pyramidal form was made out. The several platforms composed convenient ample stages on which to raise the massive stones employed in the construction. This mode of construction was certainly practised in some of the pyramids, and most probably in all, excepting those of very small dimensions. That the Great Pyramid and others originally presented plane sides has been proved by Colonel Vyse.

On each side of the Great Pyramid is an accumulation of fragments of stone and mortar which have fallen down from the summit and sides of the building, and have composed a very compact mass, which rises, in the centre, to about fifty feet above the base. The sand of the desert has contributed but little to augment these slopes of rubbish, which are nearly of the same height on each side of the pyramid. That on the northern side forms a convenient acclivity to the entrance.

The ascent to the summit of the Great Pyramid is not dangerous, though rather tedious, as the description of the exterior must have shown. At, or near, any of the angles, there is, on almost every course, or range of stones, a secure and wide footing; but some of the steps are breast-high; and these, of course, are awkward masses to climb. I had fully determined to attempt the ascent; but the wind was so high during the period of our visit, that I dared not do so. On some other occasion I hope to be more fortunate.

Many stones have been thrown down from the top of the Great Pyramid, which consequently wants about twenty-five feet (or perhaps something more) of its original height; for, without doubt, it terminated in a point. It appears, therefore, that its original height was, at the least, four hundred and eighty feet. It is worthy of remark that Diodorus Siculus describes the top of the pyramid as being six cubits (or nine feet) square; Pliny states it to have been, in his time, twenty-five feet; or, according to some copies of his work, fifteen feet; the latter of which readings must be considered the more correct. Several courses of stone have been thrown down in later ages; so that now, on arriving at the summit, there is a platform thirty-three feet square, upon which, near the eastern edge, are a few stones yet remaining of two upper courses. Upon these the names of many travellers are cut. The platform is quite flat; the stones being well joined and cemented. The ascent to the summit generally occupies between fifteen and twenty minutes.

The view from the summit of the Great Pyramid is described by my brother as being of a most extraordinary nature. On the eastern side the eye ranges over an extensive verdant plain, watered by numerous canals, and interspersed with villages erected upon mounds of rubbish, and surrounded by palm-trees. In the distance is the Nile; beyond which are seen the lofty minarets and citadel of Cairo, backed by the low yellow range of Mount Mukattam. Turning towards the opposite side, the traveller beholds a scene exactly the reverse: instead of palm-groves and corn-fields, he sees only the undulating sandy hills of the great Lybian Desert. The view of the second pyramid, from this commanding situation, is extremely grand. A small portion of the third pyramid is also seen; with one of the small pyramids on its southern side. The space which lies on the west of the Great Pyramid, and north of the second, is covered with oblong tombs, having the form of truncated pyramids; which from that height appear like patches of gravel. The head of the Great Sphinx, and the distant pyramids of Aboo-Seer, Sakkárah, and Dahshoor, are seen towards the south-south-east.

About half an hour or more after sunset, the gloom contributed much to the grandeur and solemnity of the scene. On one occasion my brother ascended the Great Pyramid about two hours before daybreak, and waited upon the summit until sunrise. He found it extremely cold, and the wind, sweeping up the northern side of the pyramid, sounded like a distant cataract. The second pyramid was at first faintly discernible, appearing of vastly more than even real magnitude. Soon after, its eastern side was lighted up by the rising moon; and the effect was truly sublime.

On the second day after he had taken up his quarters at the pyramids, during the visit to which I have referred, he went out without his pistols; and in the evening one of his guards reproved him for having done so. "How easy," he observed, "would it be for one of our people (the Bedawees) to rob you, and, if you resisted, to murder you, and throw you down one of the mummy-pits, and who would ever know what was become of you?" On the following day he ascended the Great Pyramid alone, but not unarmed. While on the summit, he perceived a solitary Arab, making towards the pyramid, from the west. He began to ascend the south-western angle, and when he arrived about half-way up, little thinking that my brother's telescope was directed towards him, he stopped, and took out a pistol from a case which was slung by his side, looked at it, and then continued the ascent. As it was evident that the fellow had no good intentions, my brother called to him, and desired him to descend; but he either did not hear him, or would not obey. My brother then discharged a pistol, to show him that he was not without the means of defence. Upon this, he immediately began to return, and having reached the base, walked slowly away into the desert.

Under the present government, travellers seldom are subjected to any danger from the natives in this or any other part of Egypt; but from the crowding and importunity of the Arab guides at the pyramids they generally suffer much annoyance. They are always attended for a considerable distance, sometimes even from El-Geezeh, by a party of Arabs who are in the habit of extorting money from the traveller on the top of the Great Pyramid before they will suffer him to descend. A few days ago, a gentleman of distinction bargained with some of these men to attend him to the summit of the Great Pyramid; and when they had done so, they claimed the promised payment, saying that they had fulfilled their engagement. Being afraid to descend without their aid, he was compelled to submit to their exactions, and paid them five dollars.

It is pitiable to observe the haste which most of the travellers to and from India are obliged to make, if able to visit the pyramids at all: some arrived during our stay, ran up the Great Pyramid, descended as rapidly, spent a few minutes within it, and disappeared in a little more than an hour.

LETTER XXVI

February, 1844

MY DEAR FRIEND,

THE entrance of the Great Pyramid[1] is over the sixteenth course, or layer of stone, about fifty feet above the base; a slope of rubbish, as I said before, leading up to it.[2] It is nearly in the centre, or equidistant from either angle of the northern side of the pyramid: the eye would hardly discover that it is not *exactly* so; though really twenty feet, or rather more, to the eastward of the centre. The opening of the pyramid seems to have been attended with considerable difficulty; a vast number of stones having been torn down above and before the aperture. An inclined plane before the entrance forms an angle of twenty-six degrees and a half with the horizon, being in the same place with the floor of the first passage. The size of the stones above the entrance, and the manner in which they are disposed, are worthy of remark. There is no granite at the entrance of the pyramid; all the blocks are of limestone. Before the traveller enters the pyramid, he should divest himself of some of his clothes (for the heat of the interior is oppressive) and resume them immediately on coming out, to prevent any check of perspiration. The passage by which we enter the Great Pyramid is only four feet high, and three feet six inches (almost exactly two ancient Egyptian cubits) in width, and we are consequently obliged to descend in a crouching position. It is lined above and below and on each side with blocks of limestone,[3] of a more compact kind than that of which the pyramid is mainly constructed. This superior kind of stone appears to have been brought from the quarries on the eastern side of the Nile, directly opposite the site of Memphis; for stone of the same quality is not found nearer; and Herodotus, and several other ancient writers, inform us that the quarries of the Arabian mountains[4] supplied materials for the construction of the pyramid. Indeed, they assert that the pyramid was entirely built of stones from these quarries; but this, evidently, was not the case: the stone of which the structure is mainly composed was quarried from the rock in its neighbourhood. The nicety with which the stones are

---

[1] See *b* in the accompanying section.
[2] See *a* in the section.
[3] Some travellers, their memories deceiving them, have described this passage as lined with *granite*; others have asserted that it is of *white marble*.
[4] The mountains on the east of the Nile are so called by ancient Greek and Roman writers, and those on the west the "Lybian Mountains."

united in the sides of the first passage is very remarkable. In some parts the joint cannot be discerned without a close and minute examination. In the flooring of this passage, and of all the sloping passages in this pyramid, notches have been roughly cut, like steps, to prevent the feet from slipping; but I found them very far from producing the desired effect, being now polished by the naked feet of the guides. These notches have been the work of modern explorers. At the distance of nearly seventy feet (measuring from the outer surface of the huge block above the entrance) we find that one of the stones which form the roofing of the passage has been hewn away precisely at the point where the second passage branches off in an ascending direction (see the letter c in the section). Here we discover the square end of a granite block, which closes the entrance of the second passage, being exactly fitted to fill up the aperture. The persons who opened the pyramid, being unable to remove this obstacle, have made a forced communication with the ascending passage. At the distance of eighty feet (from the entrance of the pyramid) is the forced aperture, on the right side of the passage (see d in the section). It has been made by hollowing out the roofing, and cutting away the upper part of the side of the lower passage.

Here the explorer must light his candle (if he have not done so before), and having ascended through this opening, finds himself in a large place, which appears like a natural cavern in a rock. We now see the upper end of the granite block before mentioned, or of a second block. Above it is another, of which a part has been broken off. Above this the passage (e f) is seen clear of other incumbrances, running upwards, but in the same southern course as the first, or descending passage. It is of the same dimensions as the first, and has the same inclination; but its sides and roofing are very rough, and consequently it has the appearance of having been cut through solid rock, which is not really the case. It is a hundred and nine feet long (measuring from the southernmost of the granite blocks above mentioned), and the flooring projects a foot and a half in the same direction. The ascent of this passage is rather fatiguing. On emerging from it, we find ourselves at the foot of the Grand Passage (see f m in the section).

This great passage, ascending to the principal chamber, is, in comparison with those which lead to it, wide and lofty. Its length being great, and its sides and every part of it blackened, as if by smoke, the further extremity was invisible to us as we stood at the lower end; and its whole appearance singularly imposing. On our right, as we stood here, we observed the entrance, or mouth, of what has been called "the well" (g). There we also, at the lower end of the Grand Passage, remarked some Arabic inscriptions, rudely cut with a chisel. These, I believe, were first noticed by Sir Gardiner Wilkinson. My brother read them to me thus—"Ezbek and Beybars have been here." "Beybars and Kalaoon El-Elfee have been here." "Sultán Mohammad. . . . Sa'eed." These three persons were Memlook sultáns of Egypt, who reigned in the latter half of the thirteenth

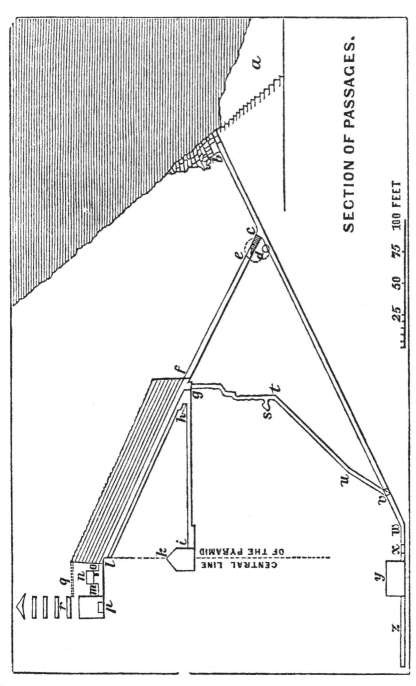

SECTION OF PASSAGES.

25 50 75 100 FEET

CENTRAL LINE
OF THE PYRAMID

century, at which period, it appears, the Great Pyramid was open; if these inscriptions be genuine, which my brother is a little inclined to doubt.

Under the grand, ascending passage, runs another, which is horizontal, low, and narrow. The entrance of the latter (*h*) is fifteen feet three inches from the projection of a foot and a half before mentioned. This passage is three feet eleven inches high, and three feet five inches wide. I found almost as much difficulty in proceeding here as I had in ascending and descending the sloping passages; the dust and the heat together being here especially oppressive. It continues of the same dimensions to the distance of ninety-three feet. Here we find a descent of one foot eight inches in the floor; so that the remainder of the passage is nearly high enough for a person of middling stature to walk along it without bending down the head. At the distance of a hundred and ten feet nine inches (from its entrance) it terminates (see *i* in the section) at the eastern corner of the north side of a chamber, which is nineteen feet long, and seventeen feet broad (see *k*). This has been called by some travellers the "Queen's Chamber;" from the supposition that the queen of the founder of the pyramid was buried in it. The roof is formed of long blocks of stone, leaning against each other. The height of the chamber, to the commencement of the roof, is thirteen feet and a half; and to the summit, about seven feet more. The floor, sides, and roof are constructed of the same kind of limestone as the passages. In the eastern end (not in the middle, but rather to the right) is a high and narrow recess, five feet wide at the bottom, but becoming narrower towards the top, like the sides of the Grand Passage. It is three feet five inches deep. Within it, four feet from the floor, is the entrance of a forced passage, four feet wide. At the commencement it is square, and smoothly cut; but further on it becomes irregular; and at the distance of fifty feet it terminates at a hollow space, wider and more irregular than the rest. In this chamber and forced passage there is little to detain us. We return to the Grand Passage.

Above the entrance of the horizontal passage which leads to the chamber above described, is a perpendicular (marked *h* in the section). This perpendicular, together with the height of the said passage, is seven feet three inches. The flooring then ascends in the same direction as the other ascending passage; at an angle of twenty-six degrees and a half. At the distance of three feet five inches is another perpendicular or step of only eight inches, above which the floor has the same inclination again; and notches have been cut in it to facilitate the ascent, which is not easily performed unless without shoes. There is a bench of stone on each side all along the passage, and in the tops of these benches are oblong holes at short intervals; their use is unknown. The width of the passage (including the benches, which are one foot eight inches and a half square), is six feet ten inches; about four ancient Egyptian cubits. The sides of the passage are composed of nine courses of stone from the benches upwards. The stone is of the same kind as that of which the lower passages are constructed. Some travellers have supposed it to be *white marble*, but no marble is found in any part of the pyramid. The two lower courses are even with each other, but each course above projects three inches beyond that below it; and so does each corresponding course at the upper and lower ends of the passage. The length of the whole passage is a hundred and fifty-eight feet. At the distance of five feet and one inch before we reach the upper end, we ascend another perpendicular of two feet eleven inches. The floor beyond is horizontal, forming a small platform (see *l* in the section). From this commences a horizontal passage three feet seven inches and a half in height, and three feet five inches and a half in width (see *m*). Within it, on the right, is the entrance of a *forced* passage, made in search for other chambers than those already known. At the distance of four feet five inches (from the entrance of the *true* passage), commences an open space above (see *n*), the upper part of which is nearly twice as wide as the passage, and nine feet eight inches in length: but the passage below is contracted again to its former height by a kind of portcullis, formed of two blocks of granite one above another, each one foot three inches thick; these have been let down from the space above between two small projections on each side which form a pair of grooves. Beyond this, the passage (which is here of *granite*), is open as before, to the space above, and there are grooves for the reception of three other portcullises of granite, by which the architect thought that he should for ever prevent access to the mysterious chamber which contains the sarcophagus; but these have been broken and their fragments carried away. The passage beyond (see *o*), is of its former dimensions, and continues so to the distance of eight feet five inches, its whole length, from the top of the Grand Passage, being twenty-two feet and a half. It terminates at the eastern extremity of the north side of the Grand Chamber (see *p* in the section).

The dimensions of the Great Chamber are especially worthy of remark: the length is thirty-four feet four inches and a half; just twenty ancient Egyptian cubits; the width exactly half that measure. The height is about two feet more than the width. It is entirely constructed of red granite. Near the western end is the sarcophagus; which is also of red granite. It is seven feet and a half in length, three and a half in breadth, and the sides are half a foot thick. No hieroglyphics nor sculptures of any kind adorn it either within or without; its sides are perfectly plain and polished, and its form is simply that of an oblong chest, in every way rectangular. Its lid has been carried away, as well as its original contents; and we find in it nothing but dust and small fragments of stone. It has been much injured at one of its corners by a number of travellers, who have broken off pieces to carry away as memorials. When struck with anything hard, or even with the hand, it sounds like a bell. It rests upon a block of granite considerably larger than any of the other blocks of which the floor is composed.

Why was such an enormous mass placed there? The alabaster sarcophagus in the great tomb opened by Belzoni in the valley of Beebán-el-Mulook, at

Thebes, closed the entrance of a deep descent of steps, which has never been explored to its termination: the soft and crumbling nature of the rock through which it is cut rendering any attempt to clear it out extremely dangerous. The enormous mass of granite under the sarcophagus in the Great Pyramid may have been placed there for a similar purpose, or to cover the mouth of a vault or pit; so that, in case any violater of the sacred edifice should succeed (notwithstanding the portcullises of granite), in effecting an entrance into the Great Chamber, he might, on discovering the sarcophagus, believe the object of his search to be accomplished. An excavation has been made (I believe by Col. Howard Vyse), beneath this huge stone, but it seems hardly to have been carried sufficiently far. The sides of the chamber are formed of six regular courses of granite blocks, which are united with the greatest exactness, and their surfaces are perfectly even and polished, without hieroglyphics or any other inscriptions or ornaments. In the northern side near the corner of the entrance is a small aperture, and opposite to it in the southern side is another. Col. Vyse discovered the termination of each of these, in the exterior of the pyramid: they seem to have been designed for the purpose of ventilation. The roof of the chamber consists of nine long granite blocks which extend from side to side. The half only of the stone at each end is seen, the other half resting on the wall.

Returning from this chamber we stop at the platform at the upper end of the Grand Passage (see *l* in the section).[1] Here we observe at the top of the eastern wall (that is on the left of a person facing the end of the passage), at the height of twenty-four feet, a square aperture which is the entrance of another passage (*q*). Small notches have been cut at the corner all the way up, for the reception of the ends of short pieces of wood, which were thus placed one above another so as to form a kind of ladder. These have been taken away, and the ascent without them is difficult and dangerous. When my brother was here alone some years ago, two Arabs contrived to climb up by means of the little notches, and took with them a strong rope, the end of which he tied round him, and so they drew him up to the top. As soon as he was freed from the rope they demanded of him a present, threatening that if he refused they would descend and leave him there. Though my brother laughed at their threats, they would not for some minutes confess that they were joking. The passage in which he found himself is only two feet four inches square. It turns immediately to the right, and to the distance of a few feet it continues square and of the same dimensions as before, but much clogged with dirt; afterwards it becomes irregular both in direction and in the construction of its sides, and it was difficult for my brother to drag himself along it, while numbers of bats escaped from within and flew against his face. At the distance

---

[1]There is a remarkable echo in this passage, on account of which it is a custom of travellers to fire a pistol or gun here.

of twenty-four feet the passage terminates at the north-east corner of a large but low place (*r*). This chamber (if such it may be called) was discovered by Mr. Davison, who was British Consul at Algiers, and who visited Egypt with Mr. Wortley Montague in 1763 and 4, and it is called by the discoverer's name. It is directly above the Grand Chamber, and is of the same width as that chamber, but four feet longer. The long granite blocks which compose the roof of the lower chamber form the floor of this, and the first and last of these blocks are here seen entire. The upper surface of each of them is very rough, and they are not all of the same thickness. The roof also of this place is formed of long blocks of granite eight in number. The height is scarcely more than three feet. In the south-east corner is a small forced passage which ascends a few feet. The second roof above the Grand Chamber was made to secure the lower roof, which otherwise might have been broken down by the superincumbent masses. Col. Vyse discovered over Davison's chamber three others similar to it one above another, and above the uppermost of these another with a pointed roof; and in making this discovery he made one of much greater importance, that of two hieroglyphic names, rudely inscribed as quarry-marks; one of them certainly the name of the founder, as before mentioned; the other, according to some, a variation of the same name; according to others, the name of a predecessor or successor of the founder.

I scarcely need tell you that I did not descend what is called the well. It was explored by Mr. Davison, and afterwards in 1801 by Col. Coutelle; but its termination and use remained involved in uncertainty and mystery, until it was cleared out in 1817 by Caviglia. On the right of the lower end of the Grand Passage two feet below the floor, are three low steps occupying a space of four feet and a half in length. Beyond them is the mouth of the first shaft which is two feet two inches square. Here are little notches roughly cut in the sides in which to place the fingers and toes, and as the space is narrow, a person may descend without the aid of a rope, as my brother did, but he found it difficult and dangerous to do so. The ascent is attended with less danger, and seems precisely like climbing a chimney. At the depth of a few feet it becomes very rugged and irregular, and continues so for nearly fifty feet. After descending rather more than sixty feet, an aperture is seen on the southern side, which is the entrance of a kind of grotto (*s*) between five and six feet high, and about three times as long, turning to the right. It is hollowed out in a vein of coarse but compact gravel, and the well, in consequence of this vein, is lined with masonry for the space of a few feet above and below the grotto. Where the masonry ceases (*t*) the well takes a sloping direction and continues so to the bottom; but towards the bottom (see *u* in the section) the slope becomes more steep. All the sloping part is cut through the solid rock below the foundation of the pyramid, and is of a square form. At the bottom of the well (*v*) is a horizontal passage six feet long, communicating with the first passage, two hundred and twelve feet below the aperture by which one ascends to the second passage.

The first passage of the pyramid from the aperture last mentioned, continues in the same direction, and is of the same dimensions, but is cut through the solid rock, and is not lined with masonry. The aperture which communicates with the bottom of the well is two feet ten inches broad. It is on the right of a person descending the first passage. This passage continues in the same direction to the distance of twenty-three feet further (see w in the section), beyond which it is horizontal, and so low and incumbered with rubbish, that the explorer is obliged to drag himself along in a prostrate position. At the distance of sixteen feet nine inches there is a recess (*x*) on the right side three feet four inches deep, and six feet five inches wide. Four feet and a half beyond this, the passage terminates at the eastern extremity of the north side of a large excavated chamber (*y*).

The Great Excavated Chamber is nearly under the centre of the pyramid. It is twenty-seven feet broad, and sixty-six feet long. The roof is flat, but the floor is very uneven. At the entrance the chamber is fifteen feet high; towards the western end the rock rises perpendicularly half-way towards the ceiling, and there are masses of strange forms, but not altogether irregular, rising still higher, and nearly touching the top of the chamber. In the floor at the lower end is a wide hollow space nearly filled with rats' dung. Immediately opposite the entrance is a level passage (*z*), low and narrow, running towards the south; it terminates abruptly at the distance of fifty-five feet. The floor of the chamber is just a hundred feet below the level of the external base of the pyramid. It appeared evident to my brother that this great chamber was an unfinished excavation. Mr. Salt thought otherwise: "He had flattered himself that it would turn out to be that described by Herodotus as containing the tomb of Cheops, which was insulated by a canal from the Nile; but the want of an inlet, and its elevation of thirty feet above the level of the Nile at its highest point, put an end to this delusive idea." This great chamber was discovered by Caviglia, of whose operations in the Great Pyramid, and in the neighbouring tombs, an interesting account is given in the 19th vol. of the 'Quarterly Review.' After having explored the well, and endeavoured, in vain, to draw up the rubbish with which the lower end was filled, he turned his attention to the clearing of the first passage of the pyramid, which, until that time, had been supposed to terminate just below the aperture which communicates with the second passage. In the prosecution of this work (which was one of much difficulty, as the passage was choked with large fragments of stone), he discovered the communication with the bottom of the well, and, continuing his operations, soon after entered the Great Excavated Chamber.

Such is the description of all that is now known of the interior of the Great Pyramid. It has been calculated that there might be within this stupendous fabric, three thousand seven hundred chambers, each equal in size to the Sarcophagus Chamber, allowing the contents of an equal number of such chambers to be solid, by way of separation.[1] Yet this enormous pile seems to have been raised merely as a sepulchral monument, to contain, perhaps, one single mummy, not a particle of which now remains in the place in which it was deposited with so much precaution;[2] unless there be yet undiscovered any other receptacle for the royal corpse than the sarcophagus in the Granite Chamber. Herodotus and Diodorus Siculus assert that the building of the Great Pyramid occupied about twenty years, and according to the former, a hundred thousand men—according to the latter three hundred and sixty thousand men—were employed in its construction.

The Great Pyramid is surrounded, on three sides, by almost innumerable tombs. On the east are three small pyramids; and on the same side, and on the west and south, are many oblong tombs, flat-topped, and with sides inclining inwards. Some persons who have been unreasonable enough to doubt whether the pyramids are sepulchral monuments, must, I think, be convinced of their error by the discoveries of Colonel Vyse: long before which, my brother found bones and mummy-rags in the principal pyramid of Sakkárah.

---

[1] Quarterly Review—vol. 19, page 401.
[2] Most ancient authors who have described this monument assert, in opposition to Diodorus, that its founder was buried in it.

LETTER XXVII

February, 1844

My Dear Friend,

I fear that I might weary you if I gave you a description of the other pyramids as full as that of the first; and, as they are far less interesting, I would pass them over entirely; but a few remarks respecting them, some of which I owe to my brother, I do not refrain from offering, as I think they will interest you. It is no trifle, I assure you, for a woman to explore the interior of the Great Pyramid. My mind continued so impressed with the difficulties of this undertaking, for some time, that I could not forget them, even in my dreams. The examination of the others is somewhat less arduous.

The name of the founder of the Second Pyramid, commonly called that of Chephrenes, still remains involved in some degree of doubt. But in some of the tombs in the neighbourhood, we find a king's name, in hieroglyphics, which, according to different dialects, may be read Khephré or Shefré; and it seems highly probable that the king to whom this name belongs was the builder of the pyramid in question.

This pyramid is but little inferior in magnitude to the first. From some points of view, it even appears more lofty, as it stands on ground about thirty feet higher than that on which the first rests, and its summit is almost entire. A large portion of its smooth casing remains on the upper part, forming a cap which extends from the top to about a quarter of the distance thence to the base. Notwithstanding this, Arabs often ascend to its summit; and many European travellers have done the same.† In its general construction, this pyramid is inferior to the first; and its interior is less remarkable. By a sloping passage, similar to the first in the Great Pyramid, but cased with granite, and then by a long horizontal passage hewn through the rock, broken by two perpendicular descents, and sloping ascents, we reach the Great Chamber. This is similar in form of the "Queen's Chamber" in the Great Pyramid, and contains a plain sarcophagus of granite, among blocks of the same material lately torn up from the floor, in which the sarcophagus was embedded.

---

†Lane did not attempt the ascent, for, as he says, "The mere contemplation of it affected me with giddiness" (Lane, *Description*, 178).

‡Lane informs us that one of the bones found in the sarcophagus, "when brought to England, was discovered to have belonged—not to a human being, but—to a cow, or a bull; or, in other words, to a representative of the goddess Isis, or of the god Apis" (Lane, *Description*, 179).

Several Arabic inscriptions are scrawled with charcoal upon various parts of this chamber. Most of these were written before the opening of the pyramid by Belzoni, and are nearly illegible; generally recording the visits of Arabs, and in the modern Arabic characters. My brother could not find any date among them. From his manuscript notes, I copy the following observations respecting one of these inscriptions which has excited especial attention: consisting of two lines, written in the same characters as the rest, and with the same material, but not so imperfectly legible. "Belzoni particularly remarked these two lines, and took a Copt scribe to copy them; but this man did not faithfully execute his task: he concluded that the second line was a continuation of the first, which is far from being certain, and gave a transcript in which he presumed to restore what was defective in the original. His transcript has been thus translated by Mr. Salame: 'The Master Mohammed Ahmed, lapicide, has opened them; and the Master Othman attended this (opening); and the King Alÿ Mohammed at first (from the beginning) to the closing up.' This inscription has exceedingly puzzled the learned Orientalists of Europe; and great pains have been taken to find out who was the king mentioned in it, and at what period he reigned. It unfortunately happens that the first line is almost wholly defaced; a traveller having scribbled his name over it: the two first words, however, have not been written over; and I must pronounce it very uncertain whether they are as in the transcript above-mentioned, and consequently, whether the inscription contain any mention of the 'opening' of the pyramid. But the second line, which is the more important, has not been defaced like the first; and the greater part of it is so plain that it can hardly be read otherwise than thus: 'El-Khaleel 'Alee, the son of Mohammad . . . has been here;' or, in the order of the Arabic words, 'Has been here El-Khaleel 'Alee, the son of Mohammad . . .' It is quite evident that the word which Belzoni's copyist makes 'el-melik,' or 'the King,' is a proper name. Another inaccuracy in the copy published by Belzoni is the omission of the word signifying 'son,' after ''Alee.' Thus we find that this inscription (instead of recording the visit of a king, or perhaps, even alluding to the opening of the pyramid) is probably nothing more than the Arabic scrawls which are seen in great numbers on many of the monuments of Egypt. It, and others similar to it, are of some interest, however, as showing that the pyramid was open at a comparatively late period."[†]

The third pyramid, commonly attributed to Mycerinus, or Mencheres, was opened by Colonel Vyse, who found in it the mummy-case of its founder, bearing the hieroglyphic name of Menkaré. This pyramid, though small in comparison with the first and second, its base being about three hundred and thirty feet, and its perpendicular height about two hundred, is

---

[†]A simplified copy from Lane with omission of texts in Arabic script (Lane, *Description*, 180–81).

a very noble monument. Its construction is excellent; and it was distinguished by being partly, or wholly, cased with granite. Several courses of
the granite casing-stones remain at the lower part. The chamber in which
the sarcophagus was found, and the entrance-passage, are formed of granite; and the roof of the former is composed of blocks leaning together, and
cut so as to form an arched ceiling. The sarcophagus was lost at sea, on its
way to England. The third pyramid was the first that I entered; and highly
was I gratified by the view of its interior, after I had summoned courage to
crawl through its entrance, which was almost closed by huge masses of
stone.[†]

Adjacent to the pyramids which I have mentioned are several others; but
these are comparatively insignificant; and I shall not attempt to describe
them: nor shall I undertake to give you a detailed account of any of the
numerous tombs to which I have before alluded. Most of these lie in a large
space to the west of the Great Pyramid, and north of the second; and are, with
few exceptions, disposed in regular lines, from north to south, and from east
to west; their walls, like the sides of the pyramids, facing the four cardinal
points. Some of them are nearly buried in the drifted sand; and many are
almost entirely demolished. Some contain no chambers above ground; but
have a pit, entered from the roof, descending to a sepulchral chamber. Others
contain narrow chambers within their walls, adorned with painted sculptures
in low relief, representing agricultural and other scenes. Most of these are of
the same age as the Great Pyramid. In one of them, which is of that age, are
represented persons engaged in various arts, carpenters, makers of papyrus-
boats (probably like the ark in which Moses was exposed), agricultural
employments, the wine-press, eating, dancing, &c. Among the subjects in
this tomb, we find two men sitting at a tray which is supported by a low
pedestal, and loaded with food: one is holding a fowl in his left hand; and,
with his right, tearing off one of the wings: the other is holding a joint, and
about to bite off a piece. Each of these persons is almost naked: had they more
clothing, they would exhibit a true representation of two modern Egyptians
at their dinner or supper.[‡] There are also many sepulchral grottoes, excavated
in the rock, in the neighbourhood of the pyramids. In one we find representations of the flocks and herds of the principal occupant, with the number of
each kind: he had 835 oxen, 220 cows with their young, 2234 he-goats, 760
asses, 974 rams. This interesting tomb is of the remote age of Khephré,
Shefré, before-mentioned. It is in the front of the rocky elevation on which the

---

[†]The description of the third pyramid is entirely by Sophia. She even differs from her
brother in the dimensions: he says its base is about 300 feet square and its height
about 180 feet. As this was the first pyramid she entered, she may have done so in
the company of Colonel Vyse.
[‡]This is one of numerous scenes described by Lane (*Description*, 186–87).

Great Pyramid stands, a little to the right of Colonel Vyse's quarters, facing the valley of the Nile.

Had I attempted a regular description of the pyramids and the monuments around them, I should have begun with the Great Sphinx, which faces the traveller approaching the Great Pyramid by the easiest route from the south-east, and lies but a short distance from that route. Its huge recumbent body, and its enormous outstretched fore legs, are almost entirely buried in sand and rubbish. The head alone is twenty feet high. The face (which lays claim to be regarded as a portrait of Thothmes IV., whom many believe to have reigned during the bondage of the Israelites in Egypt, or shortly before or after, and who may have been the very Pharaoh in whose reign the Exodus took place) is much mutilated; the nose being broken off. This loss gives to the expression of the face much of the negro character: but the features of the countenance of the ancient Egyptian, as well as the comparative lightness of complexion, widely distinguished him from the negro; and the nose of the former greatly differed from that of the latter. At first the countenance of the Sphinx, disfigured as it is, appeared to me absolutely ugly; but when I drew near, I observed in it a peculiar sweetness of expression, and I did not wonder at its having excited a high degree of admiration in many travellers. The whole of this extraordinary colossus was doubtless painted: the face still retains much of its paint, which is red ochre, the colour always employed by the ancient Egyptians to represent the complexion of their countrymen; yellow or pink being used by them for that of the Egyptian women. All that is visible of the Sphinx is hewn out of a mass of limestone rock, which perhaps naturally presented something of the form which art has given to it.†

I did not think to have written to you so much on the pyramids and the monuments around them; but having entered upon the subject, I have found it difficult to stop. So wonderful in themselves are the principal pyramids, and so impressive by reason of their remote antiquity, that all other existing works of man must, I think, in comparison with them, sink into insignificance. I could hardly believe that monuments of such stupendous magnitude, and such admirable construction, were erected several centuries before the period of the Exodus, were it not for the fact that the Tower of Babel, probably an equally wonderful edifice, was raised in an age yet earlier.

During this excursion I was gratified by observing among innumerable Arabs belonging to the villages not a single instance of blindness, a calamity so common in Cairo. These peasants seem to enjoy a very small share of this world's goods; but the exhilarating air usually blowing from the neighbouring desert has an extraordinary effect on their health and spirits.

---

†Mainly an eyewitness account by Sophia, interspersed with descriptions and remarks by Lane (*Description*, 189–91).

On the morning before our departure several well-dressed young Bedawees arrived near our tent, the sons of the sheykh of a distant village. After dismounting and loitering about for nearly an hour, they confessed to one of our party that they had ridden several miles in the hope of seeing the faces of some European ladies, who, they had been informed, were passing a few days at the pyramids, and they were seriously disappointed on finding veiled ladies only. A few weeks since these same young men enjoyed the treat of seeing an American lady who is travelling in Egypt, and who is a beautiful person. A friend of ours asked their opinion of the lady on that occasion, when they replied that her appearance was "excellent." "But," exclaimed one of the young men, "the sword! the sword! if we dared to use it, we would kill that man," alluding to the lady's companion, "whether her husband, or her brother, and take her ourselves." 'Tis well for pretty women travelling in the East that these lawless Arabs are kept under a degree of subjection by the present government.

LETTER XXVIII

March, 1844

MY DEAR FRIEND,

YOU may have heard of a famous magician in this famous city of Cairo, who, though not supposed to be possessed of art equal to that of Pharaoh's wise men and sorcerers, has perplexed and confounded several of the most intelligent travellers, by feats very nearly resembling that performed by the Witch of Endor at the request of Saul. Having inscribed a magic square upon the palm of the right hand of any young boy or girl, and poured into the centre of it a little pool of ink, he pretends by means of the repetition of certain invocations to two spirits, and by burning some small strips of paper inscribed with similar invocations, in a chafing-dish containing live coals sprinkled with frankincense and coriander-seed, or other perfume, to make the boy see in this pool of ink the image of any person, living or dead, called for by his employer. My brother has fully described his performances as witnessed by himself and several other travellers more than ten years ago, the performances of which he was himself witness were not altogether inexplicable, for some of the persons called for were not unknown to fame, and the correct description of others might have been the result of mere guessing; but the facts which he has related on the testimony of others have induced several persons whom I could name to believe them the effects of supernatural agency. The supposed mystery, however, my brother thinks he can now explain, at least so far as to satisfy any reasonable person respecting most, if not all, of the most surprising of the feats to which I have alluded.

A few weeks ago, he was requested by two English travellers, Lord N. and Major G., to witness the performances of this magician, and to act as interpreter on the occasion, in order that they might feel themselves secure from any collusion. But I must give you his own account of the exposure which this request occasioned.

"I was unwilling," he said, "to accede to the proposal made to me, and expressed a reluctance to do so; but I am glad that I at last consented. The magician tried with two boys, and with both of them he utterly failed in every case. His excuse was, that the boys were liars, and described the objects which they saw otherwise than as they appeared to them; that the feats were performed not by his own means alone, and that he was not secure from being imposed upon by others. Now if we admit that there is *still* such a thing as real magic, and we know from the Bible such was once the case, we must allow that by occasional failures this man does not show that he is not

173

a true magician, as long as he employs an agent, upon whose veracity and particular qualifications he asserts the success of his performances to depend. Partly, perhaps, from feelings of mortification, and partly with the view of upholding his reputation by urging what he had done on former occasions, he remarked to me that he was successful in the days of 'Osmán Efendee, and that since the death of that person he had been unfortunate.

"This was indeed, for him, a most unfortunate remark. The inference to be drawn from it, that the person whom he named was the main spring of his machinery, was inevitable, more especially when I considered, that in all the instances of his surprising success of which I had heard, this person served as the interpreter; and when I further reflected, that since his death, which took place nearly nine years ago, hundreds of persons had witnessed the performances of this magician, and I had been assured that his successes had been such as could not be said to be even the results of lucky guesses or mere accident, for he had almost always failed. I was at first unwilling to believe that a person whom I always regarded as an honest man, and whom I knew to have been possessed of many excellent qualities, had consented to be a means of imposition; and I remembered that, in the performances which I had myself witnessed, I ascertained that he gave no direction either by word or sign; that he was generally unacquainted in these instances with the personal appearance of the individual called for; that I took care that he should have no previous communication with the boys; and that I had seen the experiment fail when he *could* have given directions to them or to the magician. But the inferences to be derived from these circumstances, in favour of the magician, are surely outweighed by the facts which I have mentioned, resting not only upon the assertions of others, but also upon his own confession. 'Osmán perhaps considered it a light matter to practise such an artifice as that which is thus imputed to him, and perhaps was unwilling to practise it upon me, or feared my detecting him if he attempted to do so. Besides, if many of the performances of the magician had not been far more surprising than those which I witnessed, he would have gained but little notoriety. I satisfied myself that the boy employed in a case which I have mentioned in my work on the 'Modern Egyptians,' was not prompted for the part he played, by my having chosen him from a number of others passing by in the street; and I also felt satisfied that the images which he and another boy professed to have seen, were by some means produced in the ink by the magician, in consequence of their refusal to accept presents which I offered them, with the view of inducing them to confess that they did not really see what they proposed to have seen. As to the former point, I was doubtless right; but as to the latter, I now feel that I was deceived. I believe that the boys saw nothing, and that, having deceived me, they feared to confess the truth. Another difficulty, however, lies in the way of the explanation which I have proposed: two travellers (one of them M. Leon Delaborde, the other an

Englishman), both instructed by the magician of whom I am speaking, are stated to have succeeded in performing similar feats. But is it not almost certain, after what I have said, that those feats were accomplished by means of the suggestions of the interpreter or interpreters? Perhaps the same person who interpreted in the other cases which excited so much surprise did so in those also.

"I have stated all that I can for and against the magician, and leave it for others to decide upon the case. For myself, I am satisfied that his successes are to be attributed chiefly to the interpreter, but partly also to leading questions, and partly to mere guessing. Let us consider these three means as employed in one of the most remarkable cases. A number of individuals being called for, most of them (perhaps all), are correctly described. With the personal appearance of many of these individuals the interpreter is acquainted, and he is therefore able to suggest to the boy what he should say. When he has had no previous knowledge of the peculiarities of the appearance of a person called for, it has often happened that he has acquired such knowledge during the performance. One of the company, for instance, saying that he will call for such a person, adding that he is remarkable in such and such respects. When the first means cannot be employed, much may be done by the second, that is by leading questions. When a person having but one leg, or one leg shorter than another, is called for, he is perhaps vaguely described, and the boy is in consequence asked if there be anything peculiar in his legs: this question suggests to him that there *is* some peculiarity in his legs, and he probably ventures to say that he can only see *one* leg, then if this be unsatisfactory, he may add the person has turned round, and that he sees him to be *lame.* The third means (guessing) without the others is not likely to be of much service; but with them it may help to supply trifling deficiencies, and when the guessing is wrong respecting a *trifling* matter, his *error* is considered *trifling*; but when he is right, his description is often considered striking for its minute accuracy.

"The last performances of this magician in my presence were ridiculous for their complete want of success. A woman was described as a man, a tall person as short or middle-sized, the very old as of a middle age, and so on. Two boys were employed; one was very stupid and appeared much frightened, the other seemed accustomed to the performance."

A friend has just described to me the latest performance of the magician, and you can hardly conceive anything more unfortunate and absurd. He had been sent for to gratify the curiosity of a party of English travellers at the French Hotel, a frequent scene of his impositions, where he often finds a boy ready to be employed by him, familiar with his tricks, and an interpreter disposed to aid his deceptions. A donkey-boy was sent for; and after the usual preparations, Lord Auckland was named as the first person whose image was to be presented to the boy, in the mirror of ink. He was merely described as short and thin. O'Connell was next represented as short and thin, dressed in white, young, without a beard, wearing a white hat with a handkerchief tied round it (like a Frank endeavouring to preserve his head from the heat of an Egyptian summer sun), and having only one hand. Several other persons were called for, relations of individuals present, with various success; and much laughter was occasioned, which made the magician accuse the boy of not telling what he saw. Another boy was sent for; and he seemed to have been employed previously: sometimes he got on before the magician. After many ridiculous failures, the Prince of Wales was described with white hair, yellow beard, black coat, and white trousers. (Beards, I should tell you, are worn here by many European travellers.) The party agreed not to laugh; and the names of persons present were given as those of individuals whose images were required to appear. Sometimes the image described was right in being tall, but wrong in being fat: right as to coat, but wrong as to trousers: just as you would expect in cases of guessing. Five dollars were put upon a chair before the magician; but he had the presence of mind to wait for more, which, I believe, he received. I assure you he reaps a fine harvest from the pockets of travellers.

If you wish to know what the performances of this man were in earlier times, in the most remarkable instances, read an account of them in No. 117 of the "Quarterly Review;" and especially a note there, following the remarks of the reviewer. You will see, from what is there stated, that the subject was deemed worthy of serious consideration, and that a discovery of the means employed by the magician, which were thought to be of a very ingenious kind, was regarded as an interesting desideratum. That these means were not merely leading questions, and the like, as a late writer has suggested, is evident when we reflect that the magician is not known to have been even generally successful on any single occasion since the death of the interpreter 'Osmán, and it is not likely that intelligent travellers (of whom many might be named) would have been at a loss for the explanation, if such means would have sufficed.

One further remark I must make on this subject. If we give to some persons that credit which they are believed to deserve, we must admit that excited imagination, in the child employed as an agent in the deception, has sometimes produced images in the mirror of ink; but these images have been always such as the child *expected* to see. The successful performances have been supposed, by some, to have been effected by means of mesmerism; and some have attributed them to diabolical agency. As the grandest discoveries in science are often the most simple, so what appears to us at first most unaccountable is often capable of the most simple solution.

LETTER XXIX

April, 1844

My Dear Friend,

WHEN I promised you a description of the Bath, I did not anticipate that I should enter upon the subject with pleasure. Whatever others
may think of it, I confess that the operation of bathing in the Eastern manner is to me extremely agreeable; and I have found it singularly beneficial in
removing that lassitude which is occasioned by the climate. It is true that it
is followed by a sense of fatigue, but a delightful repose soon ensues; and the
consequences, upon the whole, I find almost as enjoyable as the process itself.

The buildings containing the baths are all nearly on the same plan, and are
much alike in appearance; the fronts being decorated fancifully, in red and
white, and the interiors consisting of several apartments paved with marble. I
will describe to you, in a few words, one of the best in Cairo, which I visited
with three ladies of my acquaintance,—English, Abyssinian, and Syrian.

After we had passed through two passages, we found ourselves in the first
large apartment, or chamber of repose, in which the bathers undress previously to their entering the heated chambers, and in which they dress after
taking the bath, and rest on a raised marble platform, or wide bench, on
which are spread mats and carpets. In the centre is a fountain of cold water,
over which is a dome. For a detailed account of the public baths of Cairo I
refer you to my brother's description; and shall only relate to you the scenes
through which I passed on the occasion to which I have referred.[†]

In the first apartment, each of us enveloped herself in a very long and
broad piece of drapery,—which, but for its size, I might call a scarf,—and
proceeded through a small chamber, which was moderately heated, to the
principal inner apartment, where the heat was intense. The plan of this
apartment is that of a cross, having four recesses; each of which, as well as the
central portion, is covered with a dome. The pavements are of white and
black marble, and small pieces of fine red tile, very fancifully and prettily
disposed. In the middle is a jet of hot water, rising from the centre of a high
seat of marble, upon which many persons might sit together. The pavement
of each of the recesses is a few inches higher than that of the central portion

---

[†]Lane, *Manners and Customs*, 336: "There are in Cairo, between sixty and seventy
"Hammáms," or baths, to which the public have access for a small expense. Some of
these are for men only; others, only for women and young children; and some for both
sexes; for men during the forenoon, and in the afternoon for females."

of the apartment; and in one of them is a trough, into which hot water was constantly pouring from a pipe in the dome above. The whole apartment was full of steam.

On entering this chamber a scene presented itself which beggars description. My companions had prepared me for seeing many persons undressed; but imagine my astonishment on finding at least thirty women of all ages, and many young girls and children, perfectly unclothed. You will scarcely think it possible that no one but ourselves had a vestige of clothing. Persons of all colours, from the black and glossy shade of the negro to the fairest possible hue of complexion, were formed in groups, conversing as though full dressed, with perfect *nonchalance*, while others were strolling about, or sitting round the fountain. I cannot describe the bath as altogether a beautiful scene; in truth, in some respects it is disgusting; and I regret that I can never reach a private room in any bath without passing through the large public apartment.[†]

I will turn to the more agreeable subject—the operation of the bath, which is quite luxurious. The sensation experienced on first entering the hottest chamber is almost overpowering—the heat is extremely oppressive; and at first I believed that I could not long support such a temperature; but after the first minute, I was relieved by a gentle, and afterwards by a profuse perspiration, and no longer felt in any degree oppressed. It is always necessary for each lady to send her own bathing-linen, a pair of high clogs, a large copper vessel for hot water, two copper bowls, and towels.

The first operation is a gentle kneading the flesh, or champooing. Next the attendant cracks the joints of those who desire to submit to this process. I confess I did not suffer such an infliction. Some of the native women after this are rubbed with a rasp, or rather with two rasps of different kinds, a coarse one for the feet, and a fine one for the body; but neither of these rasps do I approve. A small coarse woollen bag, into which the operator's hand is inserted, is in my opinion preferable. Next the head and face are covered with a thick lather, which is produced by rubbing soap on a handful of fibres of the palm-tree, which are called leef, and which form a very agreeable and delicate-looking rubber. It is truly ridiculous to see another under this operation. When her head and face have been well lathered, and the soap has been thoroughly washed off by abundance of hot water, a novice would suppose that at least *they* were sufficiently purified; but this is not the case: two or three of such latherings, and as many washings, are necessary before the attendant

---

[†]An interesting aspect of the Turkish bath is presented by Lady Mary Wortley Montagu, in a letter dated 1 April 1717: she sees the naked women walking and moving "with the same majestic grace which Milton describes of our general mother," and that "there were many amongst them as exactly proportioned as ever any goddess was drawn by the pencil of Guido or Titian" (*Turkish Embassy Letters*, 59).

thinks her duty to the head and face accomplished. Then follows the more agreeable part of the affair,—the general lathering and rubbing, which is performed by the attendant so gently, and in so pleasant a manner, that it is quite a luxury; and I am persuaded that the Eastern manner of bathing is highly salubrious, from its powerful effect upon the skin.

When the operation was completed, I was enveloped in a dry piece of drapery, similar to the bathing-dress, and conducted to the reposing-room, where I was rubbed and dressed, and left to take rest and refreshment, and to reflect upon the strange scene which I had witnessed. I wish I could say that there are no drawbacks to the enjoyment of the luxury I have described; but the eyes and ears of an Englishwoman must be closed in the public bath in Egypt before she can fairly enjoy the satisfaction it affords; for besides the very foreign scenes which cannot fail to shock her feelings of propriety, the cries of the children are deafening and incessant. The perfection of Eastern bathing is therefore rather to be enjoyed in a private bath, with the attendance of a practised velláneh.[†]

[†]Usually called *bellana*.

Letter XXX

April, 1844

My Dear Friend,

I REMEMBER writing, in my simplicity, that I believed Mohammad 'Alee Páshá to have but two wives; but having been introduced to another of his wives, the mother of Haleem Bey, in his hareem in the citadel, I conjecture that there is yet another, making the full Muslim allowance, namely, four wives.

The ride to the citadel is not an agreeable one, and at this time the ascent is attended with some danger, as the Páshá has directed the repair of the road leading from the Báb el Wezeer; in consequence of which heaps of stones and rubbish almost obstruct the way. I had chosen this route because it is unpaved, and my experience had made me dread the slippery paved entrance by the Great Gate, mounted, as I was, on a "high ass." Although expecting a tumble in riding over the rubbish, I could not help remarking the enormous size of some stones which had been thrown down from an old wall, so much resembling stones which lie scattered around the pyramids, that I do not doubt they are some which were transported by Karakoosh when he was employed in building the citadel.

The Kasr appropriated to the hareem of the Páshá in the citadel is a noble mansion, the finest domestic structure I have seen in Egypt. The interior is on the usual Turkish plan. On the ground floor is a spacious saloon, paved with marble of a blueish white, nearly surrounded by suites of apartments which open into it; and on the first floor are rooms on the same plan. Accompanied by my friend Mrs. Lieder, I passed from the principal entrance to a large square court, and having crossed this, we found ourselves in the lower of the two saloons. We then ascended by an ample marble staircase to the saloon on the first floor. Here a most magnificent prospect burst upon our view: three windows which are opposite the head of the stairs, command the whole of Cairo, and the plain beyond; and every object of interest to the north and west of Cairo within the reach of our sight lay in picturesque variety before our admiring gaze; the green carpet of the Delta, and the plain of Goshen, terminating the view towards the north. I would willingly have lingered here, but our attendants were impatient to conduct us into the presence of the chief lady.

We found her sitting in a room which was carpeted and surrounded by a divan, attended by three ladies. She received us with much respect and cordiality, and as I had been informed that she had the reputation of being an exceedingly haughty person, I was agreeably surprised by finding in her conversation and deportment the utmost affability and politeness. She conversed with me freely of my children, told me that her son was under twenty years of age, and introduced to my notice two nice little girls, children of the hareem, one of whom presented me with a *bouquet*. The subject of the number, health, and age of each lady's children is always the darling theme of conversation in the hareems, and truly to a mother ever agreeable. One lady asked me with perfect gravity, whether one of my boys, being thirteen years of age, was married. I conclude she meant betrothed, for the same word is used to express marriage and betrothal. I explained to her that, in England, a boy must become a man before he thinks of marriage, or even betrothal; and that if he entered into the marriage state at twenty years of age, and a girl at fifteen, they would be considered too young. The lady whom I addressed, and her companion, listened with much attention, and one of them earnestly maintained that the English were quite right in objecting to such young marriages as take place constantly in the East.

With respect to the beauties in this hareem, I can only say that one was very remarkable; and among the ornaments that I saw there, there was nothing deserving of particular notice excepting the pearl necklaces of the chief lady and two others: these were composed of the largest pearls that I have ever seen, but nearly tight round the throat.

On quitting this hareem, I was conducted by the ladies with the ceremony I have not described, which was that of holding the háberah on each side, while I crossed the saloons, and until I reached the hareem curtain. These attendant ladies, in imitation of their superiors, vied with each other in paying us every polite attention, and each and all in the hareem of the citadel were pictures of cheerfulness and good humour.

I was informed that no Franks had ever before been admitted into this hareem, and I believe it to be the case; though a portion of the same building, entered from the other side, and in which the Páshá has some rooms fitted up in the European manner, has been frequently seen by travellers. Some European ladies, a short time since, offered twenty dollars to procure admission, and were refused. I did not offer a bribe; for I never have condescended to obtain access to a hareem through the servants, and have either been introduced by my kind friend Mrs. Lieder, or paid my visit without any explanation to the slaves, and have never met with the slightest opposition. On quitting, it is necessary to give a present to the chief eunuch, or to the door-keeper.

After paying this visit, I called on my old friends, the hareem of Habeeb Efendee; and I confess I approached their house with some apprehension that, instead of their usual hearty welcome, I might meet with a cold reception, during the present state of things. England and France having lately required of the Sultán a concession which every Christian must ardently desire, but which it is almost impossible for him, as a Muslim sovereign, to grant, and the result being not yet known, it was particularly agreeable to our feelings, in visiting his near relations, to find the whole family prepared to welcome us with even more than their usual affection. The ladies in that hareem being particularly well informed, the conversation during our visit takes always a lively, and often a political turn; and as soon as we were seated yesterday, the passing events were discussed, and the question of liberty of conscience on religious subjects soon introduced. But here I must digress, to remark to you one circumstance which much pleased me. While I was in conversation with a lady who was sitting next to me, we both heard the whole company, consisting of the daughters and several visitors, suddenly rise, and, following their example immediately, I observed that the chief lady was entering the room. Very delightful is this outward respect for parents, which is not here, as in England, confined to a few of the families of the great; and when accompanied with that devotion of heart so evident in the conduct of the daughters of Habeeb Efendee. Their veneration for their amiable mother is complete; while they are permitted by her, in their conversation and manners, to indulge in the sweetest familiarity of affection.

This good lady saluted us in her usual charming manner, and took her seat, placing me, as she always has done, on her right hand; after which all resumed their places, and she listened with extreme interest to our conversation, which was translated to her into Turkish by her daughters. In common with all the Turkish ladies I have seen in this country, the wife of Habeeb Efendee speaks sufficient Arabic for the usual purposes of conversation; but when any particularly interesting topic is discussed, they all like it explained in their own language.

The eldest daughter requested to be informed particularly of the nature of the demand lately made by England and France on the Sultán; and when it was explained that he was required to protect from martyrdom such persons who, having been originally Christian, had become Muslims, and subsequently returned to their profession, she replied, with an earnestness of manner which interested my friend and me extremely, "It is but the fulfilment of prophecy! When I was a little child, I was taught that, in this year, great things would commence, which would require three years for their completion."

Surely she drew a beautiful conclusion, and under circumstances, too, of painful feelings to one strictly attached to the laws of her religion. And here I must faithfully observe, that I have not met with this lady's equal in Eastern female society, in gentleness, sweetness, and good sense; and, withal, she had decidedly a cultivated mind. The Hon. Mrs. Damer has very agreeably described this lady in her 'Tour,'[†] and has particularly mentioned her affection for her mother. I must not omit to tell you of the curiosity of

---

[†]Mrs. G.L. Damer, *Diary of a Tour in Greece, Turkey and Egypt* 1841.

the whole hareem on the subject of Mrs. Damer's book. They had been informed that she had described them, and questioned us closely on the subject. We had much pleasure in assuring them that the description in that lady's work consisted in honourable mention of her reception by the hareem, and of their agreeable manners, and perfect politeness and cordiality. They inquired the exact period of her visit, that they might perfectly recall her to their recollection. Secluded as they are, they remember the visits of Europeans as eras in their lives; and I am persuaded that they feel the pleasure they so agreeably express when we pay them a visit.

Mrs. Lieder has shown them the portrait of the present Sultán in Mrs. Damer's book; and the eldest daughter has made a copy of it in colours, very creditable to a Turkish lady. It will doubtless excite great interest in every visiter of the family; and, unless protected by a glass, it will perhaps, in the course of a few weeks, be kissed entirely away, like a miniature portrait of a Turkish grandee of which I was lately told.

LETTER I
(Second Series)

January, 1845

AFTER a residence of nearly three years in an Eastern country, in the habit of frequent and familiar intercourse with the ladies of the higher and middle classes of its population, you will probably think me able to convey some general ideas of their moral and social state. To do this, I find to be a task of extreme difficulty; though my opportunities of observation have been such as, I believe, few Englishwomen have enjoyed. In examining the effects of the peculiar position in which females are here placed, I have endeavoured to divest myself of prejudice; but altogether to lose sight of our English standards of propriety has been impossible; and as every state of society in the world has its defects, to avoid comparisons would be unnatural.

One thing that puzzles me among many others is this: that the main principle of the constitution of society prevailing now among all the Muslim nations, and even among the Eastern Christians, seems almost to receive a sanction from the practice of most of those persons whom from our childhood we have learned to regard with the greatest reverence.

In the mention of the veil we trace the Hareem system to the time of Abraham; but to what period its origin is to be referred is, I believe, doubtful. In Abraham's time it seems to have been similar to the system which has hitherto prevailed among the Arabs of the desert, and to have been much less strict than that which commonly obtains among the Arabs and other Muslims established in fixed abodes, in cities, houses, and villages. Rebekah covered not her face in the presence of Abraham's servant, the "eldest servant of his house;" but when she came before the man who was to be her husband, "she took a veil, and covered herself." In like manner, the women of the Bedawees, in general, are often careless of veiling the face before servants, and persons with whom they are familiar; and many of them have no scruple in appearing unveiled before strangers. When Abraham, or rather Abram, before the case above mentioned, went into Egypt with his wife, "the Egyptians beheld the woman, that she was very fair: the princes also of Pharaoh saw her, and commended her before Pharaoh, and the woman was taken into Pharaoh's house." After this, Abimelech also saw her, and took her.

It seems probable that the Hareem system, at this period, prevailed only, and in a lax manner, among the Semitic nations. We find no indications of it in the sculptures or paintings representing scenes of domestic life upon the ancient Egyptian monuments; some of which are anterior to the age of

184

Abraham; on the contrary, in these representations of private life we see evidences of a state of society as free, with respect to the intercourse of the sexes, as that which prevails in modern Europe. Were the ancient Egyptians a more moral people, with this freedom of the women, than the contemporary nations among whom the females were more or less secluded? I am told that the reverse appears to have been the case: that proofs of the most shocking licentiousness, or, at least, of an utter want of feeling in each sex with respect to the other, are conspicuous upon the walls of the temples and tombs throughout the valley of the Nile. But I would not refer the licentiousness, or want of delicacy, of the ancient Egyptians to the freedom allowed to their women; as I am fully satisfied that virtuous women are far more common in Christian Europe than in the Eastern Hareems. Indeed, where there is in a woman a tendency to indelicacy in words or actions, it is certainly checked by social intercourse with men; and it is as certainly promoted by seclusion from them. Eastern women, essentially virtuous, are so accustomed, among themselves, to language which, to us, is grossly indelicate, that they often use it with the utmost simplicity, even in the presence of men. This, in my opinion, is one of the worst effects of the system of the Hareem.

Do not imagine that this is the beginning of an attempt to generalize, and to unravel the perplexing difficulties presented by this strange system. It is true that I have sometimes felt inclined to try my hand at a general picture of Eastern domestic life. The persons who would figure in it would, of course, be almost all females. But I must resist the temptation; for I am sure that I should not succeed in the undertaking. You will perhaps say that this is a modest avowal. By no means is this the case, in my opinion; for I do not believe that any one who would impose upon himself such a task, could satisfy himself or others. I shall therefore content myself with offering to you detached sketches; and you may amuse yourself by trying if you can put them together so as to make a consistent whole. You will, I fancy, find them to resemble a dissected map, which some naughty child played with in such a careless manner as to lose many of the pieces; so that some of the pieces will fit together very well; others will fit only on one side; and others will not fit at all, or can only be made to suit imperfectly by turning them upside-down. To make it the more amusing to you, I shall present to you the pieces in some degree of disorder.

One important circumstance must be ever borne in mind in taking into consideration the state of Eastern society with reference to marriage; I mean the great similarity which exists in the minds of the people, both males and females. In Europe, preference depends on many causes—a woman prefers her husband for the peculiar tone of his mind, his religious opinions, and his moral code; and even his political views often form the groundwork of harmony or dissension; while his love for learning and scientific pursuits, or his talent for the fine arts, or his genius developing itself in any way, render him attractive to her, or the contrary. All these reasons for preference, or (in the absence of them) motives for dislike, exist in Europe, but have no place in the East. It is true there are a few educated Eastern men, among those who have studied in Europe; but they have no idea of communicating their information to their families, nor do they, with very few exceptions, desire the education of their ladies: therefore the notions they have acquired abroad are perhaps never discussed. It is my idea that if an Eastern husband be found by his bride, young, good-looking, and good-natured, she is perfectly satisfied, for she knows that her parents or protectors could not offer her a companion whose religious opinions and general views did not entirely coincide with her own.

It is pleasant to feel sure that there are instances, and that those instances are not uncommon, where an Eastern wife, when suitably married, gives her affection to her husband with a devotion which can hardly be surpassed, and receives from him every proof of tender and honourable love. I could give several examples of families thus happily circumstanced among our acquaintance, but they would too much resemble each other.

Among the females with whom I am acquainted, natives of this city, is one who has been for more than thirty years the wife of one husband, her first and only one, and whose home offers me much to approve and admire. Her husband seems to be possessed of much generosity, and of many other good qualities. His house, though he is a person of small income, is a kind of refuge for the destitute; not only for swarms of poor relations, but also for destitute dogs and cats; which he feeds, not with the relics or refuse of his table, but with piles of bread brought expressly for them. One of the most amiable of the traits in his wife's character is her devotion to his relations. While his mother lived, she was regarded and treated by her as her own parent; and, according to the usual custom of the East (a custom which I cannot too much applaud, and which is sufficient to make me overlook many faults in Eastern females), was always respected by her as the mistress of the house.

As another instance, I may mention a Turkish lady of rank who married many years ago to one of her own countrymen holding a distinguished position. He had about ten white slaves, who became the immediate attendants of his wife, and numerous black slaves, as inferior servants. The chief lady, an only wife, became the mother of several children, *therefore* she retained her priority both in his Hareem and in her husband's affection. Several of the white slaves became the concubines of their master, but he took no second *wife*; and I do not understand that the peace of his lady was ever disturbed by jealous misgivings. Indeed, as an Eastern wife, she had no right to admit such feelings, being especially favoured. When, as in this case, an amiable woman responds to the affection of a worthy husband, their Hareem is, in her estimation, a paradise, for she has no wish beyond the society of her own family, her husband, and her children, and no desire for amusement beyond occasional fairy-like fêtes, of which her own home is the scene. Do not mistake me when I style a man a *worthy husband* who possesses concubines; I mean worthy by comparison: and when I find some whose manners and general bearing show them to be, in a moral sense, superior to their fellows, I am induced to pity those failings which arise from education, and to lament those sins against which they have no law. Until enlightened by the truths of the Gospel, no important reformation can be effected in the Hareem system, nor in the general morals of the East; and I am inclined to think that centuries may elapse before any material change can be produced: so strong are the people's prejudices, and so firmly rooted are their habits of seclusion.[†]

You may probably ask me how I can know the happiness of these and other families. I should therefore tell you that, in this country, people do not conceal their domestic unhappiness, but invariably weary their friends and acquaintance with their complaints on this subject, whenever they have any to make.

This leads me to remark what is most extraordinary. When an Eastern husband believes himself to be dishonoured by his wife, he publishes his misfortune and disgrace to all his neighbours, and often to strangers, and the relations of each party do the same; even when such conduct may occasion a divorce, or the loss of the life of the accused. The wife, too, seems to endeavour to make the suspicion or charge to which she has become obnoxious as extensively known as she can.

A few days ago, in a house adjacent to ours, a woman was screaming from a window, "O my neighbours! O Muslims! hear what this wicked man, my husband, with whom I have lived for years, and to whom I have borne children, says of me!" Then, in none of the most delicate terms, she proceeded to explain the charge brought against her by him; while he contented himself by interrupting her with the information that the Kádee[‡] should soon set her at liberty.

In the middle and lower classes, it is not unusual for a man to be betrothed to a *little child*; and it often happens that the child, on seeing him, refuses to accept him as her husband. In such a case the man is compelled by law either to divorce the girl, or to maintain her for a certain time, limited or extended according to circumstances. Sometimes such a state of things continues for several years; but the period depends much upon the disposition of the suitor or the humour of the girl. It is a sort of probation, during which the proposed husband is permitted to visit her in the presence of her parents or guardian. Her pleasure is entirely consulted; and sometimes, being won by jewels or sweetmeats, according to her lover's resources, she will profess a growing affection for him.

[†] Urquhart thought that "the only changes that can be beneficial to Turkey, must come invisibly and slowly; and such benefits reside solely in individual instruction, in rendering literature popular and useful, in the extension of the principles, and in the application of the results of science . . . . It is only after *they* have become acquainted thoroughly with Europe, that they can know what to imitate" (*Spirit of the East*, 401).

[‡] The judge.

How strange would you think the lives of the Arab women, especially those of the lower orders! The story of one, whose early history is much the same as that of many girls in her sphere of life, will serve as an illustration. She lost her parents when a child, and was consigned to the care of a half-sister, a sort of relation with which the East abounds. At the age of thirteen she was married to a man considerably her senior, with whom she lived two years; but she was so thoroughly discontented, that at the end of that period the man divorced her by her own desire. Thus, at fifteen years of age she was seeking a second husband; and being rather pretty, and gracefully formed, she early attracted the notice of several men, but received most favourably the attentions of a remarkably plain boy, who had been brought up by the half-sister I have mentioned. He possessed a proud spirit, and an unconquerably bad temper; and under all these disadvantageous circumstances the elder sister naturally objected to his proposal. When, however, the *divorcée's* term of single life according to the Muslim law had expired,[†] the elder girl was called from home for a few days: the devoted lovers took advantage of her absence, and she found them one on her return. Although, as many have shown before, marriage is far from being here an indissoluble tie, yet it is a very serious step; and this miserable child had linked herself to wretchedness little understood in England. For a short time, things wore a decent aspect: the husband hired a coffee-shop, and took her home two piastres per day: but by degrees he neglected her, giving her no means of support; and at the end of two years, and just after the death of their only child, he deserted her. She was then about seventeen years of age, a year ago.

A young man who had for some months regarded her with admiration, and to whom she had given many opportunities of seeing her unveiled, came boldly forward, and proposed to her; asserting that he could induce her husband (if he could find him) to divorce her, by paying him a sum of money. She did not receive his proposal with indifference; but did not absolutely consent to the plan of bribing her husband. Her lover endeavoured to secure her affection by making her presents from time to time; all of which she condescendingly received; and matters went on thus for a month, at the end of which, most unexpectedly, the husband returned. Scarcely had he passed a night in his house when some kind friend informed him that he was not the happiest of men, and directed his attention to his wife's admirer. Fickle as you must acknowledge her character, or rather her conduct, to have been, there was a pulse in her heart which beat yet true to her husband; and never, but under circumstances of heartless desertion, would she for a moment have entertained a

---

[†]According to the law, a woman is not allowed to remarry another man after divorce until three menstrual periods have elapsed, to be sure there is no pregnancy. Menawhile, the divorcing husband has the right to reclaim his wife during that period if he has divorced her only twice.

preference for his good-looking rival. Now he had returned, and although I never heard that he gave any explanation of his conduct, he was with her, and that was enough: she loved him better than all the world besides. For some weeks he persecuted her most unmercifully; and in vain she protested that she preferred him before all others; he and his family reviled her almost incessantly, until, one day, she ventured to reply with some warmth to his invectives; he beat her so cruelly that she rushed from her house and sought refuge with us.

I thought then the ruffian had gone too far for forgiveness. Not at all: on the following day she returned to him, only requiring from him a promise that he would not repeat his violence. This devotion on her part met with no response; and he continued a course of torturing ill-treatment, until, in the hurry of passion, he exclaimed, "You are divorced." It was the *third* time he had done so, and the law of triple divorce is one of the strictest in the Muslim code. The girl by law was free. Had it been the first or the second time, he could have obliged her return, but now to become again his wife would be to renounce her religion; and to bring upon her head the deepest disgrace.[†] That was a time of penitence for her cruel persecutor; and he severely regretted that he had placed it in the power of his young wife to marry his hated rival. The latter naturally came forward, believing that all circumstances now at least favoured his hopes: but her constancy triumphed. She saw her husband, and saw his sorrow, and, renouncing every consideration but his happiness, she braved the torrent of abuse which poured forth upon her from every quarter; the anathemas of her sister, the reproaches of her acquaintance, and, as on her bridal day, gave her whole heart to her husband. *He* was softened: she had proved to him that he had no rival in her affections, and proved it by sacrifices even he could not gainsay; and he has become a better husband, and it is hoped a better man. He takes her home, as at first, two piastres per day; he attends to his business, and evinces something like kindness and consideration.

How strange (to our English ideas) would have been her condition had she married her admirer. Her jealous persecutor would undoubtedly have haunted her footsteps, and perhaps have threatened her life; for he sets a selfish value on the poor girl, which, in itself, has forged her fetters. And how much more strange is it to know that it is a common thing for a woman to marry a third—a fourth—I do not like to say how many husbands, while she might meet every day men to whom she had been attached by the same tie. There is one thing alone which can revise such a state of things—one holy influence—it is, and must be, Christianity.

[†]Not to "renounce her religion," but to go against the religious tenets of the law that strictly forbids a remarriage between the former husband and wife after the man has divorced the woman three times. Cohabitation would then definitely be illegal and therefore sinful.

LETTER II
(Second Series)

March, 1845

SOME of my country men seem to be inclined to regard with approbation, in several respects, the laws and customs relating to marriage, and the separation of the sexes, as prevailing in this and other Muslim countries. I think that my brother (who is not one of the persons above alluded to) has pointed out the chief advantages resulting from this state of things. After remarking that "The respect in which trade is held by the Muslim greatly tends to enlarge the circle of his acquaintance with persons of different ranks," he adds, "freedom of intercourse with his fellow-men is further and very greatly promoted by the law of the separation of the sexes, as it enables him to associate with others, regardless of difference of wealth or station, without the risk of occasioning unequal matrimonial connexions. The women, like the men, enjoy extensive intercourse with persons of their own sex."[1] Hence they enjoy a domestic quiet unknown to us, in general, in the West; and much more might doubtless be said in the way of apology for these laws and customs: but all the good that can possibly result from them is greatly outweighed by evil. Besides that greatest of all abominations sanctioned by Muslim law and usage, the custom of polygamy, and the facility of divorce,† which is its necessary consequence, there are innumerable minor kindred evils to be deplored. One of the worst of these, in my opinion, is the early marriage of boys.

It is a common thing to see a sweet intelligent youth, from whose manners and conversation the fairest promise may be deduced, growing up to the age of fourteen years, or perhaps fifteen, with his mind little tainted by example. When, however, he has attained those years, he is attacked by the Hareem of his father on the subject of marriage; and his mother especially urges upon her child the necessity of an early contract. The boy of course consents: there is something so manly in having his own Hareem, that he is far from being averse to the arrangement. He is married; and at once degenerates into a selfish, sensual character. No art is left untried, no means of fascination are neglected, no attainable luxury is unemployed to secure to his Hareem his exclusive attention. In some instances, after a lapse of years, the victim sobers down into a worthy husband; but more frequently he continues

---

[1]'*Modern Egyptians*,' Part i. Ch. 8.
†For the man.

through life the slave of self-indulgence. The change in the powers of the mind immediately consequent upon this, can hardly be imagined. The sharp, intelligent boy is quickly transformed into a dull, heavy blockhead. It is very generally observed that the promise given by the youth of mental excellence is rarely fulfilled by the man. It is curious that, though the Arabs are surprisingly quick in learning, at least four-fifths of their literature consist of little more than compilations. Talent generally lasts with them, but very seldom genius.

Boys, however, are never united to those who are older than themselves (I know but one instance of a young man being the husband of an elderly woman); while poor girls are often given in marriage to men old enough to be their grand-fathers. Most of these children accept their offered husbands from a feeling of duty towards the parents who have selected them. I need scarcely say how wretched in almost every case are the consequences of such unions. The case to which I have referred above (of an elderly woman married to a young man),was that of the sister of a grandee. She requested her brother to select for her a husband; he expressed some disgust at this proposal, but she became importunate, and he consented; and informed her that if she were determined on marrying, she should accept a certain person, whom he named. She objected to his selection, perhaps because the man he mentioned was very young; but he replied, that he was determined she should accept him, or no one. The proposed husband, on receiving the communication, could only say that he was grateful for the honour intended him; though this, you may be sure, was far from being true. Shortly, they were married; and the young Bey, on being introduced to his wife, found an elderly lady, who received him with much kindness, but who assured him that she had merely married him as a matter of form, that she had done so by compulsion, and that, considering the disparity in their years, she had provided for him a young and handsome Abyssinian slave, whom she desired he would consider his future wife. He believed her to be in earnest, and it is not surprising that he did so; for though it is very unusual for a wife to act in this manner, she appeared to apologize by noticing her own years, and his youth. He accepted the Abyssinian; and discovered, sadly too late, that the whole had been a scheme to try his allegiance. His wife has ever since requited him by taunts and revilings; and let no one suppose that the Hareem of —— Bey can, during his tormentor's lifetime, be considered as his home.

A very prevalent cause of misery in the Hareems of the great is the custom, so common among the grandees, of marrying their female relations and their emancipated female slaves to persons much beneath them in rank; for the men who are honoured by having such wives bestowed upon them seldom fail to find themselves victims of abominable tyranny; as Sir John Malcolm, in his delightful 'Sketches of Persia,' has very pleasantly shown to be the case in that country.

Another cause is the want of unanimity among the children of a Hareem in which there is a plurality of mothers. The plan of allotting a distinct suite of apartments to each wife does not separate the children of different mothers. They meet in the general saloons, in the gardens, and in the courts; and the quarrels of children grow with them into the grave disputes of youth; while envy and jealousy with regard to their mother's privileges, and their own, often increase to deadly hatred. Being but *half* brothers and sisters, they have no parents in common to whom to refer their differences; and they nurse them in their own breasts until they find some means of revenging their real or supposed wrongs. I know a great Hareem where the children of the wives and slaves are of all ages; some of the sons are nearly forty years of age; some have grown to man's estate, and some are boys. The younger ones alone are perfectly at liberty in the Hareem of their father: the elder ones have their own establishments, and seldom meet; but they are examples of envy and discord when circumstances throw them together; and their feuds will, I doubt not, ere long give rise to very deplorable consequences.

I have not hitherto touched on one most important point, the gravest of all objections to the Hareem system: that the dignity of a great Hareem cannot be supported, nor indeed can such an establishment subsist, without slaves. In such a Hareem there must be male guardians; and these the law requires to be eunuchs: there must also be female attendants; and experience has often shown that, when these are free servants, the whole family is broken up, and some members of it perhaps lose their lives, in consequence of intrigues conducted by such servants. There can be no doubt but that many of the thousands of little strangers, of every shade of complexion, who are annually brought into Egypt, forget their parents and their fatherland, and, experiencing much of indulgence and consideration, contract for their possessors nearly that affection which, under happier circumstances, would have been bestowed where Heaven first directed it. That such may be the case was lately shown to me by a remarkable instance.

A Turkish woman, residing at this time in Cairo, was left a widow some years since with one son. Her establishment consisted of several slaves and servants; and among the former was a boy who had been tenderly brought up by his mistress from a very early age, and had been emancipated. He had been carefully educated with her own son, who holds a place under the present government, and could speak and write several languages. Ascertaining that his mistress had become straitened in her circumstances since the death of her husband, and observing that her son relaxed in his duty towards her, and neglected also to perform those offices which his situation under government required, consequently that her means of comfort were reduced and her spirit broken, bethought himself that by his own exertions these evils might be mitigated. He accordingly applied for and obtained a situation as interpreter with a man of importance, who was enabled to present him with a place under government of considerable emolument after he had served him creditably during rather more than two years. In the meantime, his mistress's circumstances had become increasingly distressing: her son had forsaken her, and her heart was well-nigh broken, when, on a happy day, her slave rushed into her house, threw himself at her feet, and earnestly begged that she would honour him by sharing his good fortune. Never was consent more cheerfully given. The happy slave purchased a handsome house, into which his mistress immediately removed; and in doing so he made but one condition, that the designation of mistress should be exchanged for that of mother. He has since married; but his adopted mother has lost nothing by this circumstance. She is, and she will be as long as she lives, the chief lady of his household.

Such cases are not uncommon, but no argument deduced from instances of this kind can more than mitigate the horrors of a traffic which tears asunder the dearest, closest ties, and which gives a power over our fellow-creatures so often abused even to the death. Among all the many evils attending humanity in the present day, few exceed this making merchandise of our kind. It is true that England has raised her powerful voice, and stretched forth her successful arm, to preserve inviolate the home of the Western African, but much, ay, very much remains for her to do ere liberty will be held sacred, and the Eastern mother press her own child to her bosom, with the conviction that the tyranny of man cannot deprive her of that sweet and precious gift of God.

It often occurs to me that the blessings which we enjoy in England are very insufficiently prized until we travel in other and distant lands. What I chiefly allude to, among the blessings of England, are those which affect the people rather than the country. As far as nature is concerned, I ought not to complain of Egypt; for, with the exception of the great heat of summer, the hot winds of spring, and the occasional visits of the plague in the latter season, the climate of this country is considered by almost all who know it to be one of the finest and most salubrious in the world. The regularity of its seasons is most remarkable; and it is seldom disturbed by any frightful natural phenomena, such as hurricanes and the like. We were, however, much alarmed early in the morning of the 21st of last month, by a severe shock of an earthquake. It was perfectly dark, when we were all awoke by tremendous shaking, accompanied by a loud rumbling noise. Our house cracked fearfully, and seemed as though set upon wheels, and rapidly shaken to and fro. Some persons thought that the shock lasted three minutes: we thought that it lasted less than one minute; of course I mean from the time that it awoke us, but I can never forget the feeling of awe which possessed me then and after the shock. The motion leaving us no room for speculation, we all lay awake, longing for the morning, and fearing that we should hear of many evil results, while we considered the miserable state of the houses in general in Cairo, The morning, however, came, and brought with it no bad news.

Providentially, no person was injured further than by experiencing extreme alarm. A man and his wife, living in a neighbouring street, jumped from a first-floor window into the street, believing that if they remained in the house they should be buried in the ruins; and there, wrapped in one blanket, they remained until it became light. Whole families assembled in the courts of their houses; and an acquaintance of ours, an Englishman, so completely lost his presence of mind, that he could not for a long time remember whether he was in Egypt or not. No wonder: had I been, as he was, with only servants in the house, I might have been as much bewildered; but as such occurrences promote sociability, I and my boys made ourselves as comfortable as we could, by joining company under one musquito-net, feeling unspeakably the benefit of companionship. There is not on record any account of disastrous consequences from earthquakes in Egypt; and although this is not a proof that such will never be the case, it is an argument in favour of feeling something like security. The prophecy of our blessed Lord that "there shall be earthquakes in divers places," was instantly in my mind when awoke by that awful shock, nor did I dare to hope that the cause for alarm would so soon and so mercifully subside.

You can hardly imagine what various scenes present themselves to one looking from the window of a house in one of the great thoroughfare-streets, such as that in which we are now living, in this most strange city of Cairo; which, by the way, should no longer be called "Grand Cairo:" for it is now a city of miserable ruins, interspersed with mosques, once magnificent, but now in general falling or fallen to decay, and with comparatively few modern houses, of *which* the paltry nature of the architecture contrasts very singularly with that of the picturesque, but tottering, older dwellings among which they rise. Bridal and funeral processions very often disturb our tranquillity, the former on Mondays and Thursdays, the most propitious days for such ceremonies; the latter, almost every day.

I have read accounts of refractory Muslim saints who have, after death, resisted being carried to any place of burial excepting one on which, it is supposed by many, they had fixed their choice. A few days since I saw a procession attending the bier of one of that most singular fraternity. Instead of the usual wailing, men were shouting and women screaming for joy, and uttering the zaghareet; while the beating of drums rendered the confusion of sounds complete. Scarcely had the hundreds following the bier passed our house, when the tide of human beings seemed checked, and in another minute rushed back with impetuosity. The saint had raised his hands, they said, and the bearers of the bier felt themselves forcibly prevented from proceeding by the way they intended. The Welee had first travelled east; now he travelled west; and we concluded that he was content. But a few hours after, the procession again passed our house; the people running with the bier; and men, women, and children increasing in numbers every minute;

and I do believe that nine-tenths of the multitude believed that the bearers were super-naturally withheld from carrying the bier their own way on every occasion that they changed their course. As in the morning, so again in the afternoon, the attempt to carry their burden eastward failed; and in nearly as short a time as before, they turned and retraced their steps. When almost opposite to our house they made a stand, and that was a moment of some uneasiness; for it was possible that they might insist upon raising a tomb in the very thoroughfare, or even in our house. Such things have been done, and the tomb of a Welee has prevented the possibility of anything of consider-able size passing through some of the principal streets of Cairo. In opening the new road to the citadel, by order of the Páshá, the tomb of a Welee was taken down, but is now being rebuilt nearly in the centre of the road; because, it is said, the Páshá's sleep has been disturbed by the saint's night-ly visitations, requiring restitution of his rights. Our fears that the restless Welee would become a neighbour, were quieted by the bearers rushing for-ward as if impelled by something that seemed to urge them onward. For that night we heard no more of the saint; but on the following day we found that his bearers had had no rest but for one quarter of an hour, during which their burden was content to stay in the tomb of his parents. During that day the same game was played as on the preceding, until towards evening, when those persons most nearly interested in the arrangements of the interment commenced the preparation of a tomb, with which they pretended that he was content.

Another uncommon funeral procession, that of Khursheed Páshá, late Governor of Sennár,[†] passed our house a few days after that of the saint; and as it was the most remarkable of all such spectacles seen in Cairo since my arrival, I am induced to describe it to you. It was preceded by six camels, each bearing two boxes filled with corn and dates; above and between which sat the distributor, with a stick in his hand with which to drive off the crowd that pressed upon him, making as great a clamour as though they were all starving, and strange to say, the most decently dressed were the most impor-tunate. Then followed three camels with water, and then two buffaloes to be sacrificed at the tomb, and the flesh to be divided among the poor. These practices are always observed at the funerals of rich persons in Egypt, and I believe throughout the East. About thirty reciters of the Kur-an followed next, and about the same number of sheykhs headed a large body of Turks of the middle classes, chiefly wearing the military dress. Then followed a tribe of Chaooshes, two and two, in full uniform; and after these walked about fifty grandees of all ages. Their dresses were most picturesque; the varieties of colour they displayed rendering the group they formed by far the most strik-ing feature in the procession. There were among them some old men who

---

†In Sudan.

had doubtless seldom before walked in the streets of Cairo. One, bent with age, and apparently blind, was leaning on a youth who seemed to be his son; and many were much exhausted. They had all walked nearly a mile, and had to walk nearly a mile and a half farther; the last half-mile exposed to the burning sun. But to return to the order of the procession. Some boys walked next, each bearing a Kur-an; and they were immediately followed by a crowd of men bearing incense in silver censers, filling the streets and houses with clouds of frankincense and other perfumes; while others, carrying sprinkling-bottles of silver, showered their sweet contents around them on the more distinguished of the spectators. Then passed the bier, the appearance of which was not unusual; it was covered with a red figured Cashmere shawl, and borne by four men. The ladies, female slaves, and friends and attendants of the Hareem next folllowed, consisting of about twenty-five or thirty ladies mounted on high donkeys, and perhaps twenty slaves on ordinary donkeys, and a host on foot. All the last-mentioned screamed and wailed so loudly that the noise cannot easily be forgotten by those who have heard as well as seen a grand procession;- the mingling of noises, the reciters of the Kur-an, the chanting-boys, and the wailing-women, occasion a deafening yell hardly to be imagined. The led horses of the grandees bore up the rear, and thus concluded a spectacle as singular as almost any which can be witnessed in the streets of Cairo.

LETTER III
(Second Series)

AMONG the most singular of the customs observed in the Hareems of this country, are those which are consequent upon a death; and I think you will be entertained by an account of what is practised in a wealthy Christian Hareem on such an occasion. The scenes which I am about to describe to you were witnessed by my kind friend, Mrs. Lieder, and I shall give you the details nearly in her own words.

A few days ago, one of the richest of the Copts residing in this city sent to Mr. Lieder requesting him to send for an English physician, his wife being dangerously ill. Our friend sent immediately, but just when his messenger had returned, a servant arrived from the Copt saying that his mistress was dead. It is thus that the Copts generally act, waiting until the patient is at the point of death before they send for medical aid.

Mrs. Lieder forthwith went to the scene of mourning, and soon after her return brought me her memoranda of the strange observances which she had there witnessed. On arriving at the house, she says, I found the door thronged by the male friends of the master. I ascended to the apartments of the Hareem, and in doing so passed through the room in which the lady had died. Here everything was in a state of the utmost confusion; the bed and bed-clothes were left strewn about, evidently with intention; not a thing had been removed since the body had been washed and laid out. I then went into a large room, whence horrid screams and cries had assailed my ears; and there I found the corpse laid on a small bed or mattress on the floor, and covered with Cashmere shawls and richly embroidered crape veils. I was conducted to a place on the divan, near the head of the deceased: it was a dreadful sight, and the confusion and noise were most distressing. Two women were beating tambourines and singing dismal dirges, while about twenty ladies and hired wailing-women (such as we read of in the Scriptures) were crying aloud, and slapping, or rather beating themselves,[†] keeping time with the instruments. Other women, including the slaves, were jumping, and clapping their hands, while their bodies were bent almost double. Their performances strikingly reminded me of the American Indian dances described by Mr. Catlin, expressive of nothing less than frenzy. They continued their frantic gestures until they were nearly exhausted, when a sign was made for them to sit and rest.

[†] On the cheeks and breast.

197

Then followed the most interesting touching act of the drama. The relations sat nearest to the corpse, and each of them addressed it in turn, using
every endearing expression that love or friendship could suggest. Each held
in her hand a handkerchief, folded in the form of a bandelet; this was rapidly whirled round at the close of each address. All apostrophized the deceased;
slaves as well as relations. One cried, "Have I not loved thee, and have not
mine eyes worshipped thee?" Another, "Thou art young, my heart's treasure,
my beloved! O! thou art very young to leave thy husband, and thy mother!"
Another, a slave, cried, "I have made thy bread; must thou for ever leave thy
poor slave? O, my mistress, wilt thou no longer eat what my hands may prepare?" Then cried another slave, "Have I not cooked for thee the choicest
dainties? Wilt thou no longer remain with us? Canst thou leave us desolate?
O! come back again, my beloved! My mistress, come back, to thy wretched
slave; and she will prepare for thee sweetmeats with honey and sugar, and
perfumes, and use all her skill to please thee!" This was said by a very fat old
negro woman. One poor slave fainted several times, evidently from real affection combined with fatigue. It was astonishing that they could endure so
much excitement and exertion of mind and body.

The mother, of course, was the chief mourner. She wore a dark blue head-
veil and tób;[1] a pair of old trowsers formed part of the rest of her dress, and
around her head, over the veil above mentioned, was wound a narrow strip
of blue muslin, one of the principal insignia of mourning, as the crape hat-
band is in England. Her hands and feet were dyed with indigo. The mother-
in-law and her sisters were in like manner disfigured. I can never forget the
distracted manner in which the women of the family and the visitors conducted themselves, as, time after time, they renewed the jumping, or rather
dancing and screaming, around the corpse; how they rent their clothes, and
how they kissed the corpse, and then wept, and fell down exhausted. There
were present the ladies of all the principal scribes.[†] All of them I observed to
be in dark clothes; their tóbs, especially, were of dark and sombre hues. Pink,
and every bright colour, except blue, are considered unbecoming in the
house of mourning.

Until I had been there about an hour, I could hardly find leisure to turn my
eyes from the mourners, to examine the state of the apartment, which was
intentionally put into the utmost disorder. All kinds of broken glass, china,
and common earthenware were strewed upon the floor; and the rich Turkey
carpet, and the cushions and coverings of the divans, were all turned and
torn; the divan coverings being also intentionally soiled, smeared with indi-

---

[1] The large, loose silk dress worn over the indoor apparel and under the *habara* in
walking or riding
[†] Up until the middle of the twentieth century, Copts were customarily employed as
accountants and secretaries

go, and partly covered with bran and with strips of rag; together with broken ornaments and toys, and old books. The only thing left in its usual condition was an antique chair of dark wood inlaid with mother-of-pearl, surmounted by a canopy covered with red silk. A chair of this kind is generally found in a Copt's house; and upon it the turban is placed at bedtime. The walls were smeared with indigo;[1] and I observed the form of the Coptic cross marked in several places, expressly for the occasion, and, as it appeared to me, treated with dishonour, as though the inmates of the house were enraged even against Providence.

The time now arrived when the bridal garments of the departed young woman were brought; and the mourners whose office it was to do so began to strip the dead. I found, as I had expected, that the body had been washed, and wrapped in white cotton, but nothing further had been done. All the relations now quitted the room, leaving the body to the friends and the hired women. The first article of dress in which they clad the corpse was a pair of rich pink satin trowsers; they then put on a pair of new yellow morocco mezz (a kind of inner slipper); after this, a lace shirt; and next a magnificent long vest (a yelek) of gold brocade. Around the waist was wound a costly Cashmere shawl, and the attire was completed by a saltah (or jacket) of sky blue satin profusely embroidered with gold, together with a new faroodeeyeh (or kerchief) bound round the head, and a crape veil, one of those which I had first seen upon it. The face was fair and beautiful; characterized by a loveliness which is said to have cost the husband a very large dowry. The age of the deceased could not have been more than seventeen years. Her death was caused by childbirth, and this was the twelfth day from the commencement of her illness. While the corpse was being attired, the cries and exclamations were almost deafening, and those who surrounded it addressed it repeatedly, telling of the richness, beauty, and costliness of every article of dress, as each was put on. The next thing was to make the winding-sheet, which was a piece of satin interwoven with gold. In this the corpse, with its splendid and costly dress, was sewed up for burial.

The visitors, and I among them, now descended from the Hareem, and below we found a great number of high donkeys prepared for the friends and relations of the deceased. After most of them had mounted, the plain wooden bier was brought, and placed before the entrance of the Hareem; and the donkey-carpet upon which the deceased used to ride, and a small pillow for the head, were laid in it. The poor husband was then led forward to the bier. From the time of the death, neither he nor any of the male relations had seen the corpse. He seemed almost frantic, throwing himself upon the bier, and begging that he might be buried with his wife.

---

[1] All this description forcibly reminds me of the admirable story of the slave Káfoor, in 'The Thousand and One Nights.'

During the illness of his wife, some of the ladies of his family betook themselves to a celebrated picture of the Virgin, to address to it their prayers and complaints. This picture is in a private house, from which it is supposed it cannot be permanently removed: before it is a small table, on which candles are constantly kept burning; and it is held in great veneration. Its pretended miraculous properties are said to have been discovered by its having been transferred to a church, and found to have returned without hands, in the course of the night after its removal, to its former place! This wonderful picture the ladies above mentioned thought more likely than a physician to be a means of recovering their dying relation. As prayers addressed to it seemed unavailing, they had recourse to reproaches; crying out to it, "Do you not see the state of our dear relation? Are you blind? Are you deaf? Have you not power to heal her?—Is your power gone? You can recover her if you will! Arouse yourself!" From this and similar language, becoming enraged, they proceeded to *beating* the picture.[†]

I had no idea that persons of the higher class among the members of the Coptic Church, which was once so famous, and is still venerable for its antiquity, and for the firmness with which it has withstood persecutions too horrible to relate, could be in a state of darkness so deep as to behave in this absurd and shocking manner; and I grieve to tell you of it; but I do so that you may rejoice with me in the wise and energetic means which are employed in the present day to dispel it.

Of the numerous pupils attracted to the Missionary Institution, and the schools attached to it, in this city, a large proportion consists of children of the Copts. Here they and others enjoy the blessing of a liberal and Christian education. In the departments of the boys, the untiring zeal and excellent judgment of our highly respected friend the Reverend Mr. Lieder are in constant exercise in directing the native teachers, and labouring with them, with a devotion to which I imagine there are few parallels; while, in the female department, our dead friend Mrs. Lieder, whose life is one of extraordinary activity, and of most extensive benevolence, performs the duties of the like superintendence—duties requiring no small share of tact and knowledge, with very remarkable and gratifying success.

The Coptic Institution, to which the attention of Mrs. Lieder is principally directed, sends forth soundly educated young men to become members of the priesthood of their national Church, and has been distinguished by the high approbation of the Patriarch. Incalculable good may hence be expected to arise; for the Coptic priesthood is, in general, lamentably degraded by ignorance and superstition. In the Institution above mentioned are, at present, twenty-five pupils. Seventeen of these are boarders, who are respectably clad, and most comfortably lodged, and fed. In the boys' day-school attached

---

[†]Here end Mrs. Lieder's "memoranda."

to it, the average number of pupils attending is one hundred and twenty; composed of Christians, Jews, and Muslims; and in the girls' school, one hundred and twenty-five. Three hundred girls have left since the year 1835 (when the school was first opened),† able to read and write, and, if necessary, to earn their bread by embroidery and by other kinds of needlework; and, above all, having heard, and learned by heart, the important truths of Christianity. These girls are of different religions, like the boys.

It is interesting to observe the different countenances of Easterns of different countries in that overflowing schoolroom. Next to the well-known features of the Jewess, those of the Syrians are the most remarkable: so peculiar are the countenances of the latter, that after two were pointed out to me, I was able to separate others from those around them. In general, the Syrian girl has a high intelligent forehead, with arched eye-brows; large and long-shaped, soft, dark eyes; a fair complexion, a delicately formed aquiline nose, and small, pretty mouth. The face is long, with such a grave and sensible and thoughtful expression, that the little girl seems as though she carried an old head on young shoulders. There is no dimpled prettiness about the little Syrians; but a sort of dignified beauty, which, when matured, at the age of perhaps sixteen, is very striking: and the Syrian women retain their youthful appearance longer than any other Easterns that I know. Delicacy being their peculiar personal characteristic, they strangely contrast with the swarthy Arab child, whose good-tempered expressive mouth, and perfectly regular white teeth, comprise perhaps her only personal charms. The children of the Muslims are often sadly disfigured by weak eyes, the diseased state of which is not induced, but increased, by the most absurd superstitions.

It appears to me that most of the thousands of infants who lose their sight or drop into their graves on the very threshold of existence are rather the victims of superstition than of climate. For example, the child of an Arab girl for whom we felt interested lost his sight from an attack of ophthalmia, induced by cold, and increased by the mother's having bandaged up his eyes on the first symptom appearing, and preserved then bandaged and unwashed until they shrunk and withered in their sockets. I heard nothing of the disease having attacked the poor baby until his eyes were dark: and then it was brought to show me. It was most distressing to look upon that dear infant, and see that his Heavenly Father's best gift to his little body, that one most productive of enjoyment, was hopelessly and entirely lost. In another week, I heard that the dear child was dead; and I heard it with feelings of unmixed thankfulness to God. What had been his prospects here? Of Muslim parents, he would have been educated in a false religion, mentally and physically

---

†The first missionary school to be opened was the Anglican in 1835, superintended by Miss Haliday (who later became Mrs. Lieder, Sophia's friend). Cf. Zeinab Farid, "Education of Girls in Egypt" and Iglal Khalifa, *The Modern Feminist Movement*.

dark, to grope his way in poverty through childhood, with life's struggle before him, the child of oppressed parents who could rarely afford to lighten his burden by their presence; lonely, blind, and miserable. When I hear of the death of children under circumstances such as these, I always rejoice.

"Of such are the Kingdom of Heaven."

LETTER IV
(Second Series)

YOU may naturally be curious to know how the ladies of Cairo amuse themselves and their friends during those long visits which occupy nearly the whole of a day. When not engaged in eating and drinking, the pipe serves to many, in some measure, as a pastime, and they tell trifling anecdotes. Of which I shall here give you a specimen or two.

It is a custom of merchants to meet at coffee-shops, there to talk over the news of the day, to tell of their troubles, and sometimes of their successes; and the desire of appearing in better circumstances than they are, is often evident when they are secure of being in the company only of those of similar occupation. A braggadocio of this description was one night talking of his house, his slaves, his goods, and everything but his wives; for it is not etiquette to mention them in the presence of another man; and was overheard by a beggar-woman who resorted nightly to that coffee-shop to ask alms, and who was standing concealed from the view of its inmates, until the tone of the conversation changed. She then came forward, asked charity, obtained a few paras as usual from each person, and retired to her hiding-place until it became dark, when she followed the merchant first mentioned to his house. It was situated in a miserable lane; and was as ruined and wretched as its neighbourhood. Having remarked it sufficiently, she hastily changed in some measure the manner of arranging her maláyeh (the enveloping chequered blue and white drapery which corresponds with the black silk habarah of the better classes), and assuming an altered gait, she approached the merchant's door, and asked admittance. His wife opened it, and the beggar whiningly entreated shelter for the night. The wife called to her husband to ask his permission, and he replied, "Admit her:" therefore the beggar entered, and found herself in the same apartment with the object of her inquiry. Nothing could denote the reverse of the man's boasted wealth more than the interior of his house; scanty and dirty furniture, and the absence of every indication of even comfort, met the eye and engaged the attention of his treacherous guest. His supper was prepared by his wife, who, besides himself, alone resided in his house: but the supper was only enough for two; therefore the merchant desired his wife to go to the nearest market, and purchase something for the beggar, giving her ten paras (rather more than a half-penny of our money), to lay out for the purpose. The beggar-woman supped, and slept in the house, and on the following morning asked for breakfast before she departed; when the merchant sent his willing wife to the market as on the previous night, and gave her the same sum of money to expend. The beggar breakfasted, and went her way; and at night she was at the coffee-shop as usual. As soon as the unsuspecting merchant took his seat, and with an air of great importance filled his pipe from a tobacco-purse embroidered with gold, arranged his dress to the best advantage, and called for coffee, she accosted him in the following words: "Can you tell me of a merchant who boasts in the coffee-shops of his wealth, of the number of his slaves, and of the richness of his merchandise, but whose house is as the dwelling of a scavenger, and whose property is the wind? I can tell you," continued she, "that last night he entertained a stranger, and gave his wife ten paras to provide her supper, and ten to procure her breakfast this morning." "Are you that woman?" asked the merchant in much confusion. "Yes," replied she, "and you are that merchant." It was enough, and I imagine that the poor boaster never again contributed his company to those who had heard with envy of his riches, and now gloried in his disgrace. It seems that the woman designed to steal; and being disappointed, adopted this method of revenge. This was related to me as a true story, well attested. One more will perhaps be as much as you will desire.

A man went to the market to sell a calf, and a company of thieves, forty in number, with their chief, agreed to buy it under the name of a kid. So their chief came to the owner of the calf, and asked him, "Wilt thou sell this kid for fifteen piastres?" The owner replied, "It is a calf, not a kid." Then ten of the thieves said, "O sheykh, it is a kid, not a calf: art thou blind?" and they went away. Then came ten others of them, who offered him fourteen piastres, each of them saying, "It is a kid, not a calf;" he replying "It is a calf, not a kid: are ye blind?" So the man was perplexed, and he looked at the calf, and felt its head, and its back, and its tail. One party of the thieves after another continued to come to him, each lessening the price; but he would not sell it. Then their chief came to him, and said to him, "Wilt thou sell this kid for seventeen piastres?" but he refused. And the chief said, "I have guests with me and I have offered thee more than the kid is worth, because I desired to slaughter it for them." But still he would not. And the chief said, "Wilt thou sell it for twenty?" He answered, "I will, on the condition that thou give me its tail." And he replied "Granted." So the man went with them, and he took its tail, after it had been slaughtered, and gave it to a carpenter, to knock into it a hundred nails. He then took the tail, and having disguised himself in the dress of a woman, went to the abode of the forty thieves after sunset. And he whispered to the chief of the thieves, and said, "My husband desires to take another wife in addition to me; and he has a jar full of pieces of gold; those I wish you to take from him, that he may give up the idea of marrying another wife; so send thy people to take it, and remain thou with me lest their object should be discovered." And he sent them. Now there was in the house a great pulley, and a rope hanging down; so the owner of the calf said, "What is this?" The chief answered, "It is a swing with which we amuse ourselves." By thy life," said the owner of the calf, "put thyself in it, and show me how thou swingest." So he put himself in it, and the other drew him up. He then pulled out the tail of the calf and said to him, "Is this the tail of a calf, or the tail of a kid?" And he beat him severely, and departed. Presently the thieves, his companions, returned, and found him intoxicated without wine: and when he recovered, they said unto him, "What hath happened to thee?" He answered, groaning, "The woman is the owner of the calf;" and he related to them the story: on hearing which they said, "If we see him again, we will contrive means to slay him." He then said to them, "Bring me a physician." And they brought him one, who, when he saw him, said to him, "Thou hast been beaten: I will cure thee; but thou canst not be cured save by forty things, from forty different shops; and he wrote forty papers, for each of the thieves one, and on each paper he wrote, "An accursed, the son of an accursed. Into whose hands soever of the druggists this paper shall fall, if he do not buffet the bearer and spit in his face, ..." He then gave the papers to the thieves, desiring them to bring him the drugs; and when they were gone, he took forth the tail of the calf, and said to the patient, "Is this the tail of a calf, or the tail of a kid?" and he beat him again, until he was nearly dead, and left him. And when his companions had received the buffetings, and the spittings in their faces, they came to him, and found him like one dead; and when he had recovered, he told them what had befallen him, and that the physician was the owner of the calf. They, also, told him what had befallen to them. He then said to them, "Take me forth into the desert, put me in a tent, and range yourselves round it; and whatsoever you see coming, whether it be a woman, or a physician, or a dog, or a cat, or a kite, be sure that it is the owner of the calf." So they took him forth, put him in a tent, and ranged themselves round him. But as to the owner of the calf, he watched their motions at a distance, and knew them when he saw them round the tent from afar. And there passed by him a man, to whom he said, "Take this piece of gold, as the price of thy blood, and go to the company sitting round that tent, and say to them, 'I am the owner of the calf.' But beware lest they overtake thee, for if they do, they will slay thee, in which case this piece of gold will be the penalty for thy blood." And the man did so, and fled: and they all pursued him. And while the thieves were pursuing him, the owner of the calf came to the tent, and producing the tail to the sick man, said to him, "Is this the tail of a calf, or the tail of a kid?" And he beat him until his soul almost issued forth from his body; and he went away. And when the party returned, they found him, as it were, at the point of death. He told them what had befallen him, and said to them, "Prepare me a tomb, and put me into it alive, and give out that you have buried me, that the owner of the calf may persecute me no longer." So they put him in a tomb, and sat around him conversing until the sixth hour of the night, when they departed to their abode. The owner of the calf then came to him and said. " Is this the tail of a calf, or the tail of a kid?" The sick man said to him sighing, "Even in the tomb dost thou come to me?" He replied, from the Excellent Book, "Verily the punishment of the world to come shall be more grievous:" and was about to beat him again; but he said to him, "I make a vow of repentance to thee." And he accepted his vow, and the man fulfilled it well; beginning by paying him ten times the value of the calf.

Being in a humour for telling stories, I add one with which I was amused a few days ago, during a visit much more agreeable than are those of my Eastern friends.

It is seldom a novelty to a European to make a present; but it is a curious novelty to observe the manner in which a gift is received by an Eastern, in many cases. A distinguished gentleman, who had spent some years in Egypt, being on the point of returning to Europe, asked the advice of a judicious friend of ours with regard to the present he should give to those with whom he had been particularly concerned, and whom he had already handsomely remunerated. After the consultation, when everything appeared to our friend to be satisfactorily arranged, it was proposed that in addition to the gift of a gun and a bag of dollars to a camel proprietor, some silver bullets should be cast, and presented with the gun, as a polite accompaniment. Our friend assured him that the delicacy which suggested such a present would be neither understood nor appreciated by the "Sheykh of the camels;"[1] and that if he were resolved to add the value of the bullets, it would be better to do so in the form of money. It was, however, a favourite project; and the proposer was not disposed to abandon it: the bullets were cast, and the traveller waited with his presents at the house of our friend, who desired the attendance of those who were to receive his bounty. The Sheykh of the camels arrived first, and when the usual salutations had passed, he was presented with his gun. He received it without one word of acknowledgment, and turned it about and examined it as though he had been making a purchase. At length he said, "I have a gun; my servant always carries it; it is a better one than this: shall he bring it up to show it to you?" This our friend forbade. The bullets were then given him. "Silver bullets!" said he; "Mohammad Alee Páshá uses leaden ones. What is the use of silver bullets?" "They are only," it was replied. "intended as a handsome accompaniment to such a gun; they are not to be used in charging it; and if you do not like them, you can turn them at any time into money." This latter argument the Sheykh understood; and he weighed the bullets in his hand; but no word of thanks escaped him. Then

---

[1] Every trade and every class of artizans in Egypt has its Sheykh, or superior, by whom all its followers are controlled: thus there is a Sheykh even of the dustmen, and a troop of camels in like manner has its Sheykh.

the dollars were presented to him. Those he took out singly; he turned over every coin, counted them in the presence of his benefactor, and examined them closely. Here our friend's patience was exhausted: he had hoped that, at least, when the dollars were given, the Sheykh would express his gratitude; and he felt severely the mortification his generous companion must experience in such a disappointment of his expectations. "You shall now, " he said, "have a reckoning with *me*. When this gentleman engaged your camels for such a journey, what did you charge him, and what did you gain by him for such and such an excursion?" The Sheykh knew that he was dealing with a just and experienced person, and felt obliged to answer him with truth. The calculation was made; and it was found that the Sheykh had profited immensely by his employer. Our friend then insisted upon his making a proper acknowledgment, and leaving the house; and under these circumstances, knowing that this point was determined on by one possessing considerable influence here, he consented, and gave his tardy thanks.

It is a curious fact, and one not to be disputed, that this man was exceedingly pleased with his present; and was only endeavouring to gain every piastre he could from one who had long submitted patiently to his exactions. He only acted as most Arabs would have acted under the same circumstances.

The system of giving a present at the conclusion of an engagement with an Arab is a good one; because the hope of a backsheesh has the effect of preserving civil manners, and often fair dealing, and such a hope ought not to be disappointed.

LETTER V
(Second Series)

May, 1845

MY residence here occasions my having often friendly intercourse with persons who, according to Eastern etiquette, I must call ladies; persons born of Christian parents, and reared through childhood in the Christian profession; but now of the faith of Mohammad. I allude to those unfortunate beings who, torn from their native countries, are brought hither as slaves. One thing with respect to them, and common to them and the Memlooks, or male white slaves, very much surprises me; it is this: that they are generally far more bigoted than the rest of their co-religionists. In other respects, many of them seem to me still to have amiable dispositions, which make me to mourn the more for their unhappy lot. But it is not so with the Memlooks, among whom I frequently hear of beings more like infernal spirits than men;† monsters in cruelty and in every imaginable vice. There is also another class, very numerous in this country, somewhat similarly circumstanced; of whom some are deserving of much pity, while others cannot be too severely condemned. By the former, I mean those children of Christians, who, having early lost their parents here by death or desertion, have been easily induced to change their religious profession, and some of whom are perhaps sincere in calling themselves Muslims. Of those who have become apostates after having attained to years of discretion, many are persons of the vilest character, as you might naturally imagine; in their assumed bigotry far surpassing those who are Muslims from their birth; and behaving to their respectable Christian relations with the most abominable arrogance and tyranny. I will give you an example.

A renegade, originally an Eastern Christian, who is living in great favour with the Government, had been expecting for some time the arrival of a nephew from Syria, who left him years before, and had never heard of his apostacy. On his arrival his uncle received him with much show of affection. After conversing with him for some time, the uncle confessed his change of religion; but assured his nephew that many and great benefits had followed his profession of the faith of el Islam, recounting the advantages of his position; and concluding by conjuring him to follow his example. No argument, however,

---

†For a more balanced view of the Mamluks, see al-Jabarti. He has nothing but admiration for al-Alfi Bey (obituary A.H.1221 [A.D. 1806], vol III: 143–73), whom he calls "the last of the great Egyptian princes." On the other hand, he is critical of Murad Bey while admiring of his wife Nafisa, who died in 1816 (vol. III: 538–39).

208

availed; for the young man steadily assured him that his religion was dearer
to him than any other consideration; that no temptation should induce him
to renounce it; and that, with the help of God, he would welcome poverty
while he possessed the consolations of a Christian. The uncle finding him
inexorable, and firmly resolving to subdue, if possible, what he styled an
obstinate and rebellious spirit, had recourse to stratagem. Having desired his
nephew to take refreshment and repose, he repaired to several of his especial
Muslim friends, and collecting them in a neighbouring mosque, he told
them to wait there until he should send his nephew to call one of them by
name, when he begged that they would seize him, on the ground of his
temerity in entering a mosque, being a Christian, and compel him, on pain
of death, to renounce the faith of his fathers: "Use any means," said he, "however violent: raise a popular tumult if necessary; and do not release him until
he shall have professed himself a Muslim." Having given these directions, he
returned to his house; and after describing the mosque to his nephew, he
desired him to enter it, and call a certain person, mentioning him by name,
saying that his uncle desired to speak with him. The young man accordingly
repaired to the mosque; but, arriving at the door, he felt alarmed; for he saw
several persons within the doorway, who, in their anxiety to perform the bidding of his uncle, overshot the mark, and beckoned to him eagerly. He had
but one moment for consideration, and that proved sufficient; he appre-
hended that his life was in danger, and fled. Threading his way through intricate streets, he reached a convent. Here he threw himself at the feet of the first
person he met belonging to the place, and briefly told his story. This person
conducted him to the presence of the superior and others, to whom he related
all that had occurred, assuring them that he believed his life would be
sacrificed if he returned to his uncle, determined as he was, at all hazards, to
preserve his Christian profession. Thus resolved, he entreated them to give him
some employment in the convent; to which they replied, that all the situations
were adequately filled, therefore they could not grant his request, unless he
would undertake to become a scullion. "On my head," answered the young
Christian, in token of his readiness and fidelity; and he repaired to the kitchen,
and thankfully applied himself to his new duties. A pious man, of some
influence, residing in the convent, remarked the young stranger with deep
interest, and after he had performed for one fortnight his duties in a station so
ill-suited to his birth and expectations, succeeded in obtaining for him a lucra-
tive place of trust, to which he at once removed him. This anecdote was related
by one intimately acquainted with the circumstances of the young man.

The occurrence above related happened long before the period when the
present Sultán, yielding to the remonstrances of the Christian powers of
Europe, exempted from the penalty of death all persons who, having been originally Christians or Jews, and having become Muslims, returned to their first
faiths; therefore, if the young man whom I have mentioned had complied with

the desire of his uncle, he could not have professed himself again a Christian without losing his life, unless recommended to the notice of the Páshá.

The mildness of Mohammad 'Alee with reference to religion, in cases with respect to which the law is severe and cruel in the utmost degree, is in my opinion, his best quality. I could mention more than one instance in which, long ago, he forbade the execution of the sentence of the law upon persons who had been Muslims from their birth, and had become professed Christians, In cases of a different kind, in which religion has been concerned, he has also signalized himself by his moderation, or, if you like so to call it, by his enlightened and wise and conciliatory policy. While the Sultan's government has been insolently interposing every imaginable obstacle in the way of the erection of our church at Jerusalem, the foundation of a noble English church have been laid at Alexandria with the ready permission of Mohammad 'Alee, and with the Turkish law directly opposed to it.[†] The latter church will, it is said, be a very remarkable building. The style is said to be chiefly Byzantine; but the general character rather like that of ancient Greece and Italy. Its architect is Mr. Wild, an artist well known in England, who has been for nearly three years improving himself in his art by the study of Arabian architecture in this country; and good judges here have formed very high expectations of the results of his late investigations.

With regard to Mohammad 'Alee's religious toleration, I should observe that you can hardly conceive the hatred which it draws upon him from the Muslims in general. Their enmity to the Christians and Jews has much increased during the last few years; apparently roused to indignation at witnessing so many European innovations adopted by Turks and Memlooks in the service of the government. Occasionally it manifests itself in a manner truly ridiculous. You will scarcely believe that when Dr. Wolff was in this country, and had published some placards exhorting the Muslims to relinquish their false faith, and bestowing (in their opinions) some very disrespectful epithets upon their prophet, the principal 'Ulama held a secret council on the subject, and made him the object of a kind of mock trial, he not being present. The majority decided that sentence of death should be passed upon him for blasphemy; but a few of the less fanatical prevailed upon them to commute this sentence, and to decree that he should be flogged and banished. They knew that their decree could not be executed. This is a secret history, which I have received from a high authority.

[†]Muhammad 'Ali donated a generous tract of land in the center of Alexandria to the British Community for their "own exclusive use." The unspoken understanding was to enable them to build a church. The Church of St. Mark in the former Place des Consules (now Tahrir Square). The architect was J.W. Wild, who built it with a Basilican concept; the eclectic decorative designs in stucco have some Islamic influence. It is still in use by the Anglican community.

LETTER VI
(Second Series)

May, 1845

I TOLD you that a great marriage, which I had been invited to attend, had been put off: the preparations for it have now been commenced, and my invitation has been renewed. Some of the observances usual on the occasion of such a marriage can be witnessed only by females, the scene being the interior of the Hareem; the scenes of others are accessible only to men. Though I am obliged for a short time to defer the description of the former, I need not do the same with respect to the latter; and having, among my brother's notes, an ample account of the public ceremonials observed at one of the grandest of the marriages that have been celebrated in this city during a period of many years, I shall extract from it what I think most likely to interest you. The festival about to be described was previous to the marriage of a sister of Ahmad Páshá, a nephew of the Viceroy; and lasted nine days. Mohammad 'Alee presented to Ahmad Páshá, on this occasion, three thousand purses, equivalent to about fifteen thousand pounds; and to the bridegroom, Mukhtár Bey, who had been educated in Paris, and had lately been appointed President of the Council of State, one thousand purses, or five thousand pounds.

The scene of the festivities was the garden of the Ezbekeeyeh. It being then the season of the inundation, the large space called Birket el Ezbekeeyeh, which is of an irregular form, nearly half a mile in length, and about a third of a mile in breadth, was filled with water; and the water was unusually high. The back of the palace of Ahmad Páshá overlooks this space, which is now no longer a lake; the soil having been raised, and planted with avenues of trees. A platform of wood, supported by boats, and surrounded by little flags, to the staves of which were attached cords, with numerous lamps suspended to them, was moored about half-way between the centre of the lake and the palace. This platform was designed as a stage for fireworks; and five guns were placed upon it, and two more on the shore. The guns were fired frequently during the day-time, and more frequently during the display of the fireworks at night. There were several boats on the lake for hire; and many tents, for the sale of coffee, sweetmeats, &c., were erected on the narrow spaces between the water's edge and the surrounding houses, as well as a few swings and whirligigs. The shores of the lake, and the way leading from it to the front of the palace of Ahmad Páshá, were crowded all the day; and more especially was the palace itself, which, with the exception of a few

211

apartments, was thrown open to the public. In the court of the palace, where twelve chandeliers (two of them very large, but not handsome) were suspended, and which was covered over with red tent-cloths, &c., for shade, musicians, dancing-men, swordsmen, and others, amused the assembled crowds during the day; and refreshments, consisting of sweetmeats, coffee, sherbet, &c., were occasionally served to the people in the public rooms, high and low; for even the meanest of the people had free access; the Páshá reserving only a few rooms for himself and his friends. But the chief festivities were in the evening.

"I spent an hour (says my brother) on the shore of the lake in the evening of the first day, to see the fireworks. The place was excessively crowded. There were numerous benches and stools of palm-sticks, and strips of matting, placed along the water's edge, by the kahwegees (or keepers of the coffee-booths); as soon as a person sat on one of these, a cup of coffee was brought to him, and if he refused to take it he was not allowed to retain his seat, unless he were a person of the higher orders. Several mesh'als (or cressets) were stuck in the ground to light the company; and numbers of men were going about with cakes, nuts, and various other eatables, and with sweet drinks and water. The scene was strikingly picturesque and lively. The fireworks chiefly consisted of rockets, which were discharged one at a time, at short intervals; so that they were not very remarkable; but they had a pretty appearance, issuing from the bosom of the lake. The seven guns were occasionally fired one after another.

"From the lake I proceeded to the palace, pushing my way through dense crowds. Numerous lamps in addition to two chandeliers, were hung in the street before the palace; and the street there was covered over like the court. The court I found thronged with people, chiefly of the lower classes. A large ring was formed round a group of dancing-men; but I could not get near enough to see them. All the public apartments also were crowded with persons of every class, and in every variety of picturesque attire, from the richest to the meanest. At the door of one room I was stopped by a sentry, and told that there were only Europeans within. I found it convenient to assert my right to enter, and was admitted. Here were but a few persons, mostly Greeks, several of whom were females; some in the ordinary European dress, and others in the male costume of the Turks, which they had put on in the hope of their being mistaken for boys, as it is uncommon for females in the East to be in the company of men, or even to go out at night; but their sex was too evident.

"From the windows of this room I had a good view of what was going on in the court. A military band played several European airs remarkably well; and then a group of native musicians (alateeyeh) played some of their own airs, occasionally with the accompaniment of the voice; but there was such a confusion of noises in the court that we could not very plainly hear them.

These were succeeded by dancers, not pleasing substitutes for the dancing-girls, whose performances had been strictly interdicted between three and four months before, and many of whom, refusing to profess repentance of their dissolute lives, had been banished to Isna, in Upper Egypt. The dancers on this occasion were not the khawals, or common dancing-men of Cairo, but of a class whose dancing, dress, and appearance were nearly the same, and who differed from the khawals in little more than their appellation, which is gink. Their effeminate profession, dress, manners, and performances rendered them disgusting objects to me, and, I hope, to many others among the spectators. The gink are generally Greeks, Turks, Armenians, or Jews. In the case which I am describing, they were mostly Armenians, and about six danced at a time. They wore a tight vest, with a loose kind of petticoat, forming a compound of male and female attire, and had long hair in most instances hanging down the back in numerous plaits, and decked with the little glittering ornaments of gold generally worn by the Egyptian women of the middle and higher orders, and called safa. They used castagnettes of brass; and their dancing was, in general, similar in every respect to that of the ghawázee, or common dancing-girls; but occasionally they performed pirouettes and other exercises.

"Meanwhile, a buffoon who is a regular servant of the Páshá, dressed in a fantastical manner, and wearing a high, pointed red cap, gaudily ornamented with tinsel and bells, amused the company with ridiculous drolleries. He and several other persons, some of whom were of the meanest and dirtiest of the people, bore torches. The buffoon came up to the room of the Europeans. In this room refreshments of various kinds, liqueurs, sherbet, coffee, &c., were served to the company. The áláteeyeh, who had played in the court, also came up, and performed a concert of instrumental and vocal music. The buffoon accompanied and marred their music with his castagnettes, then sat down in the lap of an old musician, danced with his back towards the females in a very insulting manner, and performed a variety of other extravagant actions.

"At the same time, there were performances of a different kind in the court. A company of mohabbazeen (or low comedians) acted a farce, exhibiting the troubles of a hen-pecked husband. This unfortunate person, who was very fully clothed, first danced about the arena with a drawn sword. The player who personated his wife, who was a man in female attire, and to whom I must apply the feminine pronoun, came into the ring with a swaggering gait, and desired him to give her his sword, which he refusing to do, she scolded and screamed, beating her face, and then his, and thus obtained what she wanted. In the same manner she obliged him to strip off almost every article of his clothing one by one, and at last, enraged by her conduct, he beat her till she died. This foolish farce, I thought, might probably be too appropriate at a fête in celebration of the approaching marriage of a man newly elevated to rank with a woman of much higher condition; for generally in cases of this kind among the Turks, the husband is the slave of his wife. After this, a man with a lighted torch to represent a tail, ran round upon his hands and knees several times, within the ring. Such were the silly performances on the first night of this festival; these, at least, were the principal performances from sunset till past midnight. The dancers, &c. continued all the night, as well as all the day. The Páshá entertained a private party every evening during this period of rejoicing, but did not partake of the repast with them.

"The performances of the second night, and the fireworks, were so little different from those of the first, that I need not describe them. Some of the Páshá's pipes were brought to the visitors in the room appropriated to Europeans, and refreshments served as before. The buffoon, this night, was dressed as a Frank, but seemed to be ashamed of his disguise, for he was less lively.

"On the third night, after the usual performances of the gink, a háwee, or performer of slight-of-hand tricks, amused the company. The chief of his juggling performances was the putting a number of slips of white paper into a saucepan placed on a boy's head, and then taking them out dyed of various colours. No pipes were brought to the Europeans' room this night, because one of the mouth-pieces, which were all costly, had been stolen the night before, though evidently not by one of the visitors, for it was afterwards found in a room to which the Europeans had not access. Refreshments, however, were served as on the preceding nights, and more attention was given to amuse the company in this room. A military band with the ordinary Egyptian instruments, came up, and played and sang several native airs; the buffoon accompanying them with his castagnettes and drolleries. They were succeeded by a Turkish band, whose plaintive music was pleasing, but tame and poor after that of the Egyptians. Then a party of hired native musicians performed for nearly an hour, and in the best style.

"A full military band, meanwhile, played European airs in the court, and after they had finished, a farce was performed, the subject of which was the miseries of a man with two wives. In the better parts of this, there was nothing worthy of description; in the worse, there was a scene which made me quit the palace in disgust.

"A rocket, during the third night, set fire to a part of Ahmad Páshá palace; but did little injury. The boats and platform which composed the stage for the fireworks were therefore removed nearly to the middle of the lake on the morning of the fourth day. In the course of the next night, a silly farce was performed in the palace. The military band then played European airs, after which was a mock sword-fight, between a man and a boy, who aimed their blows too obviously at each other's shields; and another between two men; and after this a concert of Egyptian music by hired performers.

"On the fifth night, the performances in the court of the palace consisted of nothing more than a stupid play, and the dances of the gink; but the instrumental and vocal music of the áláateeyeh afforded better amusement in the room appropriated to the European visitors. In the course of this night, a little boy coming into the court, and seeming to be struck with the utmost astonishment at the number of lamps, probably having never seen anything of the kind before, expressed his wonder by a very loud exclamation. A Turkish captain, offended at his innocent ejaculations, seized the poor little fellow, and gave him a severe flogging; and a private soldier struck him with the butt-end of his musket; but Ahmad Páshá, coming down into the court while this was being done, and inquiring and learning the cause, immediately ordered that the Turk should be flogged with double severity, called out to the other soldiers to take warning by his example, and gave several saadeeyehs (little coins each the value of about ten-pence of our money) to the poor child, who would doubtless have willingly submitted to a flogging every day for such a compensation.

"On the sixth day, a rope for dancers was fixed in a wide space in the way leading from the lake to the palace of Ahmad Páshá. There were two performers here this day, a woman, and a boy about fourteen years of age; both of the class of the Ghugar, or Ghujar, which is the name given in Egypt to Gipsies. They performed twice in the day, and dense crowds assembled to view them. The rope was about eighteen feet from the ground, and the horizontal part of it very short, about twelve feet. The woman, who was profusely clad, in old, but gaudy things, and unveiled, like all the gipsy-women of Egypt, performed first, but merely walked along the rope, very slowly and timidly, supporting herself by holding the balancing pole, and resting one end of it upon the ground. The boy ascended immediately after, and did nothing surprising.

"Many of the idlers in the neighbourhood of the Ezbekeeyeh were drawn off from the scene of the festivities this day by the arrest of a Copt (who had always professed himself a Christian) for having employed a number of fikees in his house to perform a recitation of the Kur-an. He exculpated himself by asserting that he had been a Muslim in his heart for fourteen years, but had feared to incur the enmity of his relations, by avowing himself such. A white turban was put upon his head, instead of the black one which he had been accustomed to wear, and he was sent to the citadel, as is usual in cases of the kind; thence to the Kádee, to make an open profession of his faith; and back to the citadel, to receive a dress. On such an occasion, the apostate is preceded by musicians with drums and hautboys, and by a number of schoolboys, who cry as they go along, 'God aid the religion of El-Islám! God destroy the religion of the infidels!'—This morning also, an old wall on the shore of the lake of the Ezbekeeyeh, shaken by the firing of the guns, fell upon four men, one of whom was killed beneath its ruins.

"At the palace, in the evening of this day, a khowal, or Egyptian dancing-man, performed and outdid the gink, who danced at the same time in another part of the court. This man's performances were chiefly athletic, leaping through a hoop, &c. He stood on the shoulders of another man, who walked about with him for several minutes; then, still borne in the same manner, he carried a boy in his arms. Next he formed the support of a pile of five boys and men, whom, after two or three minutes, he threw down. But he excited most surprise by sustaining, apparently with his teeth, a weight of about sixty or seventy pounds. This was a cylinder of wood, with four circular plates of iron, forming part of the machine called nórag, which is used in Egypt for threshing wheat and cutting the straw. But while one of these iron plates was between his teeth, that next to it rested upon the top of his head. The full military band played European airs again; and a smaller military band performed native airs, with the instruments of the country.

"On the seventh night a farce was performed, which was rather tedious, the scenes being little more than the contract for the wife, and the bridal procession conducted in the ordinary manner of the country. To make up for the want of humour, the actors threw crackers about every minute, and ended by dancing in a ridiculous manner. Afterwards, a peasant displayed his skill in balancing tall mesh'als or cressets; one with a single receptacle for fire, and of the common size; another with five such receptacles; and a third with only one, but of more than twice the usual length. These he supported on his forehead.

"On the eighth night, which was the last of the festivities at the palace, the performances were more silly, and more unworthy of description than any of those of the preceding nights. I therefore pass them over in silence. But I have yet to describe the zeffeh, or procession of the bride to the house of the bridegroom, which took place on the ninth day, Thursday, the day most approved for such an event.

"It is usual, in cases of this kind, for the procession to follow a circuitous route, through several of the larger streets of the metropolis, and particularly through the main street of the city. In the present case, the procession, on quitting the palace, turned to the right, it being esteemed unlucky to turn first to the left, and after winding through some streets, made a circuit round the lake and its environs. It then passed through the part where most of the Franks reside, and, having proceeded thence just outside the original limits of the city, on the west and south, entered the main street by the great gate called Báb Zuweyleh. It had to pass through the greater part of the city to arrive at the bridegroom's house. I had been informed that it would pass through the main street about an hour before noon; and I went thither an hour earlier than the expected time; but I had to wait six hours before it arrived at the place where I sat.

"The leader of the procession was the chief buffoon, on horseback, with a pointed silver cap, belonging to the treasury. He gravely saluted the spectators, turning to the right and left, as he passed along, like the Kádee, and other great men; and occasionally performed the same absurd actions as the false bearded fool in the processions of the Kisweh and Mahhmil; such as pretending to write judicial decisions, &c. Next were four men, in ample scarlet robes, of the kind called benish, each mounted on a camel, and beating a pair of large kettle-drums, called nakákeer. The last of these was followed by a water-carrier, termed a keiyim, who was also, as were most of the persons, clad in a scarlet benish. A keiyim of the water-carriers is a man who, for the sake of a present, and this empty title, carries a skin filled with sand and water, of greater weight, and for a longer period, than any of his brethren will venture to do; and this feat he must accomplish without sitting down to rest, unless in a crouching posture. The keiyim of this procession began to carry his burthen, a skin of sand and water, about two hundred pounds in weight, at sunset of the preceding day, bore it in the procession, and continued to do so until sunset. This is a common custom in zeffehs of the great.

"Next followed twelve camels with saddles or housings covered with scarlet or green cloth, ornamented with shells, of the kind called cowries, and having a number of small flags, slanting forward from the forepart of each saddle, as in the processions of the Kisweh and Mahhmil: indeed, these were the same saddles, &c. that were used in those processions on the last occasions.

"Shortly after these had passed, a boat, mounted on a gun-carriage, and bearing Ahmad Páshá's chief reyyes, or boatmaster, was drawn along by a number of men. Next passed a small field-piece, which was fired in the street, before a public school-room, in which Ahmad Páshá was sitting to see his pageant. Some of the gink who had performed in the palace followed next, striking their castagnettes, and occasionally dancing: then two men on horseback; each bearing a long pole with an embroidered handkerchief tied at the top, another man bearing a tall cresset wound about with handkerchiefs: and several sakkas, to supply the spectators with water. Then followed a covered car, with open sides and back and front, drawn by four horses, and bearing the principal hired musicians who had performed at the palace. These performed also during the procession, though their music could scarcely be heard. A similar car followed, in which were the 'Al'mehs, or female singers, who had performed in the Hareem during the festivities. They were fully veiled, as ladies; and sang during the procession.

"Here were wanting what are generally seen in a zeffeh of this kind; namely, a number of cars each bearing persons of some particular manufacture or trade, all at work in their several crafts; even such as builders, whitewashers, and the like; including persons of all, or almost all, the arts and manufactures practised in the metropolis.

"After the car with the female singers followed a number of buffoons; boys and men with hobby-horses made of palm-sticks and paper; two men on stilts, which were about eight feet high; the farce-players, whose absurd performances at the palace I have described, and the greater number of the gink, with their Turkish band. Next came a company of lancers, followed by pioneers, a full military band, and a body of infantry: then several eunuchs, on horseback. These immediately preceded a train of eight shabby European carriages, which conveyed the ladies.

"Each carriage was drawn by four horses, driven by an Arab coachman, and attended by two or more eunuchs behind; and its upper part was covered with shawls, spread upon the top, and hanging down before, behind, and on either side; curtaining the windows, and concealing the ladies within. In the foremost, which was the best carriage, was the bride. Many of the female spectators raised their shrill and quavering cries of joy (called zagháreet) as the carriage passed. The train of carriages was followed by a number of drummers and hautboy-players, who accompany ordinary bridal processions: each of these was on horseback, and clad in a scarlet benish. Ahmad Páshá's chief gardener, in a canopied car, which was filled and hung about with fruit, closed the procession. The time which the procession occupied in passing the place where I sat was just half an hour."

My brother's remarks on the shabbiness of the carriages used by the grandees ten years since, lead me to tell you how different are the equipages of the present day in Cairo. Some are nearly as good as those you meet in Hyde Park; and a carriage with four beautiful grey horses in which I saw Mohammad 'Alee last week, could hardly, I thought, be surpassed in good taste.

LETTER VII
(Second Series)

Tuesday, Dec. 16th, 1845

HAVING received this evening a third invitation to witness the festivities on the occasion of the wedding of Zeyneb Hánum, and finding that they will commence on Thursday next, I must now devote my whole attention to the task of giving you a description of the novel scenes of which I am about to be a spectator.

Zeyneb Hánum is the youngest daughter of the Páshá, and her affianced husband is Kamil Páshá, lately Kámil Bey, a sort of aide-de camp and private secretary to Mohammad 'Alee. The Sultán conferred upon him the rank of Páshá when he heard that he was proposed as the future son-in-law of the viceroy of Egypt.

It has occurred to me that I should do well to give you a kind of diary of events during the eight days of the coming fête; for, excepting in such a form, I could not hope to give you a correct idea of an entertainment in every respect strange in its character to our notions of a bridal festival.

Dec. 18th.—About eleven o'clock in the morning I and my kind friend Mrs. Lieder were on our way to the palace in the citadel, in which the festivities were celebrated. We had many interruptions on the way; for several regiments were marching in procession to the Ezbekeeyeh, in which stands the palace of the bride, and to which she is to descend on the eighth day of the entertainment. These regiments were preceded and followed by very respectable military bands. One procession attended a large figure of an elephant, mounted and led by Indians in effigy: The whole (elephant and Indians) to be blown up on the eighth evening, and thus form the finale of the fireworks, which are to be exhibited during every evening in the Ezbekeeyeh. After the elephant, a large ark was drawn, on wheels, attended by musicians and drummers making a deafening noise. Whether the ark is to share the same fate as the elephant, time will show.

The route to the citadel is marked by innumerable new glass lanterns, each containing ten lamps, mostly hung on ropes extending across the streets. When we began to ascend the hill upon which the citadel stands, we found that on either side of the new road temporary pillars, of various fanciful styles of architecture, had been erected, painted in bright colours, and gaily hung with lamps. The principal features of the architecture of the arches of the gateway, and other entrances of the palace, were hung with lamps, and the court presented a very picturesque spectacle. Here were festoons of lamps, and many hung fruit-like from the trees; while the whole court was covered over with a red and white awning, producing a subdued light under a bright sunny sky. The garden was strikingly pretty, with the addition of bright lamps hung in festoons wherever they could be so arranged.

After gaining the last entrance, we passed the Hareem curtain, that impassable barrier to men, excepting the lord of the citadel, or any necessary employé; and we found the usual army of eunuchs, and female black slaves, looking out for the arrival of the European ladies, who had been invited. Passing through the lower saloon, we found the white slaves of many Hareems, gorgeously attired. With a full tide of these to accompany us, we proceeded up the staircase, and being directed, on reaching the upper great saloon, what course to pursue, we made our way through a dense crowd towards the seat of honour.

There we found the bride seated, raised upon cushions of pale pink satin, splendidly embroidered with gold. Her young brother, Mohammad 'Alee Bey, was seated by her side. On her left hand stood her Highness Nezleh Hánum, the eldest daughter of the Páshá, showering small gold and silver coins among the crowd. This circumstance accounted for the presence of, perhaps, three thousand persons, many of whom seemed very eager in striving to obtain the bounty. The coins thrown in the Hareem were pieces of five and three piastres, and silver paras mixed up with barley and salt. The reason for throwing the barley I could not learn,[†] but the salt was intended to prevent the influence of the evil eye.

On the right hand of the bride sat the mother of Sa'eed Páshá, and Nezleh Hánum appointed me a seat next to her, and Mrs. Lieder beyond me. When the shower of gold and silver ceased, the bride left the saloon, oppressed with the weight of gold and jewels, and supported by four slaves. The moment she rose, we were almost deafened by the sounds of many tambourines, and the shrill quavering cries of joy called zagháreet. The expression of her countenance was very sad, and gave rise to a report that she disliked her affianced husband. With her the crowd partially dispersed, and Nezleh Hánum sat down, and as she received her own pipe, ordered that pipes should be offered to us; but we both declined them. I was surprised by the splendour of the mouthpieces. That which was offered to me was beautifully set with diamonds, and the stem was rich with lacing of gold thread. Her Highness' pipe was the most costly I have ever seen. It was of the same description as ours; but the amber mouthpiece, splendid with diamonds, was as rich as art could make it; and the lower part of the pipe was beautifully decorated with a profusion of diamonds. The little tray in which the pipe-bowl rested was of exquisite enamel.

[†] A symbol of fertility, like rice.

Coffee was served to us in the elegant manner of the high Hareem. A silver chafing-dish, suspended by chains, and containing live charcoal, upon which boiled the coffee in a tiny pot, was carried by a slave magnificently attired; while another bore the small round silver tray, with the little coffee-cups and their exquisite jewelled stands. All were costly; but those handed to her Highness were most splendid. The zarf, or stand of the coffee-cup, was spirally inlaid with diamonds, on a ground of delicate enamel.

The saloons are built in the form of an oblong cross: the whole is matted, and the ends are furnished with divans of pale dove-coloured satin, massively embroidered with gold, and finished with a fringe of gold twist about a foot deep. The walls and ceilings throughout are painted in good taste: the arabesque and gilding of the ceilings are chaste and beautiful; and though the paintings, representing generally Turkish summer palaces, are evidences that the artists employed had no knowledge of perspective, yet they are so well arranged to represent a sort of pannelled wall, the gilding above and on either side of these paintings is delicately and tastefully applied, and owing to the age of the decorations, the prevailing colour is a pale bluish grey, so that the whole is harmonious, or, to use an artistic term, all is in good keeping.

There is a lower saloon of the same form, and these may be considered as saloons of reception. The private apartments are entered from the corners of the centre of the cross, thus making up a rectangular figure. One compartment of the cross is occupied by the grand staircase; and the best situation for seeing all that took place was in the compartment opposite to the staircase in each saloon.

The views from the windows of that palace are beautiful and highly interesting. During the time of extreme confusion occasioned by showers of gold, I turned towards a window and was much impressed by the contrast the view presented with the scene within. The cemetery of Kaïd Bey lay beneath, at some little distance in the desert. Never did the majestic beauty of that group of mosques and tombs so charm me, and never did the deep solitude and solemn stillness ever reigning among those monuments seem to me so deep and still. The city lay stretched to the left; and beyond it the green carpet spread by the inundation bordering upon the land of Goshen—the view is most imposing.

I have not yet told you of the magnificent dress of the bride. She wore a yelek and trowsers of red Cashmere embroidered with gold in a florid style, equally gorgeous and elegant, and interspersed with pearls, with a saltah (or jacket) of red velvet lined with ermine, and almost covered with embroidery of gold and jewels. Her headdress was absolutely grotesque, and of prodigious width: a pale yellow crape kerchief was bound across her forehead, and so arranged on either side as to resemble wings. On the front of this band, and on the spreading blue tassel of her tarboosh, were arranged a variety of diamond sprays, a tiara, and a crescent and star, the whole being surmounted by a small yellow bird, resembling the bird of Paradise excepting in colour, from which spread two long and curving tail-feathers, one bending down on the right, and the other on the left. She wore also a superb diamond necklace, of which I shall have more to say hereafter. Her hair was partly braided, partly dishevelled, and turned up and mingled with the blue tassel, without any regard to form or effect. Her girdle was a Cashmere shawl embroidered and fringed with gold. Nezleh Hánum was attired in a yelek and trowsers of white satin, very delicately embroidered with gold and coloured flowers. Mohammad 'Alee Bey wore a tight military jacket elaborately embroidered with gold and with tags of pearls, and full cloth trowsers. He left us soon after the bride had returned to her private apartments, that he might preside at a dinner given to the students of the Páshá's colleges. He is the youngest son of Mohammad 'Alee, now just twelve years of age. We should think it strange in Europe that a boy of that age should sit at the head of a table to which some hundreds were invited; but I doubt not he presided well, for a Turk of almost any age has a keen sense of propriety, and wonderful self-possession.

Benches were now brought forward, and six female slaves approached us, each bearing a different instrument of music, while a little band of other performers, each with a tambourine, accompanied them. The six took their seats, three on each bench, and the tambouriners stood behind them, and on either side. The musicians played and sang several Turkish airs extremely well, during about half an hour, when the crowd again thickened, and another bride advanced towards the seat of honour, preceded and followed by the girls beating their tambourines. Her head-dress was as grotesque as that of the Páshá's daughter, bedecked with a profusion of diamonds, and surmounted by black and yellow feathers. Her saltah, too, resembled that of Zeyneb Hánum, and so did the shawl she wore as a girdle, but her yelek and trowsers were of striped Cashmere embroidered with gold. She threw herself at the feet of Nezleh Hánum, and at those of the mother of Sa'eed Páshá, and then took her seat in the distinguished corner. Crowds then poured in, and Nezleh Hánum again threw a profusion of gold and silver coins among the multitude. The bride sat about ten minutes, looking completely wretched, and then retired, supported and accompanied in the same manner as her predecessor; and after having, with considerable difficulty, carried her burden of embroidery and jewels across the saloon, she fainted. Alas! poor brides! Mysterious as is the future to every girl on the eve of marriage, how tenfold grievous must be the apprehensions of her who knows nothing, but by report, of her affianced husband.

When the second bride had disappeared, and the crowd had swept away, leaving still a goodly company of hundreds, the musicians again sang and played until Nezleh Hánum rose to quit the saloon. The girls with tambourines preceded and followed her, beating their instruments as when they accompanied the brides. We now felt disposed to reconnoitre, and were soon joined by the mother of Mohammad 'Alee Bey, who gave us her usual charming welcome, and led us to the retiring-room which had been appointed for the European guests. She is really a very sweet, sunny-faced person, always in a pleasant, polite humour, and apparently always happy. She invited us to see the bridal presents, which had that morning arrived from the bridegroom, and we accompanied her into an adjoining room, where many costly and beautiful jewels, dresses, services of plate, &c., were displayed, and where others were being unpacked. The jewel-box was covered with red velvet, and decorated outside with sprays of diamonds. We were shown about twelve dresses of velvet, gros de Naples, and satin, most splendidly embroidered with gold, all in the florid style before mentioned, bordered with gold lace, plaited, and so disposed as to form a fringe of flowers and leaves nearly three inches deep. In similar dresses some of the slaves were attired on that day. Within each dress was folded a magnificent Cashmere shawl. The slippers and mezz (or inner shoes) were beautifully set with diamonds, and the straps of a pair of bath clogs were exquisitely decorated with the same precious stones. The clogs were inlaid with mother-of-pearl, and gold tassels hung from the straps. I was much pleased with two scent-bottles which were completely covered with diamonds. There were four dinner-services of silver, and a curious silver tea-service, composed of a sort of vase or urn,[†] and silver cups and saucers of the ordinary tea size. I remarked several trays of French china, and very elegant china dishes of basket-work for fruit: there were also many smaller presents on trays of silver. After admiring these costly gifts, I received an intimation that Nezleh Hánum had directed that I should have the privilege of examining the whole paraphernalia of the bride. I was therefore conducted to another apartment, where the magnificent diamond girdle, of which you have perhaps heard, was given into my hands that I might examine it closely. I have since ascertained from the best authority that the cost of all the diamonds given by the Páshá to his daughter on this occasion has been 200,000*l.*, and of these ornaments the girdle and a necklace are the most costly and splendid. The girdle cost 40,000*l.*, the necklace 37,000*l.*, the earrings 12,000*l.*, and the bracelets 10,000*l.* sterling!

The necklace is composed of large brilliants set in silver; it is said to be unequalled by any in Europe, excepting one of Lady Londonderry's. Its price was considerably enhanced by the extreme difficulty of procuring the principal diamond. I observed also several very splendid diamond rings, one of them containing a brilliant of prodigious size. It is rather singular that, with the exception of a very beautiful rosary of pearls, there were no jewels but diamonds. The sprays for the head, all of diamonds set in silver, were magnificent. A rose with buds and leaves, a sprig of jasmine, a superb crescent

---

[†]Probably a samovar.

and star, and a beautiful tiara most pleased me. Two watches set with an abundance of diamonds, and two magnificently decorated mirrors, also profusely set with diamonds, each of which cost a thousand guineas, lay among the dazzling ornaments by which we were surrounded. Of the mirrors was one of delicate enamel, almost covered with diamonds; the other, of some composition, in which diamonds were arranged in a most tasteful and costly manner.

The slaves vied with each other in showing me the whole paraphernalia, and I was constantly asked, "Have you seen this?" and "Have you examined this?" and so magnificent was everything, that I found the display to be infinitely beyond my expectations. Presently a slave came to inform me from her Highness that she had more to show me if I would follow her down stairs: of course I assented, and followed her through passages down stairs innumerable, again through passages, and again down stairs, until, at the end of a long passage, she stopped before a closed door, and calling to those within, announced my arrival. "The lady must enter alone, you must go back," answered one within. I did not quite like to lose my conductor, but I could not draw back, and could only hope that my excursion through nearly the whole range of that extensive palace might not end in an adventure. The door was very slowly and cautiously opened, and within I found three persons, two of whom were well known to me, the lady-treasurer of her highness and one of her especial companions. That lady-treasurer is one of those persons who, without any beauty of countenance, possess a charm of expression which is perfectly fascinating. Her home is in the Kasr ed-Dubárah, now generally called the Kasr en-Neel; and she was at the citadel during the festival with the hundreds of her companions, who were there as the attendants of Nezleh Hánum. Her highness is never at the citadel but on such occasions, when she is deputed by her father, the Páshá, to direct the ceremonials.

To return to my rencontre, the upshot of my expedition. This lady-treasurer was desired by her Highness to open to me the remaining treasures, and also to show me all that were already unpacked. The room in which we were was large, and nearly half the floor was covered with wrappers for the in-door apparel and riding-dresses. These wrappers were perfectly magnificent, being composed of red velvet or Cashmere, embroidered and fringed with gold; and one was elaborately worked with pearls. I think that there were about twenty of them spread for display on round baskets, with covers for coffee and sherbet, of the same costly description. There were also a similarly embroidered prayer-carpet, and two padded red Cashmere wrappers, one about the size of a hearth-rug, and the other smaller, for the head: both exquisitely worked, fringed with gold, and lined with white silk. They were to be used after the bath, by Mohammad 'Alee Páshá, when on a visit to the bride. There was also a beautiful satin coverlet for a bed, elegantly embroidered with gold. Here too, I saw a splendid variety of dresses; a variety, I mean, in respect of colour and fabric, but all embroidered, in the same florid style. The embroidery of one was richly interspersed with diamonds, and it was lined and trimmed with sable. The head-veils were all of pale-coloured gauze, of different hues, with bright stripes of gold, all of the same pattern. The mother of the bride had sent her, as a wedding-present, a little box almost covered with diamonds, but what was to be its appropriation I do not know. I much admired a chafing-dish of silver, having a raised lid, surmounted by a fanciful ornament, consisting of a variety of fire-arms in silver, and war-trumpets, crowned by the crescent and star. There was a large silver tray belonging to this chafing-dish, to replace the cover when the latter should be removed. All the smaller articles were in trays decorated with crape of many colours; and the floors of the rooms in which they were arranged were as gay as flower-gardens.

While I was engaged in examining these splendid and curious objects, a slave came and invited me to join the other European ladies, who had just arrived; and I set out to retrace my many steps. My conductor led me to the same compartment of the upper saloon in which we had seen the bride on our arrival; and I found myself in a goodly company of European ladies, with Nezleh Hánum sitting in the centre of the upper divan, as directress of the ceremonies. Her Highness shortly after rose, attended by two train-bearers, and led the way to a saloon where dinner was prepared for two hundred persons, perfectly in the European style. There was nothing on the table that could remind one of the East, excepting some bananas: plates, knives and forks, European dinner napkins, with the bread arranged in each as we have it at home, completed the illusion. The dinner was a cold collation; and it could not well be otherwise, as the kitchens, without exaggeration, are a long walk from the *salle à manger.* Nezleh Hánum did not head the table, on account of its great length, but presided at the side, and used a knife and fork, with a few side-glances at her guests, and occasional jests with those who stood behind her chair. I had a good situation near her, with the wife of Sa'eed Páshá on my left hand. That beautiful girl must not be passed over in silence. Her face and form are exquisite, and her manners perfectly graceful. Her tall slender figure is strikingly elegant; and, best of her attractions, a lovely disposition beams in her expressive countenance. She was given in marriage last year to Sa'eed Páshá, a son of Mohammad 'Alee: I can only hope that he treasures such a jewel. Few Orientals were seated; but the Páshás' wives and others holding high rank here, walked round the table during the repast: the bride herself being among them in dishabille, unobserved and unknown by the European guests, who had not yet seen her. I did not myself see her, though my eyes were wandering about in search of my too kind friend Mrs. Lieder, who, having been requested by Nezleh Hánum to assist her in attending to the comforts of the guests, was altogether negligent of her own.

Not long after the guests had taken their seats, the Hareem band entered, and commenced playing lively airs, which they continued during the dinner.

The Eastern ladies in general seemed quite at their ease; the difficulties of the knife and fork did, however, occasionally present themselves. A lady near me requested her neighbour, or her neighbour volunteered, to show her the way to her mouth; accordingly they raised the fork together, and consequently the morsel dropped. This was done without a smile; indeed it was a grave subject; for, like the Persian ambassador described by Hajji Bábá, the lady might have narrowly escaped losing an eye. Dinner, nevertheless, passed without any serious accident occurring; her Highness frequently inviting her guests to eat, and to feel themselves at home, by such phrases as these:—"In the name of God, in the name of God; O ladies! my house is yours,"[1] &c.

After dinner Nezleh Hanum led the way to a room adjoining the saloon in which we had dined; and, taking her seat in the centre of the upper end, she desired that all the ladies might be seated. The divan was a very miserable one, being awkwardly high, and sloping downwards towards the front; consequently the Europeans were either half seated, and slipping forward, or drew their feet upon the divan. Neither manner, we were led to suppose, entirely satisfied her Highness, as a lady who said that she was deputed by her, inquired whether those ladies would sit in such positions in the presence of their own sovereigns! An English lady sharply replied, "No; but they would have chairs to sit upon, and not so unsuitable a divan." A lady, however, who sat near her Highness during the whole of the first evening, asserts, that the question thus put to the European ladies was unauthorized, and appears to have arisen from some mistake: that, on the contrary, Nezleh Hánum desired that they might consider themselves at home; that all ceremony might be dismissed; that she considered the younger ladies as her children, and the elder ones as her sisters: and she requested that her feelings and wishes might be interpreted: but they were not: thus a false impression existed.

We were all much amused with six Turkish girls, who danced, or rather tumbled about, very pleasantly; appearing as though they were disciplined rompers. Had they laughed, the illusion would have been complete; but they were grave to a fault. Three of these girls were dressed in red Cashmere, and three in blue, with black velvet zones and wide gold fringe beneath these. Their dresses, in respect of form, were tight waistcoats, full white muslin sleeves, and full trowsers. These dancers turned round and round, threw back their heads, and rolled them in circles; knelt down, and rolled their heads again; sprung up, and seemed as though they were running in the air; and concluded by twisting white handkerchiefs, which they held in their hands, over their heads and under their arms alternately. A band of musicians played and sang in the Turkish manner during the dance. Six little girls succeeded those I have described: they were all Georgians, and were very interesting in appearance. The hair of each was dishevelled, and hanging down the back;

---

[1] "Bismalláh, Bismilláh, Yá Sittát, Beytee Beytkum."

and their dresses were of pink Cashmere, tight vests, and full petticoats, with three rows of gold fringe on the latter. Their dancing pleased me more than that of their predecessors. They took infinite pains, and often nearly fell down with their exertions; their pretty dark hair flying sometimes before their faces, and their shoes leaving them altogether. I quite enjoyed their performance. Another group of dancers from perhaps fifteen to eighteen years of age, dressed uniformly in European plaid silks, amused the spectators in much the same manner. The movements of the feet, which appear to be the last considered in the Turkish dance, consisted of three steps and a hop. These girls were succeeded by two 'A'lmehs, the first Arab singers of Egypt; and the band struck up some beautiful Arab airs; but on that evening the 'A'lmehs did not sing; they only danced in the Arab manner, for which performance they are also celebrated as the first of their day. The Arab dance has been sufficiently described by many travellers, therefore I need only remark that it is *extremely* disgusting.

After the performance of the 'A'lmehs, nearly all the European ladies partook of coffee and sherbet, and took their leave. I was among those who remained, intending to pass at least the following day and night. About eight others, whose carriages did not arrive, remained also, to pass the night.

LETTER VIII
(Second Series)

December, 1845

ON the departure of the European guests, we had left the room in which we had been sitting to say "good-bye" to our friends and acquaintances; and when we returned, a very curious scene presented itself. Six of the fattest old ladies of the Hareem were running after each other in a circle, in the centre of the room, disguised in chintz coats nearly fitting their round persons, with high fool's-caps on their heads. Their game consisted in snatching at each other's caps, and throwing them down, and scrambling for them; while they continued their circle, running, jumping, and tumbling. It was very absurd, for the good ladies were particularly unwieldy.

A theatrical exhibition followed, in which a scolding wife was represented by a pretty girl, while six other girls, in male attire, took part in a conversation which, being in Turkish, I could not understand. The spirit, however, of the farce seemed to be that one of the six personated the pretty girl's husband, and the other five her paramours. They successively endeavoured to approach her, while she appeared to encourage their addresses, but were each chased round the part of the saloon appropriated to these performances by the husband, caught, and then thrown down by him; or rather, after a little wrestling, they one after another obediently rolled on the floor, and then got up and walked away. When this was over, her Highness rose, the tambourine-girls preceded and followed her as before, and we all retired for the night.

We were conducted to a room which was furnished round with divans, and in the centre was arranged a very large and long musquito-curtain, of blue silk, under which, agreeably with the custom of the country, were placed, on the mat which covered the marble pavement, three large mattresses and pillows, with sheets and quilted coverlets. I mention these particulars to show you how carefully our comforts were considered; for the Easterns themselves generally sleep on their divans. We who were to share these beds were five persons; and we were all much tired, but too hungry to go to bed. Under such circumstances, I felt bold enough to ask for some supper for my companions and myself, and did so, and my request was most good-naturedly received and granted. A piece of cloth of gold was laid on the mat; a pretty Arab stool was placed upon it, and a silver tray, containing several little dishes, was brought. We supped right merrily, and the report of our good cheer taking wind, we were joined by two ladies, visitors, from another room, a mother and her daughter. I had during the day exceedingly admired those charming persons. They were Easterns, and were magnificently dressed, and wearing splendid diamonds; their whole attire was in perfect taste. When they joined our little supper-party they were in dishabille; but they were quite as beautiful with the simple white kerchiefs bound round their fair brows; and the plain cotton waistcoat and full trowsers, which formed their nightdress, became them admirably.

We were glad to go to bed, but our room was a thoroughfare, having doors opposite to each other; and persons were passing and repassing during nearly the whole night; consequently the night was far too lively to admit of much sleep. We were not aware, until the morning, that one, at least, of our comfortable quilted covers (which were as light and nearly as warm as eider-down) was of lilac satin, and beautifully adorned with a rich raised embroidery of gold.

Rising with the sun, we all felt that we should be glad if one of the many attendants who entered our room for the purpose of bidding us Good morning, should propose to bring us breakfast, when the pretty coffee-apparatus arrived, and a tiny cup of coffee was for each the portion. One of our companions asked for some bread, and two flat cakes were brought, and divided amongst us. Finding that the English really liked an early breakfast, our attendants most good-naturedly promised that everything "should be very nice for us, and plentiful, on the following day; but they had not been aware that any one ate in the morning." We went to an adjoining room, which was set apart as a private room for us, a thoroughfare, as is generally the case, most exquisitely fitted up. It is the Páshá's favourite resort in the Hareem. The divans extend nearly round the three sides of the room, leaving only the spaces for the doors opposite to each other; they are of stone-coloured satin, embroidered with gold in raised work of fruit and flowers. The divans along the end of each division of the great saloon, which adjoins this room, are of the same description.

Our now little party were scarcely seated in this beautiful room, when the eldest wife of the Páshá, a very charming and affable old lady, entered, and seeing us naturally rise to her, requested us immediately to resume our seats. When we had done so, she again most politely addressed us, assuring us of a hearty welcome, and adding that the palace was hers, and that she hoped we should remain. We had just acknowledged her kindness, when the favourite wife of Ibraheem Páshá joined our party, and conversed with us in a most amiable manner. His Hareem are distinguished for great affability, and on the occasion of this festivity the manners of his whole family who were present were delightful. Indeed, the attentions which we Europeans received from all the principal inmates of the Hareem, and from visitors and others, could scarcely have been exceeded without becoming irksome. The foremost in performing offices of kindness was the lady of

Hekekian Bey,[†] who devoted her whole attention to the guests, and who had the happy art of making us feel at home even in the great palace of the citadel. Her kind voice greeted us whenever we were near her with the friendly inquiry whether we had everything that we needed to render us comfortable, or if there were anything she could order for us; and she had a most delightful coadjutor in Madame ——, who zealously assisted her in paying polite attention to the guests with a tact it was pleasing to observe; and speaking admirably French, Italian, and Arabic, with some knowledge of Turkish, was delightfully qualified for her kind office, and was never at a loss in conversation with either Europeans or Easterns.

After a short chat with the ladies just mentioned in the room particularly appropriated to us, we proposed seeing and hearing what might be going forward in the great saloon below. On our arriving at the marble staircase, we heard the Arab female band in full concert; and when we reached the first landing, and, turning, saw nearly the whole saloon, how heartily we wished that such a fairy-like scene could be transferred to canvas, and that thus our friends in England might be enabled to form some idea of Eastern magnificence. Trite as is the remark, I cannot help observing that the sight which here presented itself to me most strikingly reminded me of the "Thousand and One nights." On the staircase stood here and there a slave gorgeously attired; and, at the foot of the staircase, grouped as if for artistic effect, were ladies and slaves, whose dresses displayed such a combination of rich and delicate colours, and such variety of magnificent embroidery, while on their heads and waists glittered innumerable jewels, that they unknowingly presented so splendid an effect as beggars all description. In the centre of the great saloon sat a circular group of Arab musicians on cushions on the mat, with every variety of instrument used in the country, all beautifully picturesque in form, and daintily inlaid with mother-of-pearl and dark wood. These women were all wearing the white head-veil, bound across the forehead and under the chin in the sphinx-like fashion so generally adopted by the Arab women, and hanging entirely over their backs. You will imagine that in their picturesque simplicity of attire they formed a striking contrast and pleasing relief to the gorgeous splendour of the ladies of the Hareem. Beyond this circle was the opposite compartment of the saloon, extending far away, with its row of windows, and crimson satin gold-embroidered divan across the end. Upon that divan sat all the elder members of the Páshá's family; Nezleh Hánum being in the right-hand corner. Forming a row on each side of the compartment were the ladies of Efendees belonging to the Páshá's household. The elders were simply attired; but the Efendees' wives were very splendidly adorned, and the attendant slaves magnificently apparelled.

[†]Hekekian Bey and his wife, Armenians, were friends of Lucie Duff Gordon and are mentioned in her *Letters from Egypt* (1862–69).

Finding that we were expected to join the party in that part of the saloon, we did so, and looked back with admiration on the scene through which we had passed. The dresses of the day before were laid aside for others infinitely more costly and beautiful: indeed the splendour displayed on that second day in the hundreds of rich dresses and decorations, could hardly, I think, be surpassed; and, curiously enough, *every* article of dress was different from those worn on the day before; even the diamonds were changed for others which were more costly, in many cases. The dancing-girls, the little group of six, in pink Cashmere trimmed with gold fringe, alone retained their former dresses during the whole festivity, and their doing so had a very pleasing effect, for they were identified by their pretty dresses, and the very uniformity amidst so much variety was relieving to the eye. Two of the Arab band rose from their cushions; and I was surprised to recognise, when they came forward without their tarhahs, or head-veils, the two 'A'lmehs of the preceding evening. They were tastefully attired, and a diamond crescent and star glittered on the right brow of each. One wore also a charm, contained in a little box very elegantly set with diamonds, and hung on a silk cord which passed over her left shoulder and under her right arm. Their dancing was odious; but they were not merely dancers on this occasion: they sang in turns, and their melody was so charming, there was such a wild sweetness in the airs they sang, the quality of their voices was so singularly rich, and their execution was so wonderful, that had I possessed ears without eyes, the treat which they afforded would have been complete. As it was, I could listen without looking at them, and thus intensely enjoy the vocal performances of those remarkable songstresses. It is really wonderful that there should be a great similarity between their style of singing and that which one hears in the streets of Cairo, and yet that the effect of their performances should be so enchanting. They were succeeded by the young girls in pink and gold; and their innocent romping dance pleased us, as it never failed to do; but soon the 'A'lmehs took their places, and they continued dancing for some time, joined by three others.

Weary of the sound of their castagnettes, and annoyed by their performances, my friend Mrs. Lieder and I were quite relieved by hearing the tambourines beaten merrily as Nezleh Hánum rose and retired to her private apartments. It was always pretty to see those tambourine-girls preceding and following her whenever she changed her place, beating their instruments in time, and really giving to her movements a martial air. We, too, thought that a change might be agreeable, and passing to the upper saloon, we walked through the apartments, and backwards and forwards in the saloon, wondering when breakfast or dinner would be announced. At half-past twelve our appetites were so sharpened by the pure air which the inhabitants of the citadel enjoy, that we became rather anxious for some refreshment. At one o'clock we found that a *déjeûné à la fourchette* was prepared for the Europeans, and it was proposed that we should dine at six. Thus they conformed to the common hours of the Franks, and prepared a profusion of dishes; while the simple English habit of taking light and frequent meals was not understood by our Eastern hostess.

We returned to the lower saloon after dinner, and found the 'A'lmehs dancing. A young girl in male attire, dressed as a page, directed the entertainment. She held in her hand a black baton, to the upper end of which were attached numerous little silver bells; she called on and off the dancers and singers, and ushered in new comers, and conducted them to her Highness' presence. She is about twelve years of age, and possesses and exercises a degree of delegated authority which is remarkable. It was droll to hear her shout for a change in the performances, and it surprised me to find that she possessed the power of extending or cutting short any amusement. The circle of Arab musicians remained all day, playing and occasionally singing in the centre of the saloon, only varying their airs according as the singing or dancing was Arab or Turkish. The Turkish dancers succeeded the 'A'lmehs, each carrying a wooden sword and shield; and they turned round and round, striking first their own shields, and then each other's swords and shields, with much dexterity, beating time to the Turkish airs which were played by the band. During that day the elder ladies of nearly all the great Hareems arrived.

In our wanderings through the palace, we found ourselves in a spacious and beautiful room, having in the centre a fountain. It is a pity that the magnificent silver fountain, lately presented to the Páshá by the East India Company, is not there. Its present place in the Kasr en Neel is not worthy of it, the palace is so very inferior to that of the citadel. The room above mentioned in the citadel is an oblong chamber paved with marble, the surface of each slab containing sixteen square feet, with an oval marble tank in the centre measuring eighteen feet by ten, from the middle of which rise three shallow vases, one above another, in the upper edges of which are perforations whence the water flows into as many oval basins beneath. These vases form a tall pinnacle, the lower one being large, the second smaller, and the upper one smaller still. There are also marble receptacles for water-bottles which are beautifully constructed, and resemble the fountain in form. There is one large recess in the room, surrounded by windows, and furnished with a mat and divan.

I had reason to repent my wanderings on that day, for I was saddened by witnessing grief I had no power to assuage. It being very cold, I engaged Madame —— as my companion for a quick walk through the corridors for the sake of gaining warmth; and we were cheerfully conversing, when our attention was painfully arrested by finding a little girl sitting on the floor, resting her head heavily on her hands, while the tears rolled down beneath her fingers. We begged to know the cause of her distress, and gently tried to remove her hands; but to no purpose. She only pressed them closer to her face, and gave us no reply. On inquiry, we found that she was a new slave,

and either her grief for the loss of friends, or her fears for the future, over-
whelmed her. Her sorrow was too deep for sympathy. My walk was spoilt,
and my day too; and the recollection of that little girl is still painful to me.

The afternoon passed much as the preceding had done. A sixth 'A'lmeh
disguised as a clown joined the five of the morning, and cleverly enough imitated and ridiculed their gestures. Among the companions we liked best was
a lady of most agreeable manners, who told me that she was the wife of
Mohammad 'Alee, and mother of the late Seleem Bey. It was estimated that
during the whole week of the festivity the daily average number of females
in the palace was seven thousand, and there was a constant low sound among
those thousands like that of the waves of the sea when heard from a short distance. At six o'clock we were summoned to dinner, which was served in the
same manner as the first; and after dinner the Turkish dancers and the
'A'lmehs resumed their performances, which they continued until about
eleven o'clock, when six costly Cashmere shawls were presented to the
'A'lmehs, and she who acted the part of the clown wound hers round the
fool's-cap which she wore. The evening concluded with theatrical amusements. The first farce was much the same as that I have described, with this
difference, that a green folding frame was brought forward, and so arranged
as to form a sort of enclosure, which the virago called her house, and in which
she welcomed several lady-gentlemen visitors, who where ever and anon
turned out by her jealous and offended husband. The second farce was a representation of a bath, into which so many claimed admittance that it became
impossible to accommodate one half of them. One applicant disguised as a
Darveesh (in Arabic, Darweesh) gave no very cleanly reason for requiring the
bath; the conversation during that evening being a mixture of Arabic and
Turkish, I was able to understand the drift of the performance. The people
were however so long in the bath, that I and Mrs. Lieder left them to settle
their pretended differences, and went to bed.

We found the blue silk curtain arranged as on the previous night. Three
mattresses were under it, and our party would occupy but two; we therefore
expected company for the night, and were not disappointed.

I lay awake for some hours, for, in truth, I was in wretched spirits, and little
disposed for sleep. The trouble of the poor slave was swallowed up in one far
more grievous. A eunuch belonging to one of the great hareems had, in the
evening of the preceding day, snatched from the head of his mistress a diamond spray. She immediately missed it, and accused him of the theft. He
denied it, but a peasant woman who happened to be present asserted that she
saw him take it. He was stripped, and the diamonds were found on his person. It was his third offence, and there was no tribunal to which he could
appeal. He was the property of his master, and his life was in his hands. He
was condemned to be beaten, and then to be put into a sack, and thrown into
the Nile; and the order was executed. I heard of it in the evening, and in the

morning of that day the poor fellow had been drowned. Had we but known it before his life was gone, we might have petitioned for him, and I do believe that our petition would have been granted; for the evident desire to afford gratification to the European guests was apparent in every thing. Would to Heaven we had been able to save him!

During each of the nights in the palace, there were but two quiet hours, from about two to four o'clock, owing to the irregularity of the Easterns in their seasons for taking rest. At about two hours after midnight, a lady raised our curtain, and asked if there remained room for her. We replied that one bed was unoccupied; and she immediately dropped off her slippers only, and crept into bed full dressed; her rich embroidery of gold glittering by the subdued light which the candles threw within our curtain. After very little sleep, we were truly glad to see the gleam of day. Our stranger-companion rose with us; and taking off her yelek and saltah, arranged afresh her lace shirt, and put her apparel on again. This was all the freshening she desired in the morning; and she came to breakfast without even washing her hands.

Our breakfast consisted of toast and butter and tarts, with the usual little cups of coffee; but the coffee-bearer remarked, "A number of such cups will make one large one; and I will pour as long as you like." We did not, however, tax her. Our Eastern companion helping herself to some toast, a bystander exclaimed, "The toast is for the *English* ladies." She immediately replaced it; but we begged she would oblige us by sharing our breakfast, and she did so gladly, for the toast was a novelty.

After breakfast, all was bustle and activity: the Páshá had arrived, and was in the fountain-room above mentioned, and the bride was going down to kiss his hand. All the visitors arranged themselves in the upper saloon to see her pass, and descend the stairs. We were well placed, and had an excellent view of her. Before she appeared, the shrill zagháreet and loud beating of tambourines announced her to be on her way. The dancers in pink and gold appeared first, each with a tambourine, and dancing and turning round with much spirit; then a band of musicians; and then some more little dancers. Nezleh Hánum followed them with attendants and trainbearers, all again in new dresses. Then walked the bride, supported on the right hand by her mother, and on the left hand by the wife of Sa'eed Páshá. The bride's face was perfectly colourless, and she appeared to sustain her trouble, and the weight of her ornaments, with great difficulty. The beautiful face of Sa'eed Páshá's wife, excepting that her expressive countenance beamed with deep feeling, was like that of a marble statue. I have seldom seen such a change; on that morning she looked as though she were a bride herself; and an *Eastern* one too. While the bride was passing down the stairs, her mother stopped her to place an additional diamond spray on her head-dress, which was already nearly covered with diamonds, as she was really wearing at one time all the head-ornaments I have described to you. She also wore the magnificent girdle;

otherwise her dress was the same as that in which I had seen her first. She was followed by about thirsty slaves, gorgeously attired; and then the second bride followed, attended similarly, and wearing also the same dress in which she had first appeared. Crowds passed down the staircase with them, and crossed the lower saloon; but Nezleh Hánum, and the brides, with their immediate attendants, alone entered the room where the Páshá awaited their arrival. They remained with him about ten minutes, when he left the palace, and they retraced their steps, attended as when they descended. The whole aspect of this second procession was the same as that of the first, excepting that those most nearly concerned looked as though they had passed through a painful ordeal.

Intending to return on that day (Saturday) to spend Sunday at home, and to see my dear ones, and finding my kind friend in the same mind, we both prepared for departure, as soon as the brides had repassed; and, now at home, I must tell you of the entertainment the Páshá gave his male guests, and of the out-door fantasia. By the way, this word fantasia is one of the most useful of all words here; every decoration, however applied, every entertainment, musical or otherwise, is styled a fantasia.

Mohammad 'Alee Páshá entertained a different select dinner-party on the several days of the festivity. Among the persons invited by him were the consuls, and many of the European travellers and residents in Egypt. On one day the principal 'Ulama dined with him; and in the evening, after dinner, he led these grave and dignified personages into an apartment which had been fitted up as a theatre, to witness there the performances of a company of European actors! It was the first time, they say, that any of them had been present at such a scene; and we may reckon their adventure among the greatest of all the European innovations which occurred during the festivities.

On the morning of the first day of the festivities, while I was preparing to go to the citadel, the bridegroom's presents, which I have described to you, were conveyed to Zeyneb Hánum with some pomp from her future abode in the Ezbekeeyeh. A friend who witnessed it described it to me as follows:— One of the Páshá's military bands headed the train, followed by a regiment of lancers. Then came a number of military officers on foot, bearing on their heads the trays of sweetmeats; and, after these, the carriages in which the jewels, plate, dresses, &c. were deposited. Each carriage was drawn by four horses, and covered with green velvet fringed with gold. On either side of each walked three officers in scarlet and gold. Some more officers bearing trays of sweetmeats followed the carriages, and another regiment of lancers and a military band closed the procession.

On each night there are theatrical performances at the citadel, and tickets are sent to the Europeans and to as many Easterns as can be accommodated. Three hundred cooks are employed daily to prepare excellent food for the poor in the palace of the Ezbekeeyeh. The long route from the Ezbekeeyeh to the citadel, extending about two miles, is hung with large lanterns, each containing ten well lighted lamps, and the Ezbekeeyeh, the citadel, and many of the principal houses were illuminated. The great irregular place called the Ezbekeeyeh, where the palace of the bride is situated, being of large extent, nearly half a mile in its greatest length, and about a third of a mile in its greatest width, is the chief scene of the out-door amusements. Its conversion, from a spacious lake into a pleasant garden, surrounded by a canal, and crossed by several roads, is now almost complete. Here, near to each extremity of its main road, which traverses it from west to east (from the side of the palace of the bride, and the exterior of the city, towards the heart of the metropolis), are erected two large and lofty triumphal arches. These are illuminated with a profusion of small lamps. The road between them is bordered by illuminated pillars, and by small globe-shaped lanterns of red and white paper. Many hundreds of this kind of lamp are also hung upon cords between the trees which border the whole tract of garden-ground and the several roads: and a large screen which conceals the front of the principal part of the bride's palace is hung with a vast number of similar lights. The general aspect of the place at night is singularly beautiful and picturesque.

During each day wrestlers, rope-dancers, and musicians entertain the people in several places; but the great focus for amusement is the Ezbekeeyeh. Every night there is a display of an abundance of rockets and other very good fireworks; therefore while I am in the Hareem I have the satisfaction of knowing that my dear children have amusements which they much enjoy. At the top of a very high soaped pole in the Ezbekeeyeh a shawl and ten pounds have been placed, to be the property of any one who can climb to the top. Many and earnest have already been the attempts of the poor people to obtain this boon; but they have fallen down like stones after gaining a certain height. During each day there are frequent discharges of artillery from the citadel and other parts, and the cannons thunder over the city at least four times each day.

On Monday a curious procession took place; the jewels and almost the whole paraphernalia of the bride being pompously conveyed from the citadel to the Ezbekeeyeh. The jewels were uncovered, as well as many other costly things. The following account I have received from friends, for I did not witness it. At an early hour the route from the Ezbekeeyeh to the citadel was densely crowded, and thousands were gazing from the windows and roofs of the houses. It was headed by an excellent military band playing European airs. A regiment of lancers next followed. The bridegroom took his seat at a window of the Páshá's stables, near the Ezbekeeyeh; and I should think it was as amusing a circumstance as any attending the procession to see one so nearly concerned in the stirring events of the time climb up to such a place, followed by his attendants, that he might have a good view of the property of his future wife. He was dressed in the present Constantinople style, with a diamond badge. He is a manly and good-looking person, apparently about thirty years of age. His horse was handsomely caparisoned. A number of officers in the uniform of the regular troops followed the lancers in the procession. Their dresses were beautifully embroidered, and they formed a very picturesque body. Many Muslim school-boys passed next, chanting suitable passages from the Kur-an. Then followed men on stilts, clad in short vests and long full petticoats; and next the Páshá's band on horseback, dressed in scarlet and gold, and playing European airs; and a troop of the lancers. The zagháreet from the hundreds of women in the streets, in the houses, and on the house-tops, was sometimes almost stunning, but had a joyous sound, although it did not mingle harmoniously with the European airs. A regiment of cuirassiers, never seen before by many of the oldest residents in Cairo, passed next; and then, some wrestlers, clad in leather drawers, and with their bodies oiled. Several regiments of foot-soldiers followed these, bearing red and white silk flags with the crescent and star on each. Another military band and a numerous company of well-dressed and well-mounted officers. A hundred and fifty men, handsomely attired, bearing on their heads covered trays tastefully ornamented with coloured crape and ribbons, divided into two companies; the first, consisting of forty, with a number of eunuchs, preceded and followed the carriages in which were conveyed, exposed to public view, the jewels, plate, &c. The latter part of the train consisted of a troop of cavalry, a large body of infantry, a military band, a troop of lancers, another of cuirassiers, and another military band. There was little in the procession to remind one of the old fashioned Eastern pageants. No police seemed to be employed to maintain order, and I did not hear that such persons were required.

LETTER IX
(Second Series)

ON Tuesday morning Mrs. Lieder returned with me to the palace, where we were received with distinguished politeness by Nezleh Hánum, and warmly welcomed by many. The consideration shown to us by the lady-treasurer, and all connected with the Kasr-en-Neel, was but a confirmation of what I have before remarked to you, that my dear friend Mrs. Lieder had, during her residence in Egypt, completely won their confidence and affection. She had much of prejudice to overcome when she was introduced into the Hareem of Mohammad 'Alee; but before many weeks had passed, a general feeling pervaded the minds of its members that the English lady desired their good, and they looked with pleasure for the hour of her arrival. That feeling has grown into affection; and I have always seen them welcome her as though she were a near relation. On the day of our return their cordiality was particularly manifested, because Mrs. Lieder had not led them to suppose she should return when she quitted the Hareem on Saturday.

Until breakfast was announced, Turkish and Arab dancers, and a full Arab band, filled up the hours. At one o'clock breakfast was prepared, and the mother of Mohammad 'Alee presided. Much credit is due to the Europeans who had the ordering of the refreshments for the guests. Everything was so quietly and so well arranged for the many hundreds who visited the palace, that it was matter of surprise to me how it was managed. Had the entertainment been Turkish, there were too many hands to prepare it; but being entirely European, the inmates of the Hareem could only help as they were directed, and consequently the responsibility of pleasing the guests fell entirely upon the Europeans employed.

On descending to the lower saloon we found a group of Turkish dancers; they were succeeded by the 'A'lmehs, who danced and sang alternately. During their performances, eight interesting-looking little girls arranged themselves in a row, waiting a signal for beginning their lively dance. They were dressed in black Cashmere richly embroidered with gold, and they wore black silk caps, each with a long tassel of pearls, which hung over the left ear. These caps were very picturesque, and the dishevelled hair of those pretty little dark-eyed Georgians harmonized well with the dégagé style of their headdress.

Nezleh Hánum was much pleased by an expression of approbation which fell from a lady with whom I have the pleasure of being acquainted, and her Highness requested me to return the compliment for her; and added, while she looked with a smile at the European ladies who were her guests, "The ladies who are visiting us are beautiful; our house is theirs, and I thank them for their company."

The queen of beauty, the wife of Sa'eed Páshá, presided at the dinner at six o'clock, and most gracefully did the honours of the table. There were more Europeans on that day than on any day previous, excepting the first of the entertainment. After each meal coffee was offered, and frequently during each day. We descended after dinner to the lower saloon, where we found the Arab band seated in the centre as usual, with hundreds of auditors, and, in her usual place, her Highness Nezleh Hánum, with the elder ladies of the Páshá's family, the 'A'lmehs dancing before them. Soon after our entrance, those admirable songstresses delighted us with their Arab airs, so singing that the great saloon seemed filled with music, as though by a full orchestra; and yet their tones so modulated that they fell sweetly on the ear. The taller set of the Turkish dancers came forward when the singing of the 'A'lmehs ceased, and as they danced, the musicians who accompanied them sang some Turkish airs. One thing I thought quite a pity;— the Turkish dancers on that occasion, for the first time during our visit, imitated the disgusting dancing of the 'A'lmehs: it perfectly spoilt those hitherto innocent-looking dancers, whose graceful romping before was really pleasant to witness. Enough of this subject. They were succeeded by an exceedingly fat old lady, who, disguised as a man, wearing a chintz surtout and high fool's-cap, came running forward, bearing a tray of sweetmeats. She was soon followed by the actresses of the former evenings, to whom she offered the sweetmeats for sale. One scolded her, another cheated her, a third stole her sweetmeats, and a fourth threw her on the ground with her tray, and left her bewailing the loss of her sweets and the blows she had received. While loudly lamenting, a light footstep near her put her on the alert, and she jumped on her feet just in time to secure one of her persecutors, who came to steal more of her dainties, and to bestow upon the culprit an apparently hearty beating. Becoming liberal, she afterwards allowed some to be taken by two whom she favoured, while she capriciously punished others. Thus occupied, we left her; for the night was exceedingly cold, and the wind whistled through that great saloon fearfully to those who, having mercifully passed through the great heat of summer, find an Egyptian winter severe, and dare not risk exposure to its really piercing cold unless protected by substantial additional clothing. The Easterns are wise in this respect, and scruple not at all to put on the most simple wrapper in the most distinguished company. Their simple wrappers, however, are costly; for, although very rarely embroidered, excepting sometimes with black, they are generally lined with fur. I do not refer to the saltah; these are generally exquisitely and elaborately embroidered; but to a jacket of the same form, considerably larger, the sleeves extending to the hands, and the jacket itself being ungracefully long. The Constantinople winter-coat for ladies, which much resembles the modern great-coat of England, having a high collar, being cut to fit the back, and often extending to the knees, is also worn in winter by many ladies. But I have quite run away on the subject of these surtouts, and must go back to tell you of our night arrangements.

We found in our usual sleeping-room two mattresses, &c., under a musquito-net of blue crape; and always counting our party for the night by the number of our mattresses, we found that we should have but two companions, a friend and her little girl. I had requested that the doors of our room might be locked for the night, and my request was granted. Both the doors were locked, one without, the other within. The key, however, of one door remained outside, and we were no sooner quiet than it softly opened, and two Eastern ladies came gently in, and, taking two divan cushions as pillows, laid themselves down on the divan, and rolled themselves round, taking off their girdles, and, with them, covering themselves entirely, so that each resembled a large round bundle in a Cashmere shawl. Towards morning another entered, and endeavoured to open the second door. Poor soul! she really was in rather an inconvenient position; having remained longer than she had intended witnessing the amusements, and being very sleepy, she desired to pass through to her bed-room. There was another way, it is true, but a very long and cheerless route down many stairs, through many passages, and up many stairs again; but this she was reluctant to take at two o'clock in the morning, and when all the lights of those staircases and passages had nearly burnt their last. The stranger fretted and then scolded, not at us, but at those who had taken so much care of the English ladies; and the fretting and scolding engaged the good lady long enough to have brought her considerably on her way by the long route. When she was gone I fell asleep, but our friend who shared the protection of our musquito-net was kept awake by the intrusion of several persons, who, having put out our light, remained for some time in the room. I mention these trifling particulars to give you some idea of the night-habits, or rather, the absence of any habits of comfort during the nights in the Hareems. It is not only on occasions of festivity that their hours of rest are thus irregular; although they are especially so at those times, the chief entertainment being during the nights. It is their general practice to take a siesta after dinner; and it depends upon the length of that afternoon's nap whether a night's rest is to be partially or fully enjoyed, or, as in some cases, altogether dispensed with.

Our night being passed, we rose as usual with the sun; and by and by a slave entered with a tray containing a number of tumblers; another followed her bearing a large basin full of something very hot, and in which was a very large ladle; then came a third with toast and butter. The pretty stool was brought, and the tray set upon it; the toast and butter placed in the middle, and a glass set before each person; and ere this ceremony was concluded,

several friends had joined us, and we formed a cheerful circle, while the two
first-comers of the previous night remained as round and as immovable on
the divan as when they first composed themselves to sleep. When the ladling
commenced, we were all glad to find that what had appeared to be, from the
strange manner in which it was served up, brown soup, proved to be excellent café-au-lait. How much may we be deceived by appearances! A singular
scene awaited us in the lower saloon after breakfast. Hearing that the Páshá
had arrived, we all descended, and found the saloon almost deserted; and he,
as before, was in the fountain-room. Several eunuchs were stationed at every
door to prevent ingress to the saloon; but we, being of course unmolested,
chose an excellent situation for seeing the Páshá pass. After a short time he
walked through, leaning on the arm of his daughter Nezleh Hánum. He was
looking remarkably well, his white beard forming a picturesque appendage
to his expressive countenance. As soon as he had passed, the many doors of
the saloon were thrown open, and the rush of women from all sides could
only be compared to the breaking in of a flood of water: it was fearful. We
soon learnt the cause: the Páshá had dropped gold coins (exactly equivalent
to our guineas) as he walked through. It is much to be deplored that he not
only suffers the barbarous custom of throwing money, but sanctions it by his
own example. The consequences are always frightful when it is practised in
a great Hareem, to which free access is given to all classes of women during
a festivity, or during a procession, in the close and crowded streets of an
Eastern city. It is altogether inconsistent with the enlarged views entertained
by Mohammad 'Alee on the subject of civilization.

On the morning of this day (Wednesday), the last day of the festivities in
the Hareem, almost all the European ladies who had dined in the palace on
the first day came again, and many more arrived from Alexandria. It was the
seventh day, that on which the hands of the bride are dyed with henna after
taking the bath, according to ancient custom, and the day before she is
introduced to the bridegroom. Among the newly arrived Easterns on this
and the two previous days was a little girl, apparently about six years of age:
her dress was embroidered with gold, and her head adorned with jewels in
the most costly manner; and she was attended by a little negro slave, who
sometimes walked behind her, and sometimes by her side, talking and
laughing with the great little lady, and always bearing her long and glittering train. The familiarity and the respect of such young attendants are
very remarkable; and the child who is at once the slave and companion of her
little mistress, is almost invariably a favourite with her lady's parents.

The crowds by which the palace was thronged during the festivities
were such as to cause some apprehension as to the security of the building;
consequently, some architects or surveyors were summoned to inspect the
upper saloon. It happened that, when they arrived, Mrs. Lieder was passing
across the saloon, and she was suddenly surprised on seeing the army of

eunuchs rush up the staircase, and drive before them all the ladies of the
Hareem and their slaves, who happened to be there, as though they were
driving sheep; brandishing their long sticks, and enforcing the obedience of
the slaves, while they used no gentle means in expelling the ladies. In about
two minutes, no one remained in the saloon but Mrs. Lieder and the eunuchs;
and then several veiled men were ushered up, guarded and held by eunuchs.
When I say veiled, I mean that they had handkerchiefs bound over their
faces. The eunuchs stationed themselves at every door, and then the surveyors
were suffered to unveil. The mats were rolled up, and the floors and walls
examined, to see if there were any settlement. The result of the investigation
was satisfactory; but we thought it might still be feared that the evening
entertainment might endanger the building, for it was arranged that it
should be below. I should imagine that the safety of almost any building
might be endangered by the thousands which thronged the citadel.

The entertainment during the Wednesday consisted in the performances
of the 'A'lmehs, until we were invited to breakfast at one o'clock; but we had
scarcely reached the room where it was prepared, when we were informed
that the bride was going down on her way to the bath, and would remain
some time in the lower saloon. We all descended, and witnessed a very curious scene. A passage was formed by the eunuchs, from the staircase, across
the saloon, and to the seat of honour in the corner. Through this we passed,
a row of eunuchs fronting the crowd on either side, and preventing any one
entering the avenue which they had formed, excepting European ladies, and
Easterns of rank.

I was seated very near to the place prepared for the bride. The guns thun-
dered from the citadel, and were answered from the fort on Mount
Mukattam; and when their echo was hushed, we heard the zaghâreet from a
distant chamber in the palace; it gradually drew nearer, when the merry tambourine was heard, and soon the dancing-girls in pink and gold were seen on
the great staircase, followed by many magnificent-dressed attendants, in the
midst of whom the bride slowly descended. As she approached us we saw
that her jewels, which had been paraded in the Ezbekeeyeh, were again on
her person; and her dress on this occasion made them look more brilliant and
more magnificent than ever. Her head-dress was still the same, excepting
that innumerable narrow slips of flat gold, about two feet long, were appended to it on either side before her ears[†]: behind her ears, two short tails of sable.
A head-veil of lavender-coloured gauze striped with gold hung from the back
of her head-dress. She wore the splendid diamond girdle and necklace, and
all the jewels for her head were disposed, or rather crowded together, on
her cap and headkerchief. Her yelek and trowsers were of pale green silk,

---

[†]Commonly known as *talli*, which are strips of tinsel, still worn by brides up to the
1930s.

gorgeously embroidered and fringed with gold; and her saltah of red velvet, adorned with gold and jewels, and lined with fur.

She took the seat of honour, and several magnificently-dressed persons fanned her as she sat. The showering of gold then commenced; and it was on this occasion thrown by all the ladies nearly connected with Mohammad 'Alee and his family. The rush, wherever it was thrown, was perfectly over-whelming to many hundreds; and not far from us a poor little child of three years of age was trodden to death! Most thankful were we that we did not hear of the death of the dear child, and of the distress of its poor mother, until some time after the evil had occurred; nor did we hear its cries. The rush for the money being always in directions from the part where we (the Europeans) were sitting, as it was thrown by Eastern ladies who were among us, we were in perfect security; but egress would have been impossible during that tumult. I thought that the bride looked less miserable than on the pre-vious days, and when one of her fanners accidentally struck her on her face, she smiled. The passage was cleared in the same manner by the eunuchs for the entrance of the second bride. She came attended in the same manner as the Páshá's daughter, and the same scene was enacted. Her head-dress, too, was the same as before, with the addition of the flowing strips of gold; and her yelek and trowsers were of white silk, most tastefully embroidered with gold thread, and with coloured flowers and leaves. When the brides had remained about ten minutes, a way was again cleared by the eunuchs, and with a row of those guards on either side, they retired.

We were all then invited to dinner, and about three hundred sat down to table. Nezleh Hánum presided. After dinner, Turkish and Arab dancing, and the delightful singing of the 'A'lmehs, in turns amused the company. Crowds continued to pour in until midnight, when about twenty slaves came forward, each bearing in her hands a dress in a piece of cloth of gold. These, it was said, were presents to be dispensed in honour of the principal bride. One branch of the double staircase was then cleared for her descent, while the other was densely crowded, and the procession (termed the procession of the candles) commenced. A number of eunuchs slowly descended the staircase first, bearing each a large painted wax candle, about four feet long: then a blaze of innumerable candles appeared at the head of the stairs, and flowed gently down, like a river of light. This effect was produced by a number of slaves, each bearing seven or eight wax-lights, fixed in a basket decorated with gaily-coloured flowers, on a small green jar, containing, I am told, paste of henna for dyeing the hands, to give them a deep orange-red hue, which many, by a second and different application, change to black. The jars they held in their hands, and raised high over their heads. Among those slaves walked the bride, blazing with diamonds; her jewels reflecting the hundreds of lights around her. She was preceded and attended as usual by the dancers, and by girls beating their tambourines. When all the candle-bearers reached and crossed the floor of the lower saloon, the noise produced by the shrill cries of joy and the beating of the tambourines was almost deafening.

The bride remained about a quarter of an hour, and then with her attendant band, and numerous candle-bearers, she crossed the saloon, and ascended the staircase. I felt a desire to ascend to the upper saloon in order to look down upon the scene which would present itself when the second bride should descend the stairs; and I did so, but I had nearly paid very dearly for my temerity. I was not aware that, during the exit of the first bride, money had been thrown among the women; and I only expected to ascend with the stream. When, however, I had reached the centre of the saloon, I was, indeed, in troubled waters. Two or three torrents of human beings rushed from different directions, while the eunuchs dashed in among them, and used their whole force to preserve order. A large body of women was driven against me, and I was tossed like a ball into a crowd coming another way. Thus driven to and fro, and gaining by each convulsion a little way towards the staircase, I saw that Mrs. Lieder, whom I had lost, had just reached it in safety. I had still a few feet to gain, and I had no strength left to make my way. Finding myself close to one of the eunuchs, I threw myself upon his protection, and told him that I wanted to reach the staircase. In another moment he kindly took me, as though I had been a child, and placed me on the stairs in security.

In the upper saloon we found that all the elder eunuchs had received presents of Cashmere shawls; several had received two; and one had three or four wound around him in different directions. There, also, all the candle-bearers were waiting to attend the second bride. She soon appeared, and, with her retinue, crossed the saloon and passed down the staircase. It was pretty to look down upon the lights, the dancers, and the bride; for she too, with her jewels, gave additional light to the scene; but the spectacle was not nearly so imposing as when seen from below. We waited her return, and saw the close of the brilliant exhibition at nearly two o'clock on Christmas morning.

It now became an easier matter to make our way through the crowd. We found the lights dying away in the illuminated court of the palace; and as we drove through the streets of Cairo, the city seemed deserted. We saw but two persons on our way to the Ezbekeeyeh, and the man with the mesh'al (or cresset) running before the horses, and holding high his flaming light, was the only object of interest. The gleam cast by the burning wood on his simple but picturesque costume, made him appear as though he too were wearing a holiday garb.

The zeffeh, or procession of the bride, from the citadel to her own palace, did not take place until after church on Christmas-day: but I was so completely tired that I could not go to see it; and, therefore, I give you the description which I received from my friends.

Though all the inhabitants of Cairo seemed congregated to view it, the zeffeh was not well calculated to gratify the curiosity it excited. It was little

more than a mere display of soldiery and carriages: the former, half
Europeanized in dress; and the latter, with few exceptions, just such as are
seen in the streets of London or Paris. It was headed by a full military band
preceding three troops of lancers, and as many bands of trumpeters. These
were followed, first by a numerous body of cuirassiers; and, next, by about a
dozen field-pieces with their ammunition. Some wrestlers and mock com-
batants with swords interrupted the military train, preceding a few pioneers,
and four companies of infantry, each with its band. A very numerous body of
officers rode at their rear. Among them were Mohammad 'Alee Bey and a son
of Ibraheem Páshá, with many of the grandees of Cairo: those of highest rank
occupying the rear. Then came between thirty and forty carriages; the last of
which was the state carriage of the bride. This was surrounded by a host of
well mounted eunuchs and other officers, and by four men bearing some
orange-branches bound together and laden with fruit. It was drawn by six
horses; and its blinds were closed. The coachman of each carriage had a
Cashmere shawl placed over his right shoulder and tied at the left side. A
large body of lancers closed what may properly be called the zeffeh. The cries
of joy raised by the female portion of the spectators as the carriage of the
bride passed considerably increased the uproar, which was otherwise great.
During the procession, chaooshes threw pieces of money upon the roofs of the
lower houses, into the first-floor windows, and among the dense crowds in
the streets, and six persons were, in consequence, trodden to death! The carriage of Nezleh Hánum followed at some distance after the procession, and
after it a train of the Páshá's cooks, bearing trays of food, which they distributed to the poor.

The shawl and the money at the top of the soaped pole defied all attempts
to reach them until after the conclusion of the festivities, when the man who
placed them there succeeded in making them his prize. He did not attempt
the feat until all others who had tried the ascent were hors de combat. The
mock elephant and the ark, I am told, were conveyed back to the citadel,
instead of being blown up as was expected.

LETTER X
(Second Series)

YOU will be curious to hear of the reception of the bride by her husband. When her carriage came into the Hareem-court of her palace, Kámil Páshá was at the door to receive her; but for two hours she remained with the doors and blinds fast closed, according to the etiquette of resistance; and she would have continued to make her carriage her castle much longer, had not the press of people, who desired to know the moment of her ascent, been so great as to create an uproar outside the palace-gates. At length the carriage was opened, and Kámil Páshá approached, and, uncovering the hands and feet of the bride, kissed them both respectfully, but did not then uncover her face. Taking her in his arms, he lifted her from the carriage, carried her up stairs, and placed her on a divan in a magnificently-furnished apartment, where he left her with her attendants for some hours. Late in the evening he request-ed permission to visit her, and did so in the presence of several visitors and attendants. She was veiled when he entered the saloon; and he approached with much humility, and, after kissing her hands and feet, uncovered her face; and retiring backwards, gazed upon her for a moment; after which he drew near a second time, and kissed her hands and feet again. He then con-versed with her on various subjects for about an hour and a half, and retired to his own apartments, and for eleven days he visited his bride in the same ceremonious manner. Since that period, I understand that she has thrown off her reserve.

The festivities in the family of Mohammad 'Alee have soon given place to mourning, for two persons very nearly connected with him are hourly expected to breathe their last. The one is his third wife, and the other the widow of his son Isma'eel Páshá. To the latter the cares of the Viceroy are chiefly directed. It is a curious fact, that she is the widow of a boy who was murdered in Sennár when only sixteen years of age! Since his death, she has generally resided in Constantinople, and having considerable influence with the mother of the Sultán, she has constantly exercised it in favour of Mohammad 'Alee. His interest has been her great aim at all times. He is therefore unwilling to lose her, and clings to every hope that she may ulti-mately recover. Her two principal attendants are the bride of Kámil Páshá and another near relation of Mohammad 'Alee. Those two persons sit up with the invalid during alternate nights; and, strange to say, they and all the attendants are in deep mourning. How such an ill-timed compliment affects the mind of the sufferer I cannot tell; but of one thing I am certain, so dismal an arrangement would kill a nervous person.

The late grand wedding, to which I did not expect again to have to allude, seems to have been productive of one very bad consequence; for, since its termination, robberies have been unusually numerous in Cairo; and I think they may in a great measure be attributed to the abominable act of letting loose on the public all the criminals confined in the prisons on that occasion. The thieves of Egypt are, I believe, surpassed by none in impudence. The following instance is one of which I have just been told:—

During the absence of a family from their home, a woman entered their house, and ascended to the bath, which is in an apartment very little used in the East, excepting by the higher orders of Easterns; persons of the middle and lower classes always preferring the public baths. When the family returned, they heard the cries of an infant, and finding whence the noise proceeded, they entered the bath, and there beheld the woman with a new-born child. She immediately accosted them with the utmost effrontery, admonishing them to treat her and her infant with the greatest consideration; "For," said she, "this is the child of the inhabitant of the bath." Her speech acted like a spell upon her hearers: believing, in common with most Easterns, that every bath has its inhabitant (an efreet, or powerful genie, possessing considerable influence over the destiny of the family), the deluded people treated her with the greatest liberality, and never approached her but with fear during the three days' nursing, which is all the time an Eastern woman requires for her recovery after an accouchement. At the end of that period, the visitor contrived to secrete the jewels, and many other valuables belonging to her benefactress and family, and, with her infant, decamped, leaving the good people to lament their credulity. They never succeeded in obtaining any clue to her hiding-place.

The person who related to me this anecdote, told me also another, as follows:—

Not long since, the wife of a Magrabee set out, with her husband, on pilgrimage, bearing on her person costly jewels, generally well concealed; but a beautiful string of very choice pearls, which she carried in a bag suspended by a string passing over her right shoulder and under her left arm, was by some means seen; and before she had proceeded many miles from Cairo, she was waylaid, and stripped of her treasures. Her donkey-driver, who had quitted the caravan, and returned to his house in Cairo, was suspected of the robbery, but the guilt lay on others. The thieves who had the jewels took advantage of the suspicions formed to his prejudice, and finding his house, buried a few of the pearls under the threshold of his door, and informed the superintendant of police that there was strong reason for believing that he possessed some of the lost jewels, adding, that he had been observed scraping the earth at his door in a suspicious manner. The secreted pearls were found, and the donkey-driver was arrested and bastinaded; but no confession was elicited from him, for the poor fellow had nothing to disclose. In the meantime the informers took no care to avoid detection; upon which a shrewd fellow proposed that they should be all bastinaded. They were immediately seized, and while under the corbág they all pleaded guilty, and readily criminated each other. Thus was the poor man revenged, and his innocence asserted; but that was not sufficient compensation for the many cruel lashes which had swollen his feet, and disabled him from following his usual avocations.

One more instance of impudent thieving occurs to me:—

A woman, with a basket on her head, was stooping to drink, balancing her burden cleverly, as all the Easterns do, and drinking from a rivulet by filling repeatedly her right hand. Another woman lifted the basket from her head without her knowledge, and placing it on her own, held it with her left hand, while she, too, drank from her right. The first woman rising from her crouching posture, and finding herself light-headed, was exceedingly distressed by her loss, and complained bitterly. "Look at me," said the thief; "I never balance my basket without holding it; had you done so, you would never have lost yours." The unsuspecting woman confessed her error, and determined in future to follow such good advice.

To turn to a very different subject. I had yesterday an introduction to the Armenian bishop, who resides in this city. On my way I had some difficulties to encounter. It happened to be the last day of those devoted to the celebration of the Moolid en-Nebee (the festival of Mohammad's birthday), and I found myself most unexpectedly joining the procession of Sheykhs and attendants, en route for the house of the Sheykh el-Bekree, to assist in the performance of the Dóseh. For a description of the Moolid en-Nebee and the Dóseh, I refer you to my brother's 'Modern Egyptians.'[†] The procession I witnessed yesterday was moving at a very rapid pace, and many of the persons composing it bore large flags, most of which were green. Once riding among them, there was no escape for me, and no possibility of turning back; so I pursued my course until I reached the Ezbekeeyeh, where the wide space enabled me once more to be independent. Here was a very gay scene. Rows of tents of various colours, but chiefly green, and decorated in a picturesque manner, were arranged on either side of the road bordering the Ezbekeeyeh; and there were several swings and whirligigs, but with no one to use them, for half the crowd was in the neighbourhood of the house of the Sheykh, and the other half hurrying towards it. There were also many fanciful erections of poles and cords hung with Arab lamps and decorated with coloured flags. The Muslims have borrowed some idea from the Frank decorations employed during the late wedding, and from some of the amusements also, and again a soaped pole is erected there, with a purse of money on the top, surmounted

---

[†]Lane, *Modern Egyptians*, 451-53

by the crescent and star. I was most glad to have fairly passed the crowd, and, joining my friends, to find myself on the way to the Armenian bishop's.

We found the good bishop seated in his winter-room, wrapped in a dark cloth pelisse lined with sable. He is a venerable looking person, with a remarkably intelligent and pleasing expression of countenance. He received us in a very amiable manner, and conversed agreeably on several subjects. While we were sitting with him, a priest entered the room and joined our party. He was one of the handsomest old men I have ever seen; tall and stately in person, and mild and dignified in bearing; and having a very long and perfectly white beard. Hearing the bell toll for the afternoon service, I expressed a wish to attend it, and to see the church; and, taking our leave of the bishop, who accompanied us to the edge of the mat, and bade us farewell as he took a hand of each, we entered the church before the arrival of the officiating priests. The church is a fine lofty saloon, with six windows on either side, and outside these windows are screens of ornamental ironwork, which have a solid and handsome appearance; indeed there is an air of *bien être* about the church and appendages which is peculiar in the East as applying to all religious establishments of the Armenians. A curtain was drawn before the altar, in the front of which hung a picture representing the Crucifixion, with the three Marys at the foot of the cross. Before this picture a single lamp burns night and day. The church is matted, and on either side are arranged parallel with each other a number of oblong mattresses on which the congregation kneel. Opposite to the altar, at the other end of the church, is a raised matted portion, on which chairs are placed. From the ceiling hang several large chandeliers and a multitude of small silver lamps. There is a profusion of ornament above and around the altar, consisting of wreaths of gilt flowers and leaves; and gilt stars are scattered over a pale blue ground above the altar. The service was performed by two priests habited in cowls. It was chanted by them, assisted, or rather accompanied, by two boys, each about ten years of age. The chanting was good, and the whole service was impressive. One of the officiating priests was the noble-looking person with the white beard whom we had left with the bishop when the bell had tolled for church. After the service he approached us, and politely gave me permission to accompany him behind the curtain which concealed the altar; and I did so, leaving my shoes before stepping into their most holy place. Over the altar is hung a picture of the Virgin and the Infant Saviour, with a semi-circular glory above the picture. Before this picture also burns constantly a single lamp. In mentioning these pictures, I must remark, that the Armenians do not place upon them an undue value; the bishop carefully explains to his congregation, that such representations are never, under any circumstances, to be considered objects of worship, and that they are only placed before them to remind them of those events which so nearly concern their salvation.

You probably know that the various Christian nations of the East much resemble the Muslims in their domestic life, and general manners and habits, and in many of their superstitions; but this, I hope and expect, will not long continue to be the case. They are most willing to avail themselves of the benefit of European instruction; and many of them, who have been my neighbours, have readily adopted suggestions which I have offered with respect to the management of their children, the amelioration of whose condition is an object which I have much at heart. It is far from being thus with the Muslims. Many of these have applied to me for medicines for themselves and their children; but their abominable and disgusting prejudices have generally prevented my being of any use to them in complying with their requests. How they sometimes provoke me in cases of this kind, you may imagine from the following instance:—

A woman who frequently amused me by telling me of the quaint and clever sayings of her sister's little boy, and often mentioned the doting affection of both his parents for their only child, after visiting them recently, came to me in great distress to inform me that she had found the poor boy suffering severely from an abscess in one of his ears, and that his right eye was closed. On the following day he was sent to me, that I might see him, and tell his mother what medicine he required. How can I ever forget the sickening, but most affecting sight! The bright boy of my imagination was, I am grieved to say, almost a disgusting object; a poor creature one could not touch but with the hope of saving him: not only diseased, but unwashed, and with every appearance of having been in that miserable state for many weeks. He was quiet from weakness, and in a state of half-sleepy unconsciousness; his languid head resting heavily on the shoulder of his anxious nurse, whose cleanly appearance presented a painful contrast to his wretched condition. I prepared for him some medicine, and gave some eye-water which has always been the means of removing disease wherever we have applied it, if used before ophthalmia had grown into blindness; only requiring that the eye and ear should be washed repeatedly, and the whole body daily. Two days after, I sent to inquire how my remedies had succeeded; when I found, to my dismay, that a film had formed over the suffering eye. "Have they applied the lotion?" was my anxious inquiry. "Once only," my messenger replied; "for the child would not suffer them to use it." I was grieved and disappointed, knowing how much good my application had always, with the blessing of God, effected. I spoke as strongly as a mother who knows the value of children could speak, and begged that the foolish parents would take the help that was offered to save their child; but all to no purpose. His eye is gone; and the abscess in his ear produces a drain upon his already enfeebled constitution, which he has no stamina to meet, and I can only look forward and hope for the hour when death will put a period to his sufferings.

Since I wrote the above, I have heard of the child's death. Poor little fellow! he dreaded much the darkness of the grave; and a week before his death, affectingly said to his mother, "I am going to die, but do not put me in the grave, I shall be afraid to be there alone: it is quite dark." His mother remembered his dying words, and when his lifeless body was laid in the small chamber of the tomb belonging to his family, his mother sat beside him, and when entreated to leave the place, and suffer the entrance to be closed, she touchingly refused to move, saying, "I shall pass the night with my child; he is afraid to be alone." Such a conviction was not unreasonable on her part; for the Muslims do not believe that the soul is at once separated from the body, and call the first night after burial, "Leylet el Wahdeh," or "The Night of Solitude."

LETTER XI
(Second Series)

March, 1846

I MENTIONED in my last letter the widow of Isma'eel Páshá, whose illness had occasioned so much uneasiness to Mohammad 'Alee. She is now convalescent; but the old lady whom I also mentioned as being ill at the same time, who was once his favourite wife, died about a fortnight since. She had suffered extremely during a period of two years. On the morning of her death, Nezleh Hánum was roused by screams which proceeded from the palace of the invalid, adjoining her own palace; for the Kasr en Neel is composed of several distinct mansions, occupied by some of the elders of the Páshá's Hareem and their attendants. It was the funeral cry which had been raised by the slaves of the dying sufferer while she was yet alive. Nezleh Hánum went to her chamber, commanded silence, and directed the use of restoratives, until the object of her solicitude breathed her last. The shrieks of the immediate attendants were heard throughout the Kasr, and the death-cry which went forth from the inmates of the several palaces was heard at a considerable distance.

In the morning, some time before her death, eunuchs were dispatched to desire the attendance of every person of rank in Cairo, that the grandees and their hareems might join the funeral procession. By twelve o'clock, the Kasr was filled by those persons; the hareems being drest in the mourning colours of the country, black and blue. During the time occupied in requiring their attendance, the relations and slaves of the late lady were occupied in breaking the beautiful china and glass which had been the property of the deceased. The destruction after a death is generally proportioned to the possessions of the deceased; therefore in that case it was very extensive. The body was clad in very costly apparel, and wrapped in a Cashmere shawl: a bier was then brought, in which it was laid, and another Cashmere shawl was placed over the bier, the head of which was surmounted by a splendid diamond tiara. The grandees, on foot, followed the chanters of the Kur-an and the other persons who headed the procession: their ladies rode behind the bier on high donkeys, with a large crowd of other females. Eleven buffaloes were driven before the bier, to be slaughtered, and divided among the poor. A considerable number of camels followed, bearing bread and water for charitable distribution; and the excitement of the crowds who attended to partake of the bounty can scarcely be conceived. Such a funeral is a jubilee to the poor. The eunuchs who formed part of the procession bore sprinkling bottles containing scented waters, and censers in which were burning frankincense and other perfumes.

The interment took place in a vault in the Páshá's burial-place. A rich Cashmere shawl was spread in the vault, another was doubled as a pillow; and the body was taken out of the bier, and laid upon them. A third Cashmere shawl was placed over it, entirely covering the costly dress of the corpse. The mourners then quitted the vault, uttering the most piercing shrieks, and the door was closed.

The deceased was named "Shems-i-Safa," which admits of several interpretations; but the meaning intended is "Sun of Happiness."[†] Some say that, though she enjoyed the title and rights of a wife, she was not a wife in the strict legal sense of the term.

The funeral ceremonies of Modern Egypt strongly remind me of scenes depicted in many of the ancient tombs in this country: but I make this remark without knowing much of Egyptian antiquities except from books and drawings and museums.

I have much enjoyed looking over the very choice collection of antiquities and curiosities selected by our English resident physician, Dr. Abbott. I am not about to attempt a general description of them; but some are so very curious, and others so beautiful, that I should imagine an antiquary would find nothing so interesting in Cairo. To begin with the most antique: there are a necklace and a pair of ear-rings which were found in a jar at Dendara, and are believed to be the oldest articles of the kind in the world: they are made of gold-leaf, similar to that upon which hieroglyphics are usually found stamped: attached to the centre are three pendants of lapis lazuli, and two beads of blue glass, with an amethyst bead capped at each end with gold: but what is particularly remarkable is, that the name of Menes, the first king of Egypt, is stamped upon each of the ear-rings, and upon eight oval plates which decorate the necklace. A still more remarkable object in the same collection is a ring of uncommon interest, the well-authenticated signet-ring of Cheops. Antiquary or not, I believe that no one can see, or much more handle, that ring, without experiencing a thrill of pleasure that such a relic of the age of the Founder of the Great Pyramid should have been preserved. It is of fine gold, weighing nearly three sovereigns, and bearing the name of Shofo, the Suphis of Manetho, and the Cheops of the Greeks. This precious antique is in the highest state of preservation. It was found in a tomb near the pyramids El-Geezeh. The style of the hieroglyphics is in perfect accordance with those in the tombs about the Great Pyramid, and all the details are minutely attended to and beautifully executed. There is also, among the more ancient of the curiosities in this most rare collection, a bracelet of twisted gold, terminating with the form of the lotus-flower, very much resembling the picturesque bracelets worn by the ladies of Egypt in the present day, only that it is, strange to say, of superior workmanship. I was much pleased also with

---

[†]The literal meaning of *safa* is 'clear, cloudless.'

two beautiful gold figures of birds with human heads and extended wings, representing the departing soul. Some winged orbs, too, symbols of the good genius, are remarkable for the fine taste and exquisite workmanship displayed in their formation. Some little figures in lapis lazuli are curious specimens of beautiful ancient carving; and two bronze lizards excited my admiration most especially: they are in as perfect preservation as though finished but yesterday, and wonderfully true to nature.

INDEX